Century 21
Accounting

11e | **Advanced**
Working Papers
Chapters 1–14

Claudia Bienias Gilbertson, CPA
Retired
North Hennepin Community College
Brooklyn Park, Minnesota

Mark W. Lehman, CPA, CFE
Associate Professor Emeritus
Richard C. Adkerson School of Accountancy
Mississippi State University
Starkville, Mississippi

Australia • Brazil • Mexico • Singapore • United Kingdom • United States

CENGAGE

**Century 21 Accounting Advanced,
Eleventh Edition Working Papers, Volume 1**
**Claudia Bienias Gilbertson,
Mark W. Lehman**

SVP, GM Skills & Global Product Management:
Jonathan Lau

Product Director: Matthew Seeley

Product Manager: Nicole Robinson

Senior Director, Development: Marah Bellegarde

Product Development Manager: Juliet Steiner

Senior Content Manager: Karen Caldwell

Learning Designer: Jennifer Starr

Product Assistant: Nicholas Scaglione

Vice President, Marketing Services:
Jennifer Ann Baker

Director, Product Marketing: Jeremy Walts

Marketing Manager: Abigail Hess

Managing Art Director: Jack Pendleton

Digital Delivery Lead: Jim Gilbert

Senior Digital Content Specialist:
Jaclyn Hermesmyer

Cover image(s): Shutterstock.com

Production Management and Composition:
SPi Global

For product information and technology assistance, contact us at
Cengage Customer & Sales Support, 1-800-354-9706.

For permission to use material from this text or product,
submit all requests online at **www.cengage.com/permissions.**
Further permissions questions can be e-mailed to
permissionrequest@cengage.com.

Library of Congress Control Number: 2019933594

Student Edition ISBN-13: 978-1-337-79970-6

Cengage
20 Channel Center Street
Boston, MA 02210
USA

Cengage is a leading provider of customized learning solutions with employees residing in nearly 40 different countries and sales in more than 125 countries around the world. Find your local representative at: **www.cengage.com.**

Cengage products are represented in Canada by
Nelson Education, Ltd.

To learn more about Cengage platforms and services, register or access your online learning solution, or purchase materials for your course, visit **ngl.cengage.com.**

Notice to the Reader

Printed in the United States of America
Print Number: 04   Print Year: 2020

TO THE STUDENT

These *Working Papers* are to be used in the study of Chapters 1–14 of CENTURY 21 ACCOUNTING ADVANCED, 11E. Forms are provided for:

1. Study Guides

2. Work Together Exercises

3. On Your Own Exercises

4. Application Problems

5. Mastery Problems

6. Challenge Problems

7. Source Documents Problems

8. Reinforcement Activities 1, 2, and 3

Printed on each page is the number of the problem in the textbook for which the form is to be used. Also shown is a specific instruction number for which the form is to be used.

You may not be required to use every form that is provided. Your teacher will tell you whether to retain or dispose of the unused pages.

The pages are perforated so they may be removed as the work required in each assignment is completed. The pages will be more easily detached if you crease the sheet along the line of perforations and then remove the sheet by pulling sideways rather than upward.

TABLE OF CONTENTS

Study Guide 1

Name	Perfect Score	Your Score
Identifying Accounting Terms	24 Pts.	
Analyzing Accounting Principles, Concepts, and Procedures	20 Pts.	
Total	44 Pts.	

Part One—Identifying Accounting Terms

Directions: Select the one term in Column I that best fits each definition in Column II. Print the letter identifying your choice in the Answers column.

Contains accounting terms for Lesson 1-1.

Column I	**Column II**	**Answers**
A. account	1. Anything of value that is owned. (p. 7)	1. _____
B. accounting equation	2. An amount owed by a business. (p. 7)	2. _____
C. asset	3. Financial rights to the assets of a business. (p. 7)	3. _____
D. controlling account	4. The amount remaining after the value of all liabilities is subtracted from the value of all assets. (p. 7)	4. _____
E. double-entry accounting		
F. equities	5. The owners' equity in a corporation. (p. 7)	5. _____
G. file maintenance	6. An equation showing the relationship among assets, liabilities, and owners' equity. (p. 7)	6. _____
H. general ledger	7. Business papers from which information is obtained for a journal entry. (p. 7)	7. _____
I. journal		
J. ledger	8. The recording of debit and credit parts of a transaction. (p. 8)	8. _____
K. liability	9. A form for recording transactions in chronological order. (p. 8)	9. _____
L. owners' equity		
M. source documents	10. A journal used to record only one kind of transaction. (p. 8)	10. _____
N. special journal	11. A record that summarizes all the information pertaining to a single item in the accounting equation. (p. 9)	11. _____
O. stockholders' equity		
P. subsidiary ledger	12. A group of accounts. (p. 11)	12. _____
	13. A ledger that contains all accounts needed to prepare financial statements. (p. 11)	13. _____
	14. A ledger that is summarized in a single general ledger account. (p. 11)	14. _____
	15. An account in a general ledger that summarizes all accounts in a subsidiary ledger. (p. 11)	15. _____
	16. The procedure for arranging accounts in a general ledger, assigning account numbers, and keeping records current. (p. 11)	16. _____

Accounting terms for Lessons 1-2 and 1-3 are presented on the following page.

Directions: Select the one term in Column I that best fits each definition in Column II. Print the letter identifying your choice in the Answers column.

Contains accounting terms for Lessons 1-2 and 1-3.

Column I	Column II	Answers
A. cash discount	1. An accounting system showing accounting information for two or more departments. (p. 13)	1. _____
B. contra account	2. A business that purchases and sells goods. (p. 13)	2. _____
C. debit memorandum	3. Transferring transaction information from a journal entry to a ledger account. (p. 15)	3. _____
D. departmental accounting system	4. A form prepared by the customer showing the price deduction taken by the customer for a return or an allowance. (p. 18)	4. _____
E. merchandising business	5. An account that reduces a related account on a financial statement. (p. 18)	5. _____
F. petty cash	6. A deduction that a vendor allows on the invoice amount to encourage prompt payment. (p. 20)	6. _____
G. posting	7. A cash discount taken on merchandise purchased on account. (p. 20)	7. _____
H. purchases discount	8. An amount of cash kept on hand and used for making small payments. (p. 25)	8. _____

Part Two—Analyzing Accounting Principles, Concepts, and Procedures

Directions: Place a *T* for True or an *F* for False in the Answers column to show whether each of the following statements is true or false.

Answers

1. The accounting equation may be stated as assets = owners' equity. (p. 7)   1. _____

2. A business with many daily transactions may use special journals. (p. 8)   2. _____

3. Owners' equity accounts have normal credit balances. (p. 9)   3. _____

4. A liability account has a normal debit balance. (p. 9)   4. _____

5. Revenue accounts have normal credit balances. (p. 9)   5. _____

6. Expense accounts have normal credit balances. (p. 9)   6. _____

7. Increases in asset accounts are recorded on the credit side. (p. 9)   7. _____

8. Increases in liability accounts are recorded on the credit side. (p. 9)   8. _____

9. Increases in owners' equity accounts are recorded on the debit side. (p. 9)   9. _____

10. Decreases in revenue accounts are recorded on the credit side. (p. 9)   10. _____

11. Decreases in expense accounts are recorded on the credit side. (p. 9)   11. _____

12. In a departmental accounting system, gross profit is calculated for each department. (p. 13)   12. _____

13. A departmental purchases journal should contain a Purchases Debit column for each department. (p. 14)   13. _____

14. Individual amounts in the Accounts Payable Credit column of the purchases journal are posted at the end of each month. (p. 15)   14. _____

15. When a customer returns merchandise for credit, the customer issues a debit memorandum for the amount of the return. (p. 18)   15. _____

16. Using a check as the source document for a cash payment transaction is an application of the accounting concept Objective Evidence. (p. 20)   16. _____

17. A purchases discount is usually stated as a percentage. (p. 20)   17. _____

18. A discount is calculated on the original purchase price, even if a purchase return or allowance has been granted. (p. 21)   18. _____

19. Replenishing the petty cash fund increases the Petty Cash account balance. (p. 25)   19. _____

20. Amounts in the General Debit and General Credit columns of a cash payments journal are posted individually. (p. 26)   20. _____

1-1   WORK TOGETHER (LO3), p. 12

Determining the normal balance, increase, and decrease sides for accounts

1., 2., 3., 4.

Determining the normal balance, increase, and decrease sides for accounts

1., 2., 3., 4.

1-2 WORK TOGETHER (LO6, 7, 8), p. 19

Journalizing and posting purchases on account and purchases returns and allowances

1., 2.

PURCHASES JOURNAL

PAGE _____

	DATE	ACCOUNT CREDITED	PURCH. NO.	POST. REF.	ACCOUNTS PAYABLE CREDIT (1)	PURCHASES DEBIT		
						AUDIO (2)	VIDEO (3)	
1								1
2								2
3								3
4								4
5								5
6								6
7								7
8								8
9								9

1.

GENERAL JOURNAL

PAGE _____

	DATE	ACCOUNT TITLE	DOC. NO.	POST. REF.	DEBIT	CREDIT	
1							1
2							2
3							3
4							4
5							5
6							6
7							7
8							8
9							9
10							10
11							11
12							12
13							13
14							14
15							15
16							16
17							17

1.

ACCOUNTS PAYABLE LEDGER

VENDOR Davis Corporation   VENDOR NO. 210

DATE		ITEM	POST. REF.	DEBIT	CREDIT	CREDIT BALANCE
20-- June	1	Balance	✔			1 0 3 4 23

VENDOR National Industries   VENDOR NO. 220

DATE		ITEM	POST. REF.	DEBIT	CREDIT	CREDIT BALANCE
20-- June	1	Balance	✔			9 0 2 44

VENDOR TPC Supply   VENDOR NO. 230

DATE		ITEM	POST. REF.	DEBIT	CREDIT	CREDIT BALANCE
20-- June	1	Balance	✔			2 3 1 2 41

1-2 WORK TOGETHER (concluded)

1., 2.   **GENERAL LEDGER**

ACCOUNT Accounts Payable   ACCOUNT NO. 2105

DATE	ITEM	POST. REF.	DEBIT	CREDIT	BALANCE DEBIT	BALANCE CREDIT
20-- June 1	Balance	✔				4 2 4 9 08

ACCOUNT Purchases—Audio   ACCOUNT NO. 5105

DATE	ITEM	POST. REF.	DEBIT	CREDIT	BALANCE DEBIT	BALANCE CREDIT
20-- June 1	Balance	✔			38 4 8 9 10	

ACCOUNT Purchases Returns and Allowances—Audio   ACCOUNT NO. 5115

DATE	ITEM	POST. REF.	DEBIT	CREDIT	BALANCE DEBIT	BALANCE CREDIT
20-- June 1	Balance	✔				8 1 1 50

ACCOUNT Purchases—Video   ACCOUNT NO. 5205

DATE	ITEM	POST. REF.	DEBIT	CREDIT	BALANCE DEBIT	BALANCE CREDIT
20-- June 1	Balance	✔			28 4 8 9 08	

ACCOUNT Purchases Returns and Allowances—Video   ACCOUNT NO. 5215

DATE	ITEM	POST. REF.	DEBIT	CREDIT	BALANCE DEBIT	BALANCE CREDIT
20-- June 1	Balance	✔				6 2 1 70

Journalizing and posting purchases on account and purchases returns and allowances

1., 2.

PURCHASES JOURNAL   PAGE

	DATE	ACCOUNT CREDITED	PURCH. NO.	POST. REF.	ACCOUNTS PAYABLE CREDIT 1	PURCHASES DEBIT CLOTHING 2	PURCHASES DEBIT SHOES 3	
1								1
2								2
3								3
4								4
5								5
6								6
7								7
8								8
9								9

1.

GENERAL JOURNAL   PAGE

	DATE	ACCOUNT TITLE	DOC. NO.	POST. REF.	DEBIT	CREDIT	
1							1
2							2
3							3
4							4
5							5
6							6
7							7
8							8
9							9
10							10
11							11
12							12
13							13
14							14
15							15
16							16
17							17

1-2 ON YOUR OWN (continued)

1.   **ACCOUNTS PAYABLE LEDGER**

VENDOR Ackerman Supply   VENDOR NO. 210

DATE		ITEM	POST. REF.	DEBIT	CREDIT	CREDIT BALANCE
July 20--	1	Balance	✔			2 0 6 8 00

VENDOR Keller Corporation   VENDOR NO. 220

DATE		ITEM	POST. REF.	DEBIT	CREDIT	CREDIT BALANCE
July 20--	1	Balance	✔			1 5 2 4 50

VENDOR Peters Company   VENDOR NO. 230

DATE		ITEM	POST. REF.	DEBIT	CREDIT	CREDIT BALANCE
July 20--	1	Balance	✔			3 1 5 4 75

1., 2.   **GENERAL LEDGER**

ACCOUNT Accounts Payable   ACCOUNT NO. 2105

DATE		ITEM	POST. REF.	DEBIT	CREDIT	BALANCE	
						DEBIT	CREDIT
July 1	20--	Balance	✔				18 4 4 9 20

ACCOUNT Purchases—Clothing   ACCOUNT NO. 5105

DATE		ITEM	POST. REF.	DEBIT	CREDIT	BALANCE	
						DEBIT	CREDIT
July 1	20--	Balance	✔			68 4 8 9 60	

ACCOUNT Purchases Returns and Allowances—Clothing   ACCOUNT NO. 5115

DATE		ITEM	POST. REF.	DEBIT	CREDIT	BALANCE	
						DEBIT	CREDIT
July 1	20--	Balance	✔				1 0 8 5 15

ACCOUNT Purchases—Shoes   ACCOUNT NO. 5205

DATE		ITEM	POST. REF.	DEBIT	CREDIT	BALANCE	
						DEBIT	CREDIT
July 1	20--	Balance	✔			49 1 4 8 60	

ACCOUNT Purchases Returns and Allowances—Shoes   ACCOUNT NO. 5215

DATE		ITEM	POST. REF.	DEBIT	CREDIT	BALANCE	
						DEBIT	CREDIT
July 1	20--	Balance	✔				2 3 1 95

1-3 **WORK TOGETHER (LO9, 10), p. 27**

Journalizing and posting departmental cash payments

1., 2.

CASH PAYMENTS JOURNAL

PAGE ____

DATE	ACCOUNT TITLE	CK. NO.	POST. REF.	GENERAL DEBIT	GENERAL CREDIT	ACCOUNTS PAYABLE DEBIT	PURCH. DISCOUNT CR. CRAFTS	PURCH. DISCOUNT CR. FRAMES	CASH CREDIT

1-3 WORK TOGETHER (continued)

1., 2.   ACCOUNTS PAYABLE LEDGER

VENDOR Fulton Corporation   VENDOR NO. 235

DATE		ITEM	POST. REF.	DEBIT	CREDIT	CREDIT BALANCE
20-- June	1	Balance	✔			3 6 7 4 22

VENDOR Harris Industries   VENDOR NO. 245

DATE		ITEM	POST. REF.	DEBIT	CREDIT	CREDIT BALANCE
20-- June	1	Balance	✔			2 9 5 3 30

1., 2.   GENERAL LEDGER

ACCOUNT Cash   ACCOUNT NO. 1105

DATE		ITEM	POST. REF.	DEBIT	CREDIT	BALANCE DEBIT	BALANCE CREDIT
20-- June	1	Balance	✔			16 4 3 5 34	

ACCOUNT Supplies   ACCOUNT NO. 1405

DATE		ITEM	POST. REF.	DEBIT	CREDIT	BALANCE DEBIT	BALANCE CREDIT
20-- June	1	Balance	✔			6 4 3 2 54	

ACCOUNT Accounts Payable   ACCOUNT NO. 2105

DATE		ITEM	POST. REF.	DEBIT	CREDIT	BALANCE DEBIT	BALANCE CREDIT
20-- June	1	Balance	✔				16 4 6 2 27

ACCOUNT Purchases—Crafts   ACCOUNT NO. 5105

DATE		ITEM	POST. REF.	DEBIT	CREDIT	BALANCE DEBIT	BALANCE CREDIT
20-- June	1	Balance	✔			164 3 2 6 74	

1-3 WORK TOGETHER (concluded)

ACCOUNT Purchases Discount—Crafts   ACCOUNT NO. 5110

DATE	ITEM	POST. REF.	DEBIT	CREDIT	BALANCE DEBIT	BALANCE CREDIT
20-- June 1	Balance	✔				1 8 0 7 59

ACCOUNT Purchases—Frames   ACCOUNT NO. 5205

DATE	ITEM	POST. REF.	DEBIT	CREDIT	BALANCE DEBIT	BALANCE CREDIT
20-- June 1	Balance	✔			94 3 6 5 33	

ACCOUNT Purchases Discount—Frames   ACCOUNT NO. 5210

DATE	ITEM	POST. REF.	DEBIT	CREDIT	BALANCE DEBIT	BALANCE CREDIT
20-- June 1	Balance	✔				6 7 9 43

ACCOUNT Advertising Expense—Crafts   ACCOUNT NO. 6105

DATE	ITEM	POST. REF.	DEBIT	CREDIT	BALANCE DEBIT	BALANCE CREDIT
20-- June 1	Balance	✔			7 5 9 0 00	

ACCOUNT Miscellaneous Expense   ACCOUNT NO. 7125

DATE	ITEM	POST. REF.	DEBIT	CREDIT	BALANCE DEBIT	BALANCE CREDIT
20-- June 1	Balance	✔			3 7 6 5 86	

Journalizing and posting departmental cash payments

1-3 ON YOUR OWN (LO9, 10), p. 27

1., 2.

CASH PAYMENTS JOURNAL

PAGE 6

| | | | | GENERAL | | ACCOUNTS PAYABLE DEBIT | PURCH. DISCOUNT CR. | | CASH CREDIT |
	DATE	ACCOUNT TITLE	CK. NO.	POST. REF.	DEBIT	CREDIT		CERAMIC	STONE	
					1	2	3	4	5	6
1										
2										
3										
4										
5										
6										
7										
8										
9										
10										
11										
12										
13										
14										
15										
16										
17										
18										
19										
20										
21										
22										

1-3 ON YOUR OWN (continued)

1., 2.   ACCOUNTS PAYABLE LEDGER

VENDOR Marris Ceramics   VENDOR NO. 260

DATE		ITEM	POST. REF.	DEBIT	CREDIT	CREDIT BALANCE
20-- July	1	Balance	✔			4 0 9 8 20

VENDOR Overland Stone   VENDOR NO. 270

DATE		ITEM	POST. REF.	DEBIT	CREDIT	CREDIT BALANCE
20-- July	1	Balance	✔			3 5 6 0 50

1., 2.   GENERAL LEDGER

ACCOUNT Cash   ACCOUNT NO. 1105

DATE		ITEM	POST. REF.	DEBIT	CREDIT	BALANCE DEBIT	BALANCE CREDIT
20-- July	1	Balance	✔			12 5 3 2 12	

ACCOUNT Supplies   ACCOUNT NO. 1405

DATE		ITEM	POST. REF.	DEBIT	CREDIT	BALANCE DEBIT	BALANCE CREDIT
20-- July	1	Balance	✔			5 1 2 6 21	

ACCOUNT Accounts Payable   ACCOUNT NO. 2105

DATE		ITEM	POST. REF.	DEBIT	CREDIT	BALANCE DEBIT	BALANCE CREDIT
20-- July	1	Balance	✔				22 1 5 6 75

ACCOUNT Purchases—Ceramic   ACCOUNT NO. 5105

DATE		ITEM	POST. REF.	DEBIT	CREDIT	BALANCE DEBIT	BALANCE CREDIT
20-- July	1	Balance	✔			175 4 6 3 33	

ACCOUNT Purchases Discount—Ceramic   ACCOUNT NO. 5110

DATE		ITEM	POST. REF.	DEBIT	CREDIT	BALANCE	
						DEBIT	CREDIT
July 20--	1	Balance	✔				1 5 7 9 17

ACCOUNT Purchases—Stone   ACCOUNT NO. 5205

DATE		ITEM	POST. REF.	DEBIT	CREDIT	BALANCE	
						DEBIT	CREDIT
July 20--	1	Balance	✔			91 0 6 4 54	

ACCOUNT Purchases Discount—Stone   ACCOUNT NO. 5210

DATE		ITEM	POST. REF.	DEBIT	CREDIT	BALANCE	
						DEBIT	CREDIT
July 20--	1	Balance	✔				7 2 8 52

ACCOUNT Advertising Expense—Stone   ACCOUNT NO. 6205

DATE		ITEM	POST. REF.	DEBIT	CREDIT	BALANCE	
						DEBIT	CREDIT
July 20--	1	Balance	✔			3 6 7 0 00	

ACCOUNT Miscellaneous Expense   ACCOUNT NO. 7125

DATE		ITEM	POST. REF.	DEBIT	CREDIT	BALANCE	
						DEBIT	CREDIT
July 20--	1	Balance	✔			4 6 4 2 87	

1-1 APPLICATION PROBLEM (LO3), p. 31

Determining the normal balance, increase, and decrease sides for accounts

1., 2., 3., 4., 5.

1	2	3	4	5	6	7	8
Account Title	**Account Classification**	**Account's Normal Balance**		**Increase Side**		**Decrease Side**	
		Debit	Credit	Debit	Credit	Debit	Credit
Prepaid Insurance	Asset	✔		✔			✔

1-2 APPLICATION PROBLEM (LO6, 7, 8), p. 31

Journalizing and posting departmental purchases on account and purchases returns and allowances

1., 2.

PURCHASES JOURNAL PAGE

	DATE	ACCOUNT CREDITED	PURCH. NO.	POST. REF.	ACCOUNTS PAYABLE CREDIT (1)	PURCHASES DEBIT FLOWERS (2)	PURCHASES DEBIT GIFTS (3)	
1								1
2								2
3								3
4								4
5								5
6								6
7								7
8								8
9								9

1.

GENERAL JOURNAL PAGE

	DATE	ACCOUNT TITLE	DOC. NO.	POST. REF.	DEBIT	CREDIT	
1							1
2							2
3							3
4							4
5							5
6							6
7							7
8							8
9							9
10							10
11							11
12							12
13							13
14							14
15							15
16							16

1-2 APPLICATION PROBLEM (continued)

1., 2.   **ACCOUNTS PAYABLE LEDGER**

VENDOR Carson Growers   VENDOR NO. 210

DATE	ITEM	POST. REF.	DEBIT	CREDIT	CREDIT BALANCE
Aug. 1	Balance	✔			2 5 4 4 00

VENDOR Glade Arts Center   VENDOR NO. 220

DATE	ITEM	POST. REF.	DEBIT	CREDIT	CREDIT BALANCE
Aug. 1	Balance	✔			4 9 8 1 25

VENDOR Marlon Nursery   VENDOR NO. 230

DATE	ITEM	POST. REF.	DEBIT	CREDIT	CREDIT BALANCE
Aug. 1	Balance	✔			3 1 0 4 70

VENDOR Tennessee Crafts   VENDOR NO. 240

DATE	ITEM	POST. REF.	DEBIT	CREDIT	CREDIT BALANCE
Aug. 1	Balance	✔			4 1 9 5 80

1., 2. **GENERAL LEDGER**

ACCOUNT Accounts Payable   ACCOUNT NO. 2105

DATE		ITEM	POST. REF.	DEBIT	CREDIT	BALANCE	
						DEBIT	CREDIT
20-- Aug.	1	Balance	✔				14 8 2 5 75

ACCOUNT Purchases—Flowers   ACCOUNT NO. 5105

DATE		ITEM	POST. REF.	DEBIT	CREDIT	BALANCE	
						DEBIT	CREDIT
20-- Aug.	1	Balance	✔			68 4 8 9 60	

ACCOUNT Purchases Returns and Allowances—Flowers   ACCOUNT NO. 5115

DATE		ITEM	POST. REF.	DEBIT	CREDIT	BALANCE	
						DEBIT	CREDIT
20-- Aug.	1	Balance	✔				1 0 8 5 15

ACCOUNT Purchases—Gifts   ACCOUNT NO. 5205

DATE		ITEM	POST. REF.	DEBIT	CREDIT	BALANCE	
						DEBIT	CREDIT
20-- Aug.	1	Balance	✔			49 1 4 8 60	

ACCOUNT Purchases Returns and Allowances—Gifts   ACCOUNT NO. 5215

DATE		ITEM	POST. REF.	DEBIT	CREDIT	BALANCE	
						DEBIT	CREDIT
20-- Aug.	1	Balance	✔				2 3 1 95

1-3 **APPLICATION PROBLEM (LO9, 10), p. 32**

Journalizing and posting departmental cash payments

1., 2.

CASH PAYMENTS JOURNAL

PAGE ____

DATE	ACCOUNT TITLE	CK. NO.	POST. REF.	GENERAL DEBIT	GENERAL CREDIT	ACCOUNTS PAYABLE DEBIT	PURCH. DISCOUNT CR. GUITARS	PURCH. DISCOUNT CR. KEYBOARDS	CASH CREDIT	
				1	2	3	4	5	6	
										1
										2
										3
										4
										5
										6
										7
										8
										9
										10
										11
										12
										13
										14
										15
										16
										17
										18
										19
										20
										21
										22

1., 2.   **ACCOUNTS PAYABLE LEDGER**

VENDOR Airways Music   VENDOR NO. 210

DATE	ITEM	POST. REF.	DEBIT	CREDIT	CREDIT BALANCE
Mar. 1	Balance	✔			5 2 0 9 20

VENDOR Campbell Guitar   VENDOR NO. 220

DATE	ITEM	POST. REF.	DEBIT	CREDIT	CREDIT BALANCE
Mar. 1	Balance	✔			4 2 0 9 90

1., 2.   **GENERAL LEDGER**

ACCOUNT Cash   ACCOUNT NO. 1105

DATE	ITEM	POST. REF.	DEBIT	CREDIT	BALANCE DEBIT	BALANCE CREDIT
Mar. 1	Balance	✔			20 4 5 2 53	

ACCOUNT Supplies   ACCOUNT NO. 1405

DATE	ITEM	POST. REF.	DEBIT	CREDIT	BALANCE DEBIT	BALANCE CREDIT
Mar. 1	Balance	✔			3 6 4 3 21	

ACCOUNT Accounts Payable   ACCOUNT NO. 2105

DATE	ITEM	POST. REF.	DEBIT	CREDIT	BALANCE DEBIT	BALANCE CREDIT
Mar. 1	Balance	✔				28 5 4 6 27

ACCOUNT Purchases—Guitars   ACCOUNT NO. 5105

DATE	ITEM	POST. REF.	DEBIT	CREDIT	BALANCE DEBIT	BALANCE CREDIT
Mar. 1	Balance	✔			95 6 4 2 87	

1-3 APPLICATION PROBLEM (concluded)

ACCOUNT Purchases Discount—Guitars   ACCOUNT NO. 5110

DATE		ITEM	POST. REF.	DEBIT	CREDIT	BALANCE	
						DEBIT	CREDIT
20-- Mar.	1	Balance	✔				1 9 1 29

ACCOUNT Purchases—Keyboards   ACCOUNT NO. 5205

DATE		ITEM	POST. REF.	DEBIT	CREDIT	BALANCE	
						DEBIT	CREDIT
20-- Mar.	1	Balance	✔			104 2 5 6 89	

ACCOUNT Purchases Discount—Keyboards   ACCOUNT NO. 5210

DATE		ITEM	POST. REF.	DEBIT	CREDIT	BALANCE	
						DEBIT	CREDIT
20-- Mar.	1	Balance	✔				6 2 5 54

ACCOUNT Advertising Expense—Guitars   ACCOUNT NO. 6105

DATE		ITEM	POST. REF.	DEBIT	CREDIT	BALANCE	
						DEBIT	CREDIT
20-- Mar.	1	Balance	✔			3 6 0 0 00	

ACCOUNT Miscellaneous Expense   ACCOUNT NO. 7125

DATE		ITEM	POST. REF.	DEBIT	CREDIT	BALANCE	
						DEBIT	CREDIT
20-- Mar.	1	Balance	✔			5 2 4 7 23	

Journalizing departmental purchases and cash payments

1., 3.

PURCHASES JOURNAL

PAGE

	DATE	ACCOUNT CREDITED	PURCH. NO.	POST. REF.	ACCOUNTS PAYABLE CREDIT	PURCHASES DEBIT		
						COSTUME	FINE	
1								1
2								2
3								3
4								4
5								5
6								6
7								7
8								8
9								9

1.

GENERAL JOURNAL

PAGE

	DATE	ACCOUNT TITLE	DOC. NO.	POST. REF.	DEBIT	CREDIT	
1							1
2							2
3							3
4							4
5							5
6							6
7							7
8							8
9							9
10							10
11							11
12							12
13							13
14							14
15							15
16							16

1-M MASTERY PROBLEM (continued)

1., 3.

CASH PAYMENTS JOURNAL

PAGE

									GENERAL		ACCOUNTS PAYABLE DEBIT	PURCH. DISCOUNT CR.		CASH CREDIT
DATE	ACCOUNT TITLE	CK. NO.	POST. REF.			DEBIT		CREDIT			COSTUME	FINE	
				1		2		3		4	5	6	

1., 2.   **ACCOUNTS PAYABLE LEDGER**

VENDOR Austin Creations   VENDOR NO. 210

DATE	ITEM	POST. REF.	DEBIT	CREDIT	CREDIT BALANCE

VENDOR Destin Crafters   VENDOR NO. 220

DATE	ITEM	POST. REF.	DEBIT	CREDIT	CREDIT BALANCE
20-- Aug. 1	Balance	✔			2 6 4 3 63

VENDOR Jenkins Designs   VENDOR NO. 230

DATE	ITEM	POST. REF.	DEBIT	CREDIT	CREDIT BALANCE

VENDOR Ketler Krafts   VENDOR NO. 240

DATE	ITEM	POST. REF.	DEBIT	CREDIT	CREDIT BALANCE
20-- Aug. 1	Balance	✔			2 9 5 3 30

Name _____ Date _____ Class _____

MASTERY PROBLEM (continued)

1., 2., 3.   **GENERAL LEDGER**

ACCOUNT Cash   ACCOUNT NO. 1105

DATE	ITEM	POST. REF.	DEBIT	CREDIT	BALANCE DEBIT	BALANCE CREDIT
20-- Aug. 1	Balance	✔			14 5 4 2 87	

ACCOUNT Supplies   ACCOUNT NO. 1405

DATE	ITEM	POST. REF.	DEBIT	CREDIT	BALANCE DEBIT	BALANCE CREDIT
20-- Aug. 1	Balance	✔			3 2 5 6 37	

ACCOUNT Accounts Payable   ACCOUNT NO. 2105

DATE	ITEM	POST. REF.	DEBIT	CREDIT	BALANCE DEBIT	BALANCE CREDIT
20-- Aug. 1	Balance	✔				6 4 3 2 34

ACCOUNT Purchases—Costume   ACCOUNT NO. 5105

DATE	ITEM	POST. REF.	DEBIT	CREDIT	BALANCE DEBIT	BALANCE CREDIT
20-- Aug. 1	Balance	✔			58 6 4 5 23	

ACCOUNT Purchases Discount—Costume   ACCOUNT NO. 5110

DATE	ITEM	POST. REF.	DEBIT	CREDIT	BALANCE DEBIT	BALANCE CREDIT
20-- Aug. 1	Balance	✔				5 2 7 81

ACCOUNT Purchases Returns and Allowances—Costume   ACCOUNT NO. 5115

DATE	ITEM	POST. REF.	DEBIT	CREDIT	BALANCE DEBIT	BALANCE CREDIT
20-- Aug. 1	Balance	✔				8 2 3 44

ACCOUNT Purchases—Fine   ACCOUNT NO. 5205

DATE		ITEM	POST. REF.	DEBIT	CREDIT	BALANCE	
						DEBIT	CREDIT
20-- Aug.	1	Balance	✔			65 4 3 7 86	

ACCOUNT Purchases Discount—Fine   ACCOUNT NO. 5210

DATE		ITEM	POST. REF.	DEBIT	CREDIT	BALANCE	
						DEBIT	CREDIT
20-- Aug.	1	Balance	✔				5 2 3 50

ACCOUNT Purchases Returns and Allowances—Fine   ACCOUNT NO. 5215

DATE		ITEM	POST. REF.	DEBIT	CREDIT	BALANCE	
						DEBIT	CREDIT
20-- Aug.	1	Balance	✔				9 7 8 56

ACCOUNT Advertising Expense—Fine   ACCOUNT NO. 6205

DATE		ITEM	POST. REF.	DEBIT	CREDIT	BALANCE	
						DEBIT	CREDIT
20-- Aug.	1	Balance	✔			8 9 0 0 00	

ACCOUNT Miscellaneous Expense   ACCOUNT NO. 7125

DATE		ITEM	POST. REF.	DEBIT	CREDIT	BALANCE	
						DEBIT	CREDIT
20-- Aug.	1	Balance	✔			6 2 7 5 31	

ACCOUNT Rent Expense   ACCOUNT NO. 7140

DATE		ITEM	POST. REF.	DEBIT	CREDIT	BALANCE	
						DEBIT	CREDIT
20-- Aug.	1	Balance	✔			16 8 0 0 00	

ACCOUNT Utilities Expense   ACCOUNT NO. 7160

DATE		ITEM	POST. REF.	DEBIT	CREDIT	BALANCE	
						DEBIT	CREDIT
20-- Aug.	1	Balance	✔			5 2 7 7 94	

1-C CHALLENGE PROBLEM (LO5), p. 33

Establishing a departmental accounting system

Department	Quantity	Description	Unit Cost	Sales Price
	3	Guitar straps	$ 6.95	$ 12.95
	1	5-string banjo	149.00	299.00
	15	6-string nylon guitar strings	5.95	12.95
	1	Acoustic guitar	1,495.98	2,399.00
	50	Sheet music, recent publication mix	3.99	6.99
	25	20' electric guitar cable	8.95	19.99
	2	Wireless microphone	325.95	650.00
	5	Effects pedal	99.99	209.95
	6	Beginner guitar package	89.99	199.99
	3	Harmonica with case	159.25	249.99
	5	Bass guitar package	129.99	199.99
	2	Tom drums with stand	109.95	189.99
	6	Digital metronome	59.99	109.95
	20	5B drumsticks	4.95	9.99
	3	Acoustic electric guitar with gig bag	219.99	379.99
	4	12-string nylon guitar strings	5.95	12.95
	20	Microphone wind screens	2.99	4.95
	4	100' 8-channel audio snake	129.99	259.99
	2	Bass guitar with case	799.99	1,799.99
	15	Ear plugs	2.95	5.95
	12	5-string bass guitar strings	6.95	15.95
	3	Drum set	495.95	795.95

Codes:

_____

_____

_____

_____

1-S SOURCE DOCUMENTS PROBLEM (LO6, 8, 9), p. 34

Journalizing purchase and cash payment transactions

1., 2.

PURCHASES JOURNAL   PAGE

	DATE		ACCOUNT CREDITED	PURCH. NO.	POST. REF.	ACCOUNTS PAYABLE CREDIT 1	PURCHASES DEBIT	
							GOLF 2	TENNIS 3
1									1
2									2
3									3
4									4
5									5
6									6
7									7
8									8
9									9
10									10
11									11
12									12
13									13
14									14
15									15
16									16
17									17
18									18
19									19
20									20
21									21
22									22
23									23
24									24
25									25
26									26
27									27
28									28
29									29
30									30

1-S SOURCE DOCUMENTS PROBLEM (continued)

1., 3.

CASH PAYMENTS JOURNAL

1.

GENERAL JOURNAL   PAGE

	DATE	ACCOUNT TITLE	DOC. NO.	POST. REF.	DEBIT	CREDIT	
1							1
2							2
3							3
4							4
5							5
6							6
7							7
8							8
9							9
10							10
11							11
12							12
13							13
14							14
15							15
16							16
17							17
18							18
19							19
20							20
21							21
22							22
23							23
24							24
25							25
26							26
27							27
28							28
29							29

1-S SOURCE DOCUMENTS PROBLEM (continued)

Marchese Manufacturing
725 Dreshertown Road
Fort Washington, PA 19034

INVOICE

REC'D 05/06/ -- P662

SOLD TO: Mike's Discount Golf
8520 N. Dale Mabry
Tampa, FL 33618

DATE: 5/2/--
INV. NO. 4818
TERMS: 2/10, n/30
ACCT. NO. 2450

QUANTITY	CAT. NO.	DESCRIPTION	UNIT PRICE	TOTAL
250	8186	3-Pack tennis balls	$ 2.19	$ 547.50
30	4811	4-Pocket tennis bag, assorted colors	25.65	769.50
		TOTAL		$ 1,317.00

Perfect Score, Inc.
809 E. 12th St.
Los Angeles, CA 90021

SALES INVOICE

REC'D 05/14/ -- P663

TO: Mike's Discount Golf
8520 N. Dale Mabry
Tampa, FL 33618

NO. 16548
DATE: 5/12/--

CUSTOMER P.O.	ORDER RECEIVED	ORDER SHIPPED	SALES REPRESENTATIVE	TERMS	CUSTOMER ACCOUNT
642	4/16/--	5/11/--	MGE	2/10, n/30	1420

PART NO.	QUANTITY	DESCRIPTION	UNIT PRICE	TOTAL
156	12	Beginner short set, right	$ 69.99	$ 839.88
184	10	Terston brand set, right steel	249.99	2,499.90
185	15	Terston brand set, right graphite	349.99	5,249.85
		TOTAL		$ 8,589.63

Altman Industries
1125 Fulton Ave.
San Antonio, TX 78201

INVOICE

REC'D 05/28/ -- P664

SOLD TO: Mike's Discount Golf
8520 N. Dale Mabry
Tampa, FL 33618

NO. 895
DATE: 5/25/--
TERMS: 2/10, n/30

QUANTITY	PART	DESCRIPTION	UNIT PRICE	TOTAL
60	B-8015	80 Compression, 15-pack	$ 7.95	$ 477.00
80	B-9015	90 Compression, 15-pack	8.25	660.00
		TOTAL		$ 1,137.00

No. 57

DEBIT MEMORANDUM

Mike's Discount Golf
8520 N. Dale Mabry
Tampa, FL 33618

TO: Marchese Manufacturing
725 Dreshertown Road
Fort Washington, PA 19034

DATE: May 7, 20--

ACCT. NO. 248

QUANTITY	CAT. NO.	DESCRIPTION	UNIT PRICE	TOTAL
2	4811	4-pocket tennis bag, assorted colors damaged in transit	$ 25.65	$ 51.30

No. 58

DEBIT MEMORANDUM

Mike's Discount Golf
8520 N. Dale Mabry
Tampa, FL 33618

TO: Altman Industries
1125 Fulton Ave.
San Antonio, TX 78201

DATE: May 14, 20--

ACCT. NO. 206

QUANTITY	CAT. NO.	DESCRIPTION	UNIT PRICE	TOTAL
5	B-9015	90 Compression, 15-pack short shipment	$ 8.25	$ 41.25

1-S   SOURCE DOCUMENTS PROBLEM (continued)

NO. 738	$ 2,690.77		
Date: May 4			20 --
To: Altman Industries			
For: Purchase invoice #660 for golf equipment, $2,745.68, less 2% discount			
BALANCE BROUGHT FORWARD	8,943	72
AMOUNT DEPOSITED	Date		
SUBTOTAL	8,943	72
OTHER:		
SUBTOTAL	8,943	72
AMOUNT THIS CHECK	2,690	77
BALANCE CARRIED FORWARD	6,252	95

NO. 739	$ 103.18		
Date: May 6			20 --
To:			
For: Supplies			
BALANCE BROUGHT FORWARD		6,252	95
AMOUNT DEPOSITED	5 5 --	3,154	00
SUBTOTAL	Date	9,406	95
OTHER:			
SUBTOTAL		9,406	95
AMOUNT THIS CHECK		103	18
BALANCE CARRIED FORWARD		9,303	77

NO. 740	$ 418.15		
Date: May 8			20 --
To:			
For: Utilities			
BALANCE BROUGHT FORWARD	9,303	77
AMOUNT DEPOSITED	Date		
SUBTOTAL	9,303	77
OTHER:		
SUBTOTAL	9,303	77
AMOUNT THIS CHECK	418	15
BALANCE CARRIED FORWARD	8,885	62

NO. 741	$ 1,240.39		
Date: May 10			20 --
To: Marchese Manufacturing			
For: Purchase invoice #662 less debit memorandum 57, less 2% discount			
BALANCE BROUGHT FORWARD		8,885	62
AMOUNT DEPOSITED	5 8 --	1,485	18
SUBTOTAL	Date	10,370	80
OTHER:			
SUBTOTAL		10,370	80
AMOUNT THIS CHECK		1,240	39
BALANCE CARRIED FORWARD		9,130	41

NO. **742** $ _4,485.00_

Date: _May 16_   20--

To: _Eastern Tennis Mfg._

For: _Tennis merchandise_

BALANCE BROUGHT FORWARD	9,130	41
AMOUNT DEPOSITED Date		
SUBTOTAL	9,130	41
OTHER:		
SUBTOTAL	9,130	41
AMOUNT THIS CHECK	4,485	00
BALANCE CARRIED FORWARD	4,645	41

NO. **743** $ _1,900.00_

Date: _May 20_   20--

To: _Veteran Support Society_

For: _Tournament sponsorship_

BALANCE BROUGHT FORWARD			4,645	41
AMOUNT DEPOSITED	5	18 --	3,164	18
SUBTOTAL Date			7,809	59
OTHER:				
SUBTOTAL			7,809	59
AMOUNT THIS CHECK			1,900	00
BALANCE CARRIED FORWARD			5,909	59

NO. **744** $ _2,482.50_

Date: _May 28_   20--

To: _Lake Michigan Fabrics_

For: _Golf merchandise_

BALANCE BROUGHT FORWARD	5,909	59
AMOUNT DEPOSITED Date		
SUBTOTAL	5,909	59
OTHER:		
SUBTOTAL	5,909	59
AMOUNT THIS CHECK	2,482	50
BALANCE CARRIED FORWARD	3,427	09

NO. **745** $ _145.35_

Date: _May 31_   20--

To: _Sandy Adams, Petty Cash_

For: _Petty cash_

BALANCE BROUGHT FORWARD			3,427	09
AMOUNT DEPOSITED	5	30 20--	5,486	18
SUBTOTAL Date			8,913	27
OTHER:				
SUBTOTAL			8,913	27
AMOUNT THIS CHECK			145	35
BALANCE CARRIED FORWARD			8,767	92

No. 69

MEMORANDUM

Attached Macon Office Supply invoice #6434 is for store supplies.

Signed: _Sheila Manuel_   Date: _May 3,_   20--

No. 70

MEMORANDUM

Declare dividend of $2.00 on 5,00 shares outstanding

Signed: _Thomas Maloney_   Date: _May 31,_   20--

1-S   SOURCE DOCUMENTS PROBLEM (continued)

Invoice — Macon Office Supply

Macon Office Supply
8125 N. Dale Mabry
Tampa, FL 33618

INVOICE

TO: *Mike's Discount Golf*
8520 N. Dale Mabry
Tampa, FL 33618

DATE: *5/3/--*
INV. NO. *6434*

CUSTOMER P.O.	ORDER RECEIVED	ORDER SHIPPED	SALES REPRESENTATIVE	TERMS	CUSTOMER ACCOUNT
629	*4/10/--*	*Pick up*	*Danny S.*	*Net 30*	———

QTY	ITEM	ITEM DESCRIPTION	UNIT PRICE	TOTAL
1	*n/a*	*Custom printing of accounting documents*	$ *142.68*	$ *142.68*
		TOTAL		$ *142.68*

Invoice — Davidson Office Center

Davidson Office Center
29780 Highway 19 North
Palm Harbor, FL 34684

INVOICE

TO: Mike's Discount Golf
8520 N. Dale Mabry
Tampa, FL 33618

DATE: May 6, 20--
INV. NO. 9484
TERMS: Cash

QUANTITY	PART NO.	DESCRIPTION	UNIT PRICE	TOTAL
2	9444	Tape dispenser	$ 9.95	$ 19.90
4	1648	8" × 11" Envelopes, box of 25	12.99	51.96
3	136-48	Pens	6.20	18.60
3	136-86	White board marker, black	1.99	5.97
		SUBTOTAL		$ 96.43
		TAX		6.75
		TOTAL		$ 103.18

Statement — Southern Electric

Southern Electric
P.O. Box 1342
Tampa, FL 33602

61564

May 8, 20 --

TO: *Mike's Discount Golf*
8520 N. Dale Mabry
Tampa, FL 33618

	This Month	Last Month		
Kilowatts	*2,488*	*2,348*	*Paid this amount* ————→	$ *418.15*
per Day	*80*	*78*		

Serving Your Energy Needs Since 1948

Eastern Tennis Mfg. 1633 NW 37th Ave. Miami, FL 33125		**INVOICE**		DATE: *5/16/20--* INV. NO. *16489* TERMS: *Cash*
		TO: *Mike's Discount Golf* *8520 N. Dale Mabry* *Tampa, FL 33618*		

QUANTITY	CAT. NO.	DESCRIPTION	UNIT PRICE	TOTAL
3	*9448*	*Tennis ball machine*	*$1,495.00*	*$ 4,485.00*
		TOTAL		*$ 4,485.00*

Veteran Support Society

P.O. Box 1223
Brandon, FL 33619

TO: Mike's Discount Golf 8520 N. Dale Mabry Tampa, FL 33618	May 20, 20-- Invoice No. 4688 Terms: Cash

Hole sponsorship of golf tournament benefiting Veteran Support Society shelter project	*$ 1,500.00*
Four-player green fee	*400.00*
	$ 1,900.00

Thank you for your support!

1-S SOURCE DOCUMENTS PROBLEM (concluded)

Lake Michigan Fabrics 7542 Lakefront Avenue Evanston, IL 60204		INVOICE			
			DATE:	5/28/--	
	TO: Mike's Discount Golf 8520 N. Dale Mabry Tampa, FL 33618		INV. NO.	48942	
			TERMS:	Cash	

QUANTITY	PART	DESCRIPTION	UNIT PRICE	TOTAL	
15	B164	Golf netting	$165.50	$	2,482.50
		TOTAL		$	2,482.50

PETTY CASH REPORT

Date: May 31, 20— **Custodian:** Sandy Adams

	Explanation		Reconciliation	Replenish Amount
Fund Total			250.00	
Payments:	Supplies	64.21		
	Advertising—Tennis	50.00		
	Miscellaneous	31.14		
Less:	Total payments		145.35	→ 145.35
Equals:	Recorded amount on hand		104.65	
Less:	Actual amount on hand		104.65	
Equals:	Cash short (over)		——	→ ——
Amount to Replenish				145.35

Name	Perfect Score	Your Score
Analyzing Departmental Accounting Procedures	15 Pts.	
Analyzing Departmental Sales and Cash Receipts	13 Pts.	
Analyzing Transactions Recorded in Special Journals	12 Pts.	
Total	40 Pts.	

Part One—Analyzing Departmental Accounting Procedures

Directions: Place a *T* for True or an *F* for False in the Answers column to show whether each of the following statements is true or false.

Answers

1. Records of departmental operating expenses are necessary to determine departmental gross profit from operations. (p. 38)   **1.** _____

2. In a departmental business, each sales invoice shows the amount of merchandise sold by department. (p. 38)   **2.** _____

3. Preparing two copies of a sales invoice provides a copy for the customer and a copy for the business to use for journalizing the transaction. (p. 38)   **3.** _____

4. Each departmental sales journal entry is posted individually as a credit to the appropriate customer's account. (p. 41)   **4.** _____

5. After posting a line of a departmental sales journal, the customer number is recorded in the journal's Post. Ref. column. (p. 41)   **5.** _____

6. The vendor prepares a debit memorandum for a sales returns and allowances transaction. (p. 43)   **6.** _____

7. An account showing deductions from a sales account is known as a contra cost account. (p. 44)   **7.** _____

8. A cash discount on a sale taken by the customer is called a sales discount. (p. 47)   **8.** _____

9. A departmental cash receipts journal contains a Cash Debit column for each department. (p. 48)   **9.** _____

10. Both the debit part and the credit parts of a cash or credit card sales transaction are entered in special amount columns in a departmental cash receipts journal. (p. 49)   **10.** _____

11. Each amount in the Accounts Receivable Credit column of a departmental cash receipts journal is posted individually to the accounts receivable ledger. (p. 52)   **11.** _____

12. Each amount in the Accounts Receivable Credit column of a departmental cash receipts journal is posted when the transaction is recorded in the cash receipts journal. (p. 52)   **12.** _____

13. Each amount in the Cash Debit column of a departmental cash receipts journal is posted individually to the debit side of the Cash account. (p. 52)   **13.** _____

14. The total of each Sales Credit column of a departmental cash receipts journal is posted to a general ledger account. (p. 52)   **14.** _____

15. After the totals of special amount columns have been posted, the general ledger account numbers are written in parentheses below the totals of the special columns in the cash receipts journal. (p. 52)   **15.** _____

Part Two—Analyzing Departmental Sales and Cash Receipts

Directions: For each item below, select the choice that best completes the sentence. Print the letter identifying your choice in the Answers column.

1. One item of information available through a departmental accounting system is the (A) net income or net loss for each department (B) gross profit from operations for each department (C) administrative expenses for each department (D) total operating expenses for each department. (p. 38)

    1. _____

2. The source document for recording a transaction in a departmental sales journal is (A) a cash register tape (B) a memorandum (C) a sales invoice (D) an adding machine tape. (p. 38)

    2. _____

3. Recording all sales at the time of sale, regardless of when payment is made, is an application of the (A) Going Concern concept (B) Realization of Revenue concept (C) Matching Expenses with Revenue concept (D) Historical Cost concept. (p. 38)

    3. _____

4. When audio equipment subject to sales tax is sold on account, Accounts Receivable is (A) debited for the amount of merchandise sold (B) debited for the amount of merchandise sold plus the sales tax on the merchandise (C) credited for the amount of merchandise sold (D) not affected. (p. 40)

    4. _____

5. In a departmental business, when audio equipment is sold on account, (A) Sales is debited (B) Sales—Audio is debited (C) Sales is credited (D) Sales—Audio is credited. (p. 40)

    5. _____

6. Each amount in the Accounts Receivable Debit column of a departmental sales journal is (A) posted as a debit to a customer's account (B) posted as a credit to a customer's account (C) posted to a controlling account (D) not posted. (p. 41)

    6. _____

7. The total of each column in a departmental sales journal is (A) posted daily (B) posted weekly (C) posted at the end of the month (D) posted when the page is filled or at the end of the month. (p. 42)

    7. _____

8. The account credited when a customer returns merchandise or is granted an allowance is (A) Accounts Payable (B) Sales Returns (C) the appropriate departmental sales account (D) none of these. (p. 43)

    8. _____

9. The source document for a sales returns and allowances transaction is (A) a sales invoice (B) a debit memorandum (C) a credit memorandum (D) none of these. (p. 43)

    9. _____

10. Sales returns and allowances are posted (A) monthly to a customer's account in the general ledger (B) frequently to a customer's account in the general ledger (C) monthly to a customer's account in the accounts receivable ledger (D) to the customer's account in the accounts receivable ledger and the general ledger when the transaction is journalized. (p. 45)

    10. _____

11. A business offers a sales discount (A) because of state laws (B) to encourage early payment (C) to get repeat business from the customer (D) none of these. (p. 47)

    11. _____

12. The terms 2/10, n/30 mean (A) a 2% sales discount may be deducted if sales on account are paid within 30 days of the invoice date (B) a 2% sales discount may be deducted if sales on account are paid within 10 days (C) all sales on account must be paid within 30 days (D) B and C. (p. 47)

    12. _____

13. Credit card sales are recorded in the cash receipts journal because (A) the cash is usually deposited in the cash account in two or three days (B) government policy requires immediate payment (C) credit card companies are not included in the accounts receivable ledger (D) this procedure is the first step in collecting from credit card companies. (p. 49)

    13. _____

Part Three—Analyzing Transactions Recorded in Special Journals

Directions: In Answers Column 1, print the abbreviation for the journal in which each transaction is to be recorded. In Answers Columns 2 and 3, print the letters identifying the accounts to be debited and credited for each transaction.

SJ—Sales journal; **CRJ**—Cash receipts journal; **GJ**—General journal

Account Titles	Transactions	Answers Journal	Debit	Credit
A. Cash	**1-2-3.** Sold merchandise on account to Tom Jenkins, plus sales tax. (p. 40)	**1.** _____	**2.** _____	**3.** _____
B. Accounts Receivable				
C. Sales Tax Payable	**4-5-6.** Granted credit to Tom Jenkins for returned merchandise. (p. 43)	**4.** _____	**5.** _____	**6.** _____
D. Sales	**7-8-9.** Received cash on account from Hanna Nelson, less sales discount. (p. 48)	**7.** _____	**8.** _____	**9.** _____
E. Sales Discount				
F. Sales Returns and Allowances	**10-11-12.** Recorded cash and credit card sales, plus sales tax. (p. 49)	**10.** _____	**11.** _____	**12.** _____
G. Tom Jenkins				
H. Hanna Nelson				

2-1 WORK TOGETHER (LO2, 3, 4, 5), p. 46

Journalizing and posting departmental sales on account and sales returns and allowances

1., 2.

SALES JOURNAL

PAGE

	DATE	ACCOUNT DEBITED	SALE NO.	POST. REF.	ACCOUNTS RECEIVABLE DEBIT 1	SALES TAX PAYABLE CREDIT 2	SALES CREDIT CHAIRS 3	SALES CREDIT DESKS 4	
1									1
2									2
3									3
4									4
5									5
6									6
7									7
8									8
9									9
10									10
11									11

GENERAL JOURNAL

PAGE

	DATE	ACCOUNT TITLE	DOC. NO.	POST. REF.	DEBIT	CREDIT	
1							1
2							2
3							3
4							4
5							5
6							6
7							7
8							8
9							9
10							10
11							11
12							12
13							13
14							14

1.

ACCOUNTS RECEIVABLE LEDGER

CUSTOMER Davenport Corp.   CUSTOMER NO. 110

DATE		ITEM	POST. REF.	DEBIT	CREDIT	DEBIT BALANCE
20-- Sept.	1	Balance	✔			1 5 3 3 00

CUSTOMER Grasson, Inc.   CUSTOMER NO. 120

DATE		ITEM	POST. REF.	DEBIT	CREDIT	DEBIT BALANCE
20-- Sept.	1	Balance	✔			1 6 3 4 00

CUSTOMER LKL Products Co.   CUSTOMER NO. 130

DATE		ITEM	POST. REF.	DEBIT	CREDIT	DEBIT BALANCE
20-- Sept.	1	Balance	✔			5 2 5 00

CUSTOMER United Charities   CUSTOMER NO. 140

DATE		ITEM	POST. REF.	DEBIT	CREDIT	DEBIT BALANCE
20-- Sept.	1	Balance	✔			8 5 5 00

2-1 WORK TOGETHER (concluded)

2.   **GENERAL LEDGER**

ACCOUNT Accounts Receivable   ACCOUNT NO. 1205

DATE		ITEM	POST. REF.	DEBIT	CREDIT	BALANCE DEBIT	BALANCE CREDIT
20-- Sept.	1	Balance	✔			16 762 50	

ACCOUNT Sales Tax Payable   ACCOUNT NO. 2110

DATE		ITEM	POST. REF.	DEBIT	CREDIT	BALANCE DEBIT	BALANCE CREDIT
20-- Sept.	1	Balance	✔				7 15 75

ACCOUNT Sales—Chairs   ACCOUNT NO. 4105

DATE		ITEM	POST. REF.	DEBIT	CREDIT	BALANCE DEBIT	BALANCE CREDIT
20-- Sept.	1	Balance	✔				54 367 95

ACCOUNT Sales Returns and Allowances—Chairs   ACCOUNT NO. 4115

DATE		ITEM	POST. REF.	DEBIT	CREDIT	BALANCE DEBIT	BALANCE CREDIT
20-- Sept.	1	Balance	✔			1 955 76	

ACCOUNT Sales—Desks   ACCOUNT NO. 4205

DATE		ITEM	POST. REF.	DEBIT	CREDIT	BALANCE DEBIT	BALANCE CREDIT
20-- Sept.	1	Balance	✔				49 087 98

ACCOUNT Sales Returns and Allowances—Desks   ACCOUNT NO. 4215

DATE		ITEM	POST. REF.	DEBIT	CREDIT	BALANCE DEBIT	BALANCE CREDIT
20-- Sept.	1	Balance	✔			2 421 67	

Journalizing and posting departmental sales on account and sales returns and allowances

1., 2.

SALES JOURNAL

PAGE

	DATE	ACCOUNT DEBITED	SALE NO.	POST. REF.	1 ACCOUNTS RECEIVABLE DEBIT	2 SALES TAX PAYABLE CREDIT	SALES CREDIT 3 EQUIPMENT	4 ACCESSORIES	
1									1
2									2
3									3
4									4
5									5
6									6
7									7
8									8
9									9
10									10
11									11

GENERAL JOURNAL

PAGE

	DATE	ACCOUNT TITLE	DOC. NO.	POST. REF.	DEBIT	CREDIT	
1							1
2							2
3							3
4							4
5							5
6							6
7							7
8							8
9							9
10							10
11							11
12							12
13							13
14							14

2-1 **ON YOUR OWN (continued)**

1.   **ACCOUNTS RECEIVABLE LEDGER**

CUSTOMER Mason Dent   CUSTOMER NO. 110

DATE		ITEM	POST. REF.	DEBIT	CREDIT	DEBIT BALANCE
20-- Oct.	1	Balance	✔			6 4 0 62

CUSTOMER Mountain Pass High School   CUSTOMER NO. 120

DATE		ITEM	POST. REF.	DEBIT	CREDIT	DEBIT BALANCE
20-- Oct.	1	Balance	✔			1 7 2 6 00

CUSTOMER Davis Reese   CUSTOMER NO. 130

DATE		ITEM	POST. REF.	DEBIT	CREDIT	DEBIT BALANCE
20-- Oct.	1	Balance	✔			1 6 4 34

CUSTOMER Sara Stennis   CUSTOMER NO. 140

DATE		ITEM	POST. REF.	DEBIT	CREDIT	DEBIT BALANCE
20-- Oct.	1	Balance	✔			5 3 23

2. **GENERAL LEDGER**

ACCOUNT Accounts Receivable ACCOUNT NO. 1205

DATE		ITEM	POST. REF.	DEBIT	CREDIT	BALANCE	
						DEBIT	CREDIT
Oct. 20--	1	Balance	✔			10 9 8 3 64	

ACCOUNT Sales Tax Payable ACCOUNT NO. 2110

DATE		ITEM	POST. REF.	DEBIT	CREDIT	BALANCE	
						DEBIT	CREDIT
Oct. 20--	1	Balance	✔				6 3 5 23

ACCOUNT Sales—Equipment ACCOUNT NO. 4105

DATE		ITEM	POST. REF.	DEBIT	CREDIT	BALANCE	
						DEBIT	CREDIT
Oct. 20--	1	Balance	✔				87 6 2 7 23

ACCOUNT Sales Returns and Allowances—Equipment ACCOUNT NO. 4115

DATE		ITEM	POST. REF.	DEBIT	CREDIT	BALANCE	
						DEBIT	CREDIT
Oct. 20--	1	Balance	✔			3 6 5 3 44	

ACCOUNT Sales—Accessories ACCOUNT NO. 4205

DATE		ITEM	POST. REF.	DEBIT	CREDIT	BALANCE	
						DEBIT	CREDIT
Oct. 20--	1	Balance	✔				27 5 4 3 16

ACCOUNT Sales Returns and Allowances—Accessories ACCOUNT NO. 4215

DATE		ITEM	POST. REF.	DEBIT	CREDIT	BALANCE	
						DEBIT	CREDIT
Oct. 20--	1	Balance	✔			2 6 4 7 97	

Name _____ Date _____ Class _____

Journalizing and posting departmental cash receipts

1., 2.

2-2 **WORK TOGETHER (LO7, 8), p. 54**

CASH RECEIPTS JOURNAL

PAGE _____

			GENERAL		ACCOUNTS RECEIVABLE CREDIT	SALES TAX PAYABLE CREDIT	SALES CREDIT		SALES DISCOUNT DEBIT		CASH DEBIT
DATE	ACCOUNT TITLE	DOC. NO.	POST. REF.	DEBIT	CREDIT			HARDWARE	LUMBER	HARDWARE	LUMBER	
				1	2	3	4	5	6	7	8	9

1.   **ACCOUNTS RECEIVABLE LEDGER**

CUSTOMER Andrews Homes   CUSTOMER NO. 110

DATE		ITEM	POST. REF.	DEBIT	CREDIT	DEBIT BALANCE
20-- Mar.	1	Balance	✔			14 8 1 4 97

CUSTOMER Estate Housing   CUSTOMER NO. 120

DATE		ITEM	POST. REF.	DEBIT	CREDIT	DEBIT BALANCE
20-- Mar.	1	Balance	✔			9 2 4 8 17
	3		G3		8 3 3 02	8 4 1 5 15

CUSTOMER Lisle Construction   CUSTOMER NO. 130

DATE		ITEM	POST. REF.	DEBIT	CREDIT	DEBIT BALANCE
20-- Mar.	12		S3	2 4 7 3 61		2 4 7 3 61
	16		G3		3 2 5 51	2 1 4 8 10

2-2 WORK TOGETHER (continued)

2.   **GENERAL LEDGER**

ACCOUNT Cash   ACCOUNT NO. 1105

DATE		ITEM	POST. REF.	DEBIT	CREDIT	BALANCE DEBIT	BALANCE CREDIT
Mar. 20--	1	Balance	✔			14 5 8 9 15	

ACCOUNT Accounts Receivable   ACCOUNT NO. 1205

DATE		ITEM	POST. REF.	DEBIT	CREDIT	BALANCE DEBIT	BALANCE CREDIT
Mar. 20--	1	Balance	✔			32 1 5 4 67	
	3		G3		8 3 3 02	31 3 2 1 65	
	16		G3		3 2 5 51	30 9 9 6 14	

ACCOUNT Sales Tax Payable   ACCOUNT NO. 2110

DATE		ITEM	POST. REF.	DEBIT	CREDIT	BALANCE DEBIT	BALANCE CREDIT
Mar. 20--	1	Balance	✔				4 8 5 15
	3		G3	5 8 12			4 2 7 03
	16		G3	2 2 71			4 0 4 32

ACCOUNT Sales—Hardware   ACCOUNT NO. 4105

DATE		ITEM	POST. REF.	DEBIT	CREDIT	BALANCE DEBIT	BALANCE CREDIT
Mar. 20--	1	Balance	✔				22 1 8 4 17

ACCOUNT Sales Discount—Hardware   ACCOUNT NO. 4110

DATE	ITEM	POST. REF.	DEBIT	CREDIT	BALANCE DEBIT	BALANCE CREDIT
20-- Mar. 1	Balance	✔			3 2 4 94	

ACCOUNT Sales—Lumber   ACCOUNT NO. 4205

DATE	ITEM	POST. REF.	DEBIT	CREDIT	BALANCE DEBIT	BALANCE CREDIT
20-- Mar. 1	Balance	✔				29 4 8 1 31

ACCOUNT Sales Discount—Lumber   ACCOUNT NO. 4210

DATE	ITEM	POST. REF.	DEBIT	CREDIT	BALANCE DEBIT	BALANCE CREDIT
20-- Mar. 1	Balance	✔			6 1 4 19	

2-2 ON YOUR OWN (LO7, 8), p. 54

Journalizing and posting departmental cash receipts

1., 2.

CASH RECEIPTS JOURNAL

PAGE ____

			GENERAL		ACCOUNTS RECEIVABLE CREDIT	SALES TAX PAYABLE CREDIT	SALES CREDIT		SALES DISCOUNT DEBIT		CASH DEBIT
DATE	ACCOUNT TITLE	DOC. NO.	POST. REF.	DEBIT	CREDIT			FLOWERS	PLANTS	FLOWERS	PLANTS	
				1	2	3	4	5	6	7	8	9
1												
2												
3												
4												
5												
6												
7												
8												
9												
10												
11												
12												
13												
14												
15												
16												
17												
18												
19												
20												
21												

1.   **ACCOUNTS RECEIVABLE LEDGER**

CUSTOMER Bakersville Gardens   CUSTOMER NO. 110

DATE		ITEM	POST. REF.	DEBIT	CREDIT	DEBIT BALANCE
20-- Apr.	1	Balance	✔			1 1 4 7 05

CUSTOMER Grendon Clinic   CUSTOMER NO. 120

DATE		ITEM	POST. REF.	DEBIT	CREDIT	DEBIT BALANCE
20-- Apr.	1	Balance	✔			4 1 4 19
	5		G3		3 5 20	3 7 8 99

CUSTOMER Hillside Manor   CUSTOMER NO. 130

DATE		ITEM	POST. REF.	DEBIT	CREDIT	DEBIT BALANCE
20-- Apr.	1	Balance	✔			6 1 5 17

CUSTOMER Platte Hotels   CUSTOMER NO. 140

DATE		ITEM	POST. REF.	DEBIT	CREDIT	DEBIT BALANCE
20-- Apr.	18		S4	8 4 1 95		8 4 1 95
	22		G5		2 9 4 33	5 4 7 62

2-2 ON YOUR OWN (continued)

2. **GENERAL LEDGER**

ACCOUNT Cash · ACCOUNT NO. 1105

DATE		ITEM	POST. REF.	DEBIT	CREDIT	BALANCE DEBIT	BALANCE CREDIT
Apr.	1	Balance	✔			6 4 9 8 17	

ACCOUNT Accounts Receivable · ACCOUNT NO. 1205

DATE		ITEM	POST. REF.	DEBIT	CREDIT	BALANCE DEBIT	BALANCE CREDIT
Apr.	1	Balance	✔			18 4 8 9 69	
	5		G3		3 5 20	18 4 5 4 49	
	22		G3		2 9 4 33	18 1 6 0 16	

ACCOUNT Sales Tax Payable · ACCOUNT NO. 2110

DATE		ITEM	POST. REF.	DEBIT	CREDIT	BALANCE DEBIT	BALANCE CREDIT
Apr.	1	Balance	✔				8 9 5 21
	5		G3	2 15			8 9 3 06
	22		G3	1 7 96			8 7 5 10

ACCOUNT Sales—Flowers · ACCOUNT NO. 4105

DATE		ITEM	POST. REF.	DEBIT	CREDIT	BALANCE DEBIT	BALANCE CREDIT
Apr.	1	Balance	✔				14 8 9 4 11

ACCOUNT Sales Discount—Flowers   ACCOUNT NO. 4110

DATE		ITEM	POST. REF.	DEBIT	CREDIT	BALANCE DEBIT	BALANCE CREDIT
20-- Apr.	1	Balance	✔			6 9 49	

ACCOUNT Sales—Plants   ACCOUNT NO. 4205

DATE		ITEM	POST. REF.	DEBIT	CREDIT	BALANCE DEBIT	BALANCE CREDIT
20-- Apr.	1	Balance	✔				16 9 9 4 08

ACCOUNT Sales Discount—Plants   ACCOUNT NO. 4210

DATE		ITEM	POST. REF.	DEBIT	CREDIT	BALANCE DEBIT	BALANCE CREDIT
20-- Apr.	1	Balance	✔			1 0 4 15	

2-1 APPLICATION PROBLEM (LO2, 3, 4, 5), p. 58

Journalizing and posting departmental sales on account and sales returns and allowances

1., 2.

SALES JOURNAL

PAGE

	DATE	ACCOUNT DEBITED	SALE NO.	POST. REF.	ACCOUNTS RECEIVABLE DEBIT (1)	SALES TAX PAYABLE CREDIT (2)	SALES CREDIT CHAIRS (3)	SALES CREDIT TABLES (4)	
1									1
2									2
3									3
4									4
5									5
6									6
7									7
8									8
9									9
10									10
11									11

GENERAL JOURNAL

PAGE

	DATE	ACCOUNT TITLE	DOC. NO.	POST. REF.	DEBIT	CREDIT	
1							1
2							2
3							3
4							4
5							5
6							6
7							7
8							8
9							9
10							10
11							11
12							12
13							13
14							14

1.   **ACCOUNTS RECEIVABLE LEDGER**

CUSTOMER Elrod Clinic   CUSTOMER NO. 110

DATE		ITEM	POST. REF.	DEBIT	CREDIT	DEBIT BALANCE
20-- May	1	Balance	✔			9 4 5 25

CUSTOMER Lincoln City Schools   CUSTOMER NO. 120

DATE		ITEM	POST. REF.	DEBIT	CREDIT	DEBIT BALANCE
20-- May	1	Balance	✔			2 4 8 5 30

CUSTOMER Anna Patrick   CUSTOMER NO. 130

DATE		ITEM	POST. REF.	DEBIT	CREDIT	DEBIT BALANCE

CUSTOMER Keller Stendal   CUSTOMER NO. 140

DATE		ITEM	POST. REF.	DEBIT	CREDIT	DEBIT BALANCE
20-- May	1	Balance	✔			3 2 1 5 84

2-1 APPLICATION PROBLEM (concluded)

2.   **GENERAL LEDGER**

ACCOUNT Accounts Receivable   ACCOUNT NO. 1205

DATE		ITEM	POST. REF.	DEBIT	CREDIT	BALANCE DEBIT	BALANCE CREDIT
20-- May	1	Balance	✔			16 4 5 8 02	

ACCOUNT Sales Tax Payable   ACCOUNT NO. 2110

DATE		ITEM	POST. REF.	DEBIT	CREDIT	BALANCE DEBIT	BALANCE CREDIT
20-- May	1	Balance	✔				5 5 1 19

ACCOUNT Sales—Chairs   ACCOUNT NO. 4105

DATE		ITEM	POST. REF.	DEBIT	CREDIT	BALANCE DEBIT	BALANCE CREDIT
20-- May	1	Balance	✔				151 1 9 4 92

ACCOUNT Sales Returns and Allowances—Chairs   ACCOUNT NO. 4115

DATE		ITEM	POST. REF.	DEBIT	CREDIT	BALANCE DEBIT	BALANCE CREDIT
20-- May	1	Balance	✔			4 1 4 8 61	

ACCOUNT Sales—Tables   ACCOUNT NO. 4205

DATE		ITEM	POST. REF.	DEBIT	CREDIT	BALANCE DEBIT	BALANCE CREDIT
20-- May	1	Balance	✔				134 2 1 8 95

ACCOUNT Sales Returns and Allowances—Tables   ACCOUNT NO. 4215

DATE		ITEM	POST. REF.	DEBIT	CREDIT	BALANCE DEBIT	BALANCE CREDIT
20-- May	1	Balance	✔			3 4 9 5 18	

Journalizing and posting departmental cash receipts

1., 2.

CASH RECEIPTS JOURNAL

PAGE 9

DATE	ACCOUNT TITLE	DOC. NO.	POST. REF.	GENERAL DEBIT 1	GENERAL CREDIT 2	ACCOUNTS RECEIVABLE CREDIT 3	SALES TAX PAYABLE CREDIT 4	SALES CREDIT PARTS 5	SALES CREDIT TIRES 6	SALES DISCOUNT DEBIT PARTS 7	SALES DISCOUNT DEBIT TIRES 8	CASH DEBIT 9
												1
												2
												3
												4
												5
												6
												7
												8
												9
												10
												11
												12
												13
												14
												15
												16
												17
												18
												19
												20
												21

2-2 APPLICATION PROBLEM (continued)

1.

ACCOUNTS RECEIVABLE LEDGER

CUSTOMER Bob's Auto Repair   CUSTOMER NO. 110

DATE		ITEM	POST. REF.	DEBIT	CREDIT	DEBIT BALANCE
20-- June	1	Balance	✔			8 4 2 62

CUSTOMER Delta Transportation   CUSTOMER NO. 120

DATE		ITEM	POST. REF.	DEBIT	CREDIT	DEBIT BALANCE
20-- June	1	Balance	✔			3 2 2 1 94
	20		G9		2 8 0 17	2 9 4 1 77

CUSTOMER Foreign Car Center   CUSTOMER NO. 130

DATE		ITEM	POST. REF.	DEBIT	CREDIT	DEBIT BALANCE
20-- June	1	Balance	✔			3 2 4 19

CUSTOMER Sam's Service Station   CUSTOMER NO. 140

DATE		ITEM	POST. REF.	DEBIT	CREDIT	DEBIT BALANCE
20-- June	1	Balance	✔			1 8 4 2 21

2. **GENERAL LEDGER**

ACCOUNT Cash   ACCOUNT NO. 1105

DATE		ITEM	POST. REF.	DEBIT	CREDIT	BALANCE	
						DEBIT	CREDIT
20-- June	1	Balance	✔			4 2 1 8 94	

ACCOUNT Accounts Receivable   ACCOUNT NO. 1205

DATE		ITEM	POST. REF.	DEBIT	CREDIT	BALANCE	
						DEBIT	CREDIT
20-- June	1	Balance	✔			22 1 4 9 91	
	20		G9		2 8 0 17	21 8 6 9 74	

ACCOUNT Sales Tax Payable   ACCOUNT NO. 2110

DATE		ITEM	POST. REF.	DEBIT	CREDIT	BALANCE	
						DEBIT	CREDIT
20-- June	1	Balance	✔				2 2 4 8 31
	20		G9	1 7 10			2 2 3 1 21

ACCOUNT Sales—Parts   ACCOUNT NO. 4105

DATE		ITEM	POST. REF.	DEBIT	CREDIT	BALANCE	
						DEBIT	CREDIT
20-- June	1	Balance	✔				54 9 1 8 71

2-2 **APPLICATION PROBLEM (concluded)**

ACCOUNT Sales Discount—Parts   ACCOUNT NO. 4110

DATE		ITEM	POST. REF.	DEBIT	CREDIT	BALANCE	
						DEBIT	CREDIT
20-- June	1	Balance	✔			3 4 5 14	

ACCOUNT Sales—Tires   ACCOUNT NO. 4205

DATE		ITEM	POST. REF.	DEBIT	CREDIT	BALANCE	
						DEBIT	CREDIT
20-- June	1	Balance	✔				85 1 4 1 31

ACCOUNT Sales Discount—Tires   ACCOUNT NO. 4210

DATE		ITEM	POST. REF.	DEBIT	CREDIT	BALANCE	
						DEBIT	CREDIT
20-- June	1	Balance	✔			1 8 4 22	

2-M MASTERY PROBLEM (LO2, 3, 4, 5, 7, 8), p. 59

Journalizing departmental sales, sales returns and allowances, and cash receipts

1., 2.

SALES JOURNAL PAGE

						1	2	3	4	
	DATE	ACCOUNT DEBITED	SALE NO.	POST. REF.	ACCOUNTS RECEIVABLE DEBIT		SALES TAX PAYABLE CREDIT	SALES CREDIT EQUIPMENT	SUPPLIES	
1										1
2										2
3										3
4										4
5										5
6										6
7										7
8										8
9										9
10										10
11										11

GENERAL JOURNAL PAGE

	DATE	ACCOUNT TITLE	DOC. NO.	POST. REF.	DEBIT	CREDIT	
1							1
2							2
3							3
4							4
5							5
6							6
7							7
8							8
9							9
10							10
11							11
12							12
13							13
14							14

2-M MASTERY PROBLEM (continued)

1., 3.

CASH RECEIPTS JOURNAL

PAGE 9

				GENERAL		ACCOUNTS RECEIVABLE CREDIT	SALES TAX PAYABLE CREDIT	SALES CREDIT		SALES DISCOUNT DEBIT		CASH DEBIT
DATE	ACCOUNT TITLE	DOC. NO.	POST. REF.	DEBIT	CREDIT			EQUIPMENT	SUPPLIES	EQUIPMENT	SUPPLIES	
				1	2	3	4	5	6	7	8	9
1												
2												
3												
4												
5												
6												
7												
8												
9												
10												
11												
12												
13												
14												
15												
16												
17												
18												
19												
20												
21												

1.

ACCOUNTS RECEIVABLE LEDGER

CUSTOMER BLC Storage   CUSTOMER NO. 110

DATE	ITEM	POST. REF.	DEBIT	CREDIT	DEBIT BALANCE

CUSTOMER Eastern Realty   CUSTOMER NO. 120

DATE	ITEM	POST. REF.	DEBIT	CREDIT	DEBIT BALANCE

CUSTOMER Lakeland Church   CUSTOMER NO. 130

DATE	ITEM	POST. REF.	DEBIT	CREDIT	DEBIT BALANCE
20-- May 1	Balance	✔			3 1 5 74

CUSTOMER Natural Products   CUSTOMER NO. 140

DATE	ITEM	POST. REF.	DEBIT	CREDIT	DEBIT BALANCE
20-- May 1	Balance	✔			1 8 2 0 94

2-M MASTERY PROBLEM (continued)

2., 3.   **GENERAL LEDGER**

ACCOUNT Cash   ACCOUNT NO. 1105

DATE	ITEM	POST. REF.	DEBIT	CREDIT	BALANCE DEBIT	BALANCE CREDIT
May 1 (20--)	Balance	✔			6 1 8 4 19	

ACCOUNT Accounts Receivable   ACCOUNT NO. 1205

DATE	ITEM	POST. REF.	DEBIT	CREDIT	BALANCE DEBIT	BALANCE CREDIT
May 1 (20--)	Balance	✔			28 1 4 9 61	

ACCOUNT Sales Tax Payable   ACCOUNT NO. 2110

DATE	ITEM	POST. REF.	DEBIT	CREDIT	BALANCE DEBIT	BALANCE CREDIT
May 1 (20--)	Balance	✔				9 3 2 54

ACCOUNT Sales—Equipment   ACCOUNT NO. 4105

DATE	ITEM	POST. REF.	DEBIT	CREDIT	BALANCE DEBIT	BALANCE CREDIT
May 1 (20--)	Balance	✔				61 2 1 4 09

ACCOUNT Sales Discount—Equipment   ACCOUNT NO. 4110

DATE	ITEM	POST. REF.	DEBIT	CREDIT	BALANCE DEBIT	BALANCE CREDIT
20-- May 1	Balance	✔			2 4 1 10	

ACCOUNT Sales Returns and Allowances—Equipment   ACCOUNT NO. 4115

DATE	ITEM	POST. REF.	DEBIT	CREDIT	BALANCE DEBIT	BALANCE CREDIT
20-- May 1	Balance	✔			1 4 1 5 99	

ACCOUNT Sales—Supplies   ACCOUNT NO. 4205

DATE	ITEM	POST. REF.	DEBIT	CREDIT	BALANCE DEBIT	BALANCE CREDIT
20-- May 1	Balance	✔				38 4 1 0 07

ACCOUNT Sales Discount—Supplies   ACCOUNT NO. 4210

DATE	ITEM	POST. REF.	DEBIT	CREDIT	BALANCE DEBIT	BALANCE CREDIT
20-- May 1	Balance	✔			1 8 9 94	

ACCOUNT Sales Returns and Allowances—Supplies   ACCOUNT NO. 4215

DATE	ITEM	POST. REF.	DEBIT	CREDIT	BALANCE DEBIT	BALANCE CREDIT
20-- May 1	Balance	✔			1 0 9 4 61	

2-S SOURCE DOCUMENTS PROBLEM (LO2, 3, 4, 5, 7, 8), p. 59

Journalizing departmental sales, sales returns and allowances, and cash receipts

Ozark AV SHACK 5701 Madison Ave. Fort Smith, AR 72903		INVOICE		
	SOLD TO: Peter Simms 2345 S. Boston Street Fort Smith, AR 72903		DATE: 11/6/-- INV. NO.: 541 TERMS: n/30 CUST. NO.: 178	

QUANTITY	PART NO.	DESCRIPTION	UNIT PRICE	TOTAL
2	6345	54" Interactive HD television	$949.00	**$1,898.00**
		SUBTOTAL		**$1,898.00**
		TAX		142.35
		TOTAL		**$2,040.35**

Look to Ozark AV Shack for all your audio/video needs

Ozark AV SHACK 5701 Madison Ave. Fort Smith, AR 72903		INVOICE		
	SOLD TO: Janice Tillman 106 N. Plum Street Hackett, AR 72937		DATE: 11/15/-- INV. NO.: 542 TERMS: n/30 CUST. NO.: 184	

QUANTITY	PART NO.	DESCRIPTION	UNIT PRICE	TOTAL
1	948	Home theater sound system	$899.00	$ 899.00
2	732	48" SOUND BAR	149.95	**299.90**
3	733	54" SOUND BAR	199.95	**599.85**
		SUBTOTAL		**$1,798.75**
		TAX		134.91
		TOTAL		**$1,933.66**

Look to Ozark AV Shack for all your audio/video needs

Ozark AV SHACK
5701 Madison Ave.
Fort Smith, AR 72903

INVOICE

	SOLD TO:	Stan O'Brien		DATE:	11/22/--
		1406 Parkview Drive		INV. NO.:	543
		Van Buren, AR 72956		TERMS:	n/30
				CUST. NO.:	164

QUANTITY	PART NO.	DESCRIPTION	UNIT PRICE	TOTAL
1	1949	Premium in-wall surround system	$2,299.00	$2,299.00
		SUBTOTAL		$2,299.00
		TAX		172.43
		TOTAL		$2,471.43

Look to Ozark AV Shack for all your audio/video needs

Ozark AV SHACK
5701 Madison Ave.
Fort Smith, AR 72903

RECEIPT

FROM: *Daniel Campbell*

DATE: *11/6/--*
RECEIPT NO.: 569

PAYMENT METHOD	CHECK NO.	CUSTOMER ACCT. NO.	RECEIVED BY
Check	*1848*	*132*	*Sandi Blake*

DESCRIPTION	INVOICE	GROSS AMOUNT	DISCOUNT	CASH RECEIVED
On account (invoice was for video equipment)	*538*	*$1,112.31*	*$ 22.25*	*$1,090.06*
		TOTAL DISCOUNT	*$ 22.25*	
			TOTAL	*$1,090.06*

2-S SOURCE DOCUMENTS PROBLEM (continued)

Ozark AV SHACK
5701 Madison Ave.
Fort Smith, AR 72903

RECEIPT

FROM: _Stan O'Brien_

DATE: 11/7/--
RECEIPT NO.: 570

PAYMENT METHOD	CHECK NO.	CUSTOMER ACCT. NO.	RECEIVED BY
Check	944	164	Sandi Blake

DESCRIPTION	INVOICE	GROSS AMOUNT	DISCOUNT	CASH RECEIVED
On account (invoice was for audio equipment)	540	$ 349.18	$ 6.98	$ 342.20
		TOTAL DISCOUNT	$ 6.98	
			TOTAL	$ 342.20

Ozark AV SHACK
5701 Madison Ave.
Fort Smith, AR 72903

RECEIPT

FROM: _Peter Simms_

DATE: 11/15/--
RECEIPT NO.: 571

PAYMENT METHOD	CHECK NO.	CUSTOMER ACCT. NO.	RECEIVED BY
Check	532	178	Sally Richards

DESCRIPTION	INVOICE	GROSS AMOUNT	DISCOUNT	CASH RECEIVED
On account	501	$1,243.09	$ —	$1,243.09
On account	541	$2,040.35	$ 40.81	$1,999.54
		TOTAL DISCOUNT	$ 40.81	
			TOTAL	$3,242.63

Ozark AV SHACK
5701 Madison Ave.
Fort Smith, AR 72903

RECEIPT

FROM: _Janice Tillman_

DATE: 11/24/--

RECEIPT NO.: 572

PAYMENT METHOD	CHECK NO.	CUSTOMER ACCT. NO.	RECEIVED BY
Check	865	184	Sally Richards

DESCRIPTION	INVOICE	GROSS AMOUNT	DISCOUNT	CASH RECEIVED
Partial payment on account	542	$1,020.41	$ 20.41	$1,000.00

TOTAL DISCOUNT $ 20.41

TOTAL $1,000.00

Ozark AV SHACK
5701 Madison Ave.
Fort Smith, AR 72903

Credit Memorandum

TO: Daniel Campbell
152 S. Durant Street
Muldrow, OK 74948

DATE: 11/3/--

CM. NO.: 25

CUST. ID: 132

QUANTITY	ITEM NO.	DESCRIPTION	UNIT PRICE	TOTALS
1	7438	48" HD television	$499.00	$499.00
		SUBTOTAL		$499.00
		SALES TAX		37.43
		TOTAL		$536.43

Ozark AV SHACK
5701 Madison Ave.
Fort Smith, AR 72903

Credit Memorandum

TO: Janice Tillman
106 N. Plum Street
Hackett, AR 72937

DATE: 11/18/--

CM. NO.: 26

CUST. ID: 184

QUANTITY	ITEM NO.	DESCRIPTION	UNIT PRICE	TOTALS
2	732	48" Sound bar	$149.95	$299.90
		SUBTOTAL		$299.90
		SALES TAX		22.49
		TOTAL		$322.39

2-S **SOURCE DOCUMENTS PROBLEM (continued)**

TERMINAL SUMMARY		
Ozark AV Shack		
SUMMARY NO.:		32
DATE:		11/10/--
TIME:		18:30
VISA	023	
Sales		3,218.99
Sales Tax		241.42
Total		3,460.41
MasterCard	025	
Sales		3,418.13
Sales Tax		256.36
Total		3,674.49
Debit Cards	057	
Sales		6,419.36
Sales Tax		481.45
Total		6,900.81
Cash	121	
Sales		3,198.11
Sales Tax		239.86
Total		3,437.97
Totals		
Audio		7,841.91
Video		8,412.68
Sales Tax		1,219.09
Total		17,473.68

TERMINAL SUMMARY		
Ozark AV Shack		
SUMMARY NO.:		33
DATE:		11/20/--
TIME:		19:04
VISA	019	
Sales		2,814.11
Sales Tax		211.06
Total		3,025.17
MasterCard	017	
Sales		2,189.99
Sales Tax		164.25
Total		2,354.24
Debit Cards	062	
Sales		7,019.64
Sales Tax		526.47
Total		7,546.11
Cash	098	
Sales		2,991.61
Sales Tax		224.37
Total		3,215.98
Totals		
Audio		5,534.25
Video		9,481.10
Sales Tax		1,126.15
Total		16,141.50

SALES JOURNAL

PAGE

	DATE	ACCOUNT DEBITED	SALE NO.	POST. REF.	ACCOUNTS RECEIVABLE DEBIT 1	SALES TAX PAYABLE CREDIT 2	SALES CREDIT AUDIO 3	VIDEO 4	
1									1
2									2
3									3
4									4
5									5
6									6
7									7
8									8
9									9
10									10
11									11

1.

GENERAL JOURNAL

PAGE

	DATE	ACCOUNT TITLE	DOC. NO.	POST. REF.	DEBIT	CREDIT	
1							1
2							2
3							3
4							4
5							5
6							6
7							7
8							8
9							9
10							10
11							11
12							12
13							13
14							14

2-S SOURCE DOGUMENTS PROBLEM (continued)

1., 3.

CASH RECEIPTS JOURNAL

PAGE 9

DATE	ACCOUNT TITLE	DOC. NO.	POST. REF.	GENERAL DEBIT	GENERAL CREDIT	ACCOUNTS RECEIVABLE CREDIT	SALES TAX PAYABLE CREDIT	SALES CREDIT AUDIO	SALES CREDIT VIDEO	SALES DISCOUNT DEBIT AUDIO	SALES DISCOUNT DEBIT VIDEO	CASH DEBIT
				1	2	3	4	5	6	7	8	9

1. **ACCOUNTS RECEIVABLE LEDGER**

CUSTOMER Daniel Campbell   CUSTOMER NO. 132

DATE	ITEM	POST. REF.	DEBIT	CREDIT	DEBIT BALANCE
20-- Nov. 1	Balance	✔			1 6 4 8 74

CUSTOMER Stan O'Brien   CUSTOMER NO. 164

DATE	ITEM	POST. REF.	DEBIT	CREDIT	DEBIT BALANCE
20-- Nov. 1	Balance	✔			3 4 9 18

CUSTOMER Peter Simms   CUSTOMER NO. 178

DATE	ITEM	POST. REF.	DEBIT	CREDIT	DEBIT BALANCE
20-- Nov. 1	Balance	✔			1 2 4 3 09

CUSTOMER Janice Tillman   CUSTOMER NO. 184

DATE	ITEM	POST. REF.	DEBIT	CREDIT	DEBIT BALANCE

2-S SOURCE DOCUMENTS PROBLEM (continued)

2., 3.   **GENERAL LEDGER**

ACCOUNT Cash   ACCOUNT NO. 1105

DATE	ITEM	POST. REF.	DEBIT	CREDIT	BALANCE DEBIT	BALANCE CREDIT
20-- Nov. 1	Balance	✔			11 2 0 4 66	

ACCOUNT Accounts Receivable   ACCOUNT NO. 1205

DATE	ITEM	POST. REF.	DEBIT	CREDIT	BALANCE DEBIT	BALANCE CREDIT
20-- Nov. 1	Balance	✔			29 1 8 0 06	

ACCOUNT Sales Tax Payable   ACCOUNT NO. 2110

DATE	ITEM	POST. REF.	DEBIT	CREDIT	BALANCE DEBIT	BALANCE CREDIT
20-- Nov. 1	Balance	✔				2 2 1 9 94

ACCOUNT Sales—Audio   ACCOUNT NO. 4105

DATE	ITEM	POST. REF.	DEBIT	CREDIT	BALANCE DEBIT	BALANCE CREDIT
20-- Nov. 1	Balance	✔				108 1 8 4 99

ACCOUNT Sales Discount—Audio   ACCOUNT NO. 4110

DATE	ITEM	POST. REF.	DEBIT	CREDIT	BALANCE DEBIT	BALANCE CREDIT
20-- Nov. 1	Balance	✔			5 9 4 19	

ACCOUNT Sales Returns and Allowances—Audio   ACCOUNT NO. 4115

DATE	ITEM	POST. REF.	DEBIT	CREDIT	BALANCE DEBIT	BALANCE CREDIT
20-- Nov. 1	Balance	✔			6 1 4 8 28	

ACCOUNT Sales—Video   ACCOUNT NO. 4205

DATE	ITEM	POST. REF.	DEBIT	CREDIT	BALANCE DEBIT	BALANCE CREDIT
20-- Nov. 1	Balance	✔				154 8 1 9 10

ACCOUNT Sales Discount—Video   ACCOUNT NO. 4210

DATE	ITEM	POST. REF.	DEBIT	CREDIT	BALANCE DEBIT	BALANCE CREDIT
20-- Nov. 1	Balance	✔			7 1 4 19	

ACCOUNT Sales Returns and Allowances—Video   ACCOUNT NO. 4215

DATE	ITEM	POST. REF.	DEBIT	CREDIT	BALANCE DEBIT	BALANCE CREDIT
20-- Nov. 1	Balance	✔			9 1 4 8 31	

2-C CHALLENGE PROBLEM (LO7), p. 60

Journalizing departmental sales, sales returns and allowances, and cash receipts

1.

CASH RECEIPTS JOURNAL

PAGE _____

DATE	ACCOUNT TITLE	DOC. NO.	POST. REF.	GENERAL DEBIT	GENERAL CREDIT	ACCOUNTS RECEIVABLE CREDIT	SALES TAX PAYABLE CREDIT	SALES CREDIT PAINT	SALES CREDIT SUPPLIES	SALES DISCOUNT DEBIT PAINT	SALES DISCOUNT DEBIT SUPPLIES	CASH DEBIT
				1	2	3	4	5	6	7	8	9
													1
													2
													3
													4
													5
													6
													7
													8
													9
													10
													11
													12
													13

Study Guide 3

Name		Perfect Score	Your Score
	Analyzing Departmental Payroll Procedures	25 Pts.	
	Identifying Accounting Terms	11 Pts.	
	Analyzing Payroll Accounting	10 Pts.	
	Total	46 Pts.	

Part One—Analyzing Departmental Payroll Procedures

Directions: Place a *T* for True or an *F* for False in the Answers column to show whether each of the following statements is true or false.

Answers

1. Laws require employers to keep records of the payroll information and other payments related to employee services. (p. 64)   1. _____

2. Employers are required by law to withhold certain payroll taxes from employee salaries each pay period. (p. 64)   2. _____

3. The yearly report of an employee's earnings and deductions that is provided to the employee is Form W-2. (p. 64)   3. _____

4. Employers pay government agencies all payroll taxes withheld from employee salaries on an annual basis. (p. 64)   4. _____

5. By January 31, businesses must report to employees the earnings and amounts withheld for the previous calendar year. (p. 64)   5. _____

6. Payroll records must show an employee's earnings, amounts withheld, net amount paid, and the total amount of payroll taxes that a business must pay. (p. 64)   6. _____

7. Income and Medicare taxes are the only two federal taxes deducted from earnings of each employee. (p. 65)   7. _____

8. The amount of federal income tax to be withheld is determined solely by the number of withholding allowances. (p. 65)   8. _____

9. The Internal Revenue Service sets the tax base and the tax rates for the Social Security tax. (p. 65)   9. _____

10. Like Social Security, Medicare has a tax base. (p. 65)   10. _____

11. Laws for handling state, city, and county taxes vary. (p. 65)   11. _____

12. Other deductions from employee earnings include health insurance, life insurance, retirement plan contributions, and charitable contributions. (p. 65)   12. _____

13. All time worked in excess of 40 hours in any one week is considered overtime. (p. 66)   13. _____

14. Employees are paid two times the regular rate for overtime hours. (p. 66)   14. _____

15. Commissions, cost-of-living adjustments, a share of profits, and a bonus are included in an employee's earnings. (p. 67)   15. _____

16. In proving a payroll register's accuracy, the total of the Net Pay column is subtracted from the Total Deductions column. (p. 69)   16. _____

17. An employee's total earnings and deductions for the quarter are summarized on one line of the employee earnings record. (p. 73)   17. _____

18. After a biweekly payroll register has been completed, a check for the total earnings indicated on the payroll register is written for each employee. (p. 76)   18. _____

19. Transferring payroll amounts electronically from the employer's account to the employee's bank account is known as electronic funds transfer (EFT). (p. 76)

19. _____

20. Unemployment taxes are used to pay qualified workers cash benefits for limited periods of unemployment. (p. 77)

20. _____

21. Both employers and employees are required to pay a federal unemployment tax. (p. 78)

21. _____

22. The frequency of payments for federal, state, and local government taxes is determined by the amount of tax paid each year. (p. 80)

22. _____

23. If a business is classified as a monthly schedule depositor, the business must pay the total amount due by the 15th day of the following month. (p. 80)

23. _____

24. Only employers having total payroll taxes due greater than $1 million are required to use the Electronic Federal Tax Payment System. (p. 80)

24. _____

25. A memorandum with an attached receipt is the source document for a payment made using the Electronic Federal Tax Payment System. (p. 81)

25. _____

Part Two—Identifying Accounting Terms

Directions: Select the one term in Column I that best fits each definition in Column II. Print the letter identifying your choice in the Answers column.

Column I	Column II	Answers
A. automatic check deposit	1. The amount paid to an employee for every hour worked. (p. 64)	1. _____
B. electronic funds transfer (EFT)	2. A fixed annual sum of money divided among equal pay periods. (p. 64)	2. _____
C. employee earnings record	3. The number of days or weeks of work covered by an employee's paycheck. (p. 64)	3. _____
D. pay period	4. The total amount earned by all employees for a pay period. (p. 64)	4. _____
E. payroll	5. Taxes based on the payroll of a business. (p. 64)	5. _____
F. payroll register	6. A deduction from total earnings for each person legally supported by a taxpayer, including the employee. (p. 65)	6. _____
G. payroll taxes	7. The maximum amount of earnings on which a tax is calculated. (p. 65)	7. _____
H. salary	8. An accounting form that summarizes the earnings, deductions, and net pay of all employees for one pay period. (p. 68)	8. _____
I. tax base	9. A business form used to record details of an employee's earnings and deductions. (p. 73)	9. _____
J. wage	10. Depositing payroll checks directly to an employee's checking or savings account. (p. 76)	10. _____
K. withholding allowance	11. A computerized cash payments system that transfers funds without the use of checks, currency, or other paper documents. (p. 76)	11. _____

Part Three—Analyzing Payroll Accounting

Directions: For each item below, select the choice that best completes the sentence. Print the letter identifying your choice in the Answers column.

Answers

1. The Social Security tax provides insurance for (A) old-age (B) survivors (C) disability (D) all of the above. (p. 65)

   1. _____

2. In a biweekly payroll system employees are paid (A) once a week (B) twice a year (C) every two weeks (D) twice a month. (p. 66)

   2. _____

3. When employees are paid a percentage of sales in addition to their regular salary, the earnings are often referred to as (A) salary (B) pensions (C) commissions (D) wages. (p. 67)

   3. _____

4. The amount due an individual for a pay period, after deductions, is referred to as (A) regular earnings (B) overtime (C) total earnings (D) none of these. (p. 69)

   4. _____

5. When all employees have cashed their payroll checks, the balance of the payroll bank account (A) equals zero (B) equals the net pay for the period (C) equals total earnings for the period (D) none of these. (p. 76)

   5. _____

6. A payroll tax which the employer does not pay is (A) Social Security tax (B) Medicare tax (C) federal income tax (D) federal unemployment tax. (p. 78)

   6. _____

7. Social Security and Medicare taxes are paid by (A) the employees (B) the employer (C) both A and B (D) none of these. (p. 78)

   7. _____

8. A tax which is not deducted from employees' pay is (A) Medicare tax (B) state income tax (C) federal unemployment tax (D) federal income tax. (p. 78)

   8. _____

9. The frequency of employer payment of payroll taxes is determined by (A) the amount owed (B) the employer's geographic location (C) the type of business (D) none of these. (p. 80)

   9. _____

10. If the quarterly federal unemployment tax for a business is $500.00 or more, the business must (A) make the payment in the month following the end of the quarter (B) make one payment by January 31 of the following year (C) make the payment at the end of each month (D) make the payment at the end of each quarter. (p. 81)

    10. _____

3-1 WORK TOGETHER (LO2, 3), p. 74

Completing payroll records

1.

COMMISSIONS RECORD

EMPLOYEE NO. _____   EMPLOYEE NAME _____

PAY PERIOD ENDED _____   REGULAR BIWEEKLY SALARY _____

DEPARTMENT _____   POSITION _____

	Carpet	Tile	
Sales on Account	_____	_____	
Cash and Credit Card Sales	_____	_____	
equals Total Sales for the Month............................	_____	_____	
Less:			
Sales Discounts..	_____	_____	
Sales Returns and Allowances	_____	_____	
equals Total Reductions in Sales.............................	_____	_____	
Equals:			
Net Sales..	_____	_____	
times Commission Rate..	_____	_____	_____
equals Commission on Net Sales............................	_____	_____	_____

4.

EARNINGS RECORD FOR QUARTER ENDED

EMPLOYEE NO. _____ NAME _____ WITHHOLDING ALLOWANCES _____

HOURLY WAGE _____ SALARY _____ MARITAL STATUS _____ POSITION _____

DEPARTMENT _____

PAY PERIOD		TOTAL EARNINGS	DEDUCTIONS						NET PAY	ACCUMULATED EARNINGS
NO.	ENDED	1	FEDERAL INCOME TAX (2)	STATE INCOME TAX (3)	SOC. SEC. TAX (4)	MEDICARE TAX (5)	HEALTH INSURANCE (6)	RETIREMENT PLAN (7)	TOTAL (8) / NET PAY (9)	(10)
1										
2										
TOTALS										

2., 3.

PAYROLL REGISTER

SEMIMONTHLY PERIOD ENDED _____ DATE OF PAYMENT _____

EMPL. NO.	EMPLOYEE'S NAME	MARITAL STATUS	NO. OF ALLOWANCES	EARNINGS REGULAR (1)	OVERTIME (2)	COMMISSION (3)	TOTAL (4)	DEPARTMENT CARPET (5)	TILE (6)	ADMINISTRATIVE (7)	DEDUCTIONS FEDERAL INCOME TAX (8)	STATE INCOME TAX (9)	SOCIAL SECURITY TAX (10)	MEDICARE TAX (11)	HEALTH INSURANCE (12)	RETIREMENT PLAN (13)	TOTAL (14)	NET PAY (15)	CHECK NO.
22	Belizean, Thomas C.	M	4	800 00		6210 05	14210 05	3889 11	10321 94		33 00	28 42	88 11	20 61	90 00	65 00	325 14	1095 91	1
20	Foxworth, Nevaeh A.	M	1	1120 00	105 00		1225 00		1225 00		63 00	24 50	75 95	17 76	50 00	25 00	256 21	968 79	2
4	Kirkwood, Nandi P.	S	2	960 00	36 00		996 00	996 00			56 00	19 92	61 75	14 44	60 00	50 00	262 11	733 89	3
9	Marist, Brenda C.	M	3	1760 00			1760 00			1760 00	85 00	35 20	109 12	25 52	80 00	80 00	414 84	1345 16	4
																			5
																			6
																			7
																			8

3-1 ON YOUR OWN (LO2, 3), p. 75

Completing payroll records

1.

COMMISSIONS RECORD

EMPLOYEE NO. _____   EMPLOYEE NAME _____

PAY PERIOD ENDED _____   REGULAR BIWEEKLY SALARY _____

DEPARTMENT _____   POSITION _____

	Audio	Video	
Sales on Account	_____	_____	
Cash and Credit Card Sales	_____	_____	
equals Total Sales for the Month	_____	_____	
Less:			
Sales Discounts	_____	_____	
Sales Returns and Allowances	_____	_____	
equals Total Reductions in Sales	_____	_____	
Equals:			
Net Sales	_____	_____	
times Commission Rate	_____	_____	
equals Commission on Net Sales	_____	_____	_____

4.

EARNINGS RECORD FOR QUARTER ENDED _____

EMPLOYEE NO. _____   NAME _____   MARITAL STATUS _____   WITHHOLDING ALLOWANCES _____

HOURLY WAGE _____   SALARY _____   DEPARTMENT _____   POSITION _____

PAY PERIOD NO.	ENDED	TOTAL EARNINGS 1	FEDERAL INCOME TAX 2	STATE INCOME TAX 3	SOC. SEC. TAX 4	MEDICARE TAX 5	HEALTH INSURANCE 6	RETIREMENT PLAN 7	TOTAL 8	NET PAY 9	ACCUMULATED EARNINGS 10
1											
2											
TOTALS											

(DEDUCTIONS: columns 2–8)

2., 3.

PAYROLL REGISTER

SEMIMONTHLY PERIOD ENDED _____   DATE OF PAYMENT _____

EMPL. NO.	EMPLOYEE'S NAME	MARITAL STATUS	NO. OF ALLOWANCES	REGULAR 1	OVERTIME 2	COMMISSION 3	TOTAL 4	AUDIO 5	VIDEO 6	ADMINISTRATIVE 7	FEDERAL INCOME TAX 8	STATE INCOME TAX 9	SOCIAL SECURITY TAX 10	MEDICARE TAX 11	HEALTH INSURANCE 12	RETIREMENT PLAN 13	TOTAL 14	NET PAY 15	CHECK NO.
3	Avilo, Alexi P.	S	1	120000		337751	1537751		1537751		140000	6150	9533	2229	6000	8000	459912	1077839	1
10	Becker, Xavier T.	M	3	100000	7500		107500		107500		1500	4300	6665	1559	10000	12000	36024	71476	2
4	Johnson, Patrick T.	S	2	162800			162800			162800	13300	6512	10094	2361	8000	10000	50267	112533	3
8	Hu, Fang D.	M	3	128000	14400		142400	142400			4900	5696	8829	2065	10000	6500	37990	104410	4
																			5
																			6
																			7
																			8

(EARNINGS: columns 1–4; DEPARTMENT: columns 5–7; DEDUCTIONS: columns 8–14)

3-2 WORK TOGETHER (LO5, 6, 7), p. 83

Journalizing and paying payroll and payroll taxes

1.

Department	Social Security Earnings	Social Security 6.2%	Medicare 1.45%	FUTA Earnings	Federal Unemployment 0.6%	State Unemployment 5.4%	Total Payroll Taxes
Carpet							
Tile							
Administrative							
Total							

2.

CASH PAYMENTS JOURNAL

PAGE 6

	DATE	ACCOUNT TITLE	CK. NO.	POST. REF.	GENERAL DEBIT	GENERAL CREDIT	ACCOUNTS PAYABLE DEBIT	PURCH. DISCOUNT CR. CARPET	PURCH. DISCOUNT CR. TILE	CASH CREDIT	
1											1
2											2
3											3
4											4
5											5
6											6
7											7
8											8
9											9
10											10
11											11
12											12
13											13
14											14
15											15

2.

GENERAL JOURNAL

PAGE

	DATE		ACCOUNT TITLE	DOC. NO.	POST. REF.	DEBIT	CREDIT	
1								1
2								2
3								3
4								4
5								5
6								6
7								7
8								8
9								9
10								10
11								11
12								12
13								13
14								14
15								15
16								16
17								17
18								18
19								19
20								20
21								21
22								22
23								23
24								24
25								25
26								26
27								27
28								28
29								29
30								30
31								31
32								32

3-2 ON YOUR OWN (LO5, 6, 7), p. 83

Journalizing and paying payroll and payroll taxes

1.

Department	Social Security Earnings	Social Security 6.2%	Medicare 1.45%	FUTA Earnings	Federal Unemployment 0.6%	State Unemployment 5.4%	Total Payroll Taxes
Audio							
Video							
Administrative							
Total							

2.

CASH PAYMENTS JOURNAL

PAGE ___

DATE	ACCOUNT TITLE	CK. NO.	POST. REF.	GENERAL DEBIT	GENERAL CREDIT	ACCOUNTS PAYABLE DEBIT	PURCH. DISCOUNT CR. CARPET	PURCH. DISCOUNT CR. TILE	CASH CREDIT
1									
2									
3									
4									
5									
6									
7									
8									
9									
10									
11									
12									
13									
14									
15									

2.

GENERAL JOURNAL

PAGE

	DATE	ACCOUNT TITLE	DOC. NO.	POST. REF.	DEBIT	CREDIT	
1							1
2							2
3							3
4							4
5							5
6							6
7							7
8							8
9							9
10							10
11							11
12							12
13							13
14							14
15							15
16							16
17							17
18							18
19							19
20							20
21							21
22							22
23							23
24							24
25							25
26							26
27							27
28							28
29							29
30							30
31							31
32							32

3-1 **APPLICATION PROBLEM (LO2, 3), p. 87**

Completing payroll records

1.

<table>
<tr><td colspan="5" align="center">COMMISSIONS RECORD</td></tr>
<tr><td>EMPLOYEE NO. _____</td><td colspan="4">EMPLOYEE NAME _____</td></tr>
<tr><td>PAY PERIOD ENDED _____</td><td colspan="4">REGULAR BIWEEKLY SALARY _____</td></tr>
<tr><td>DEPARTMENT _____</td><td colspan="4">POSITION _____</td></tr>
</table>

	Equipment	Parts	
Sales on Account	_____	_____	
Cash and Credit Card Sales	_____	_____	
equals Total Sales for the Month...........................	_____	_____	
Less:			
Sales Discounts..	_____	_____	
Sales Returns and Allowances	_____	_____	
equals Total Reductions in Sales...........................	_____	_____	
Equals:			
Net Sales..	_____	_____	
times Commission Rate..	_____	_____	_____
equals Commission on Net Sales..........................	_____	_____	_____

4.

EARNINGS RECORD FOR QUARTER ENDED _____

EMPLOYEE NO. _____   NAME _____   MARITAL STATUS _____   WITHHOLDING ALLOWANCES _____

HOURLY WAGE _____   SALARY _____   DEPARTMENT _____   POSITION _____

| PAY PERIOD | | TOTAL EARNINGS | DEDUCTIONS | | | | | | NET PAY | ACCUMULATED EARNINGS |
NO.	ENDED	1	2 FEDERAL INCOME TAX	3 STATE INCOME TAX	4 SOC. SEC. TAX	5 MEDICARE TAX	6 HEALTH INSURANCE	7 RETIREMENT PLAN	8 TOTAL	9	10
1											
2											
TOTALS											

2., 3.

PAYROLL REGISTER

SEMIMONTHLY PERIOD ENDED _____   DATE OF PAYMENT _____

| EMPL. NO. | EMPLOYEE'S NAME | MARITAL STATUS | NO. OF ALLOWANCES | EARNINGS | | | | DEPARTMENT | | | DEDUCTIONS | | | | | | | NET PAY | CHECK NO. |
				1 REGULAR	2 OVERTIME	3 COMMISSION	4 TOTAL	5 EQUIPMENT	6 PARTS	7 ADMINISTRATIVE	8 FEDERAL INCOME TAX	9 STATE INCOME TAX	10 SOCIAL SECURITY TAX	11 MEDICARE TAX	12 HEALTH INSURANCE	13 RETIREMENT PLAN	14 TOTAL	15	
6	Bui, Duong M	S	1	148000		411142	1891142			1891142	19300	9457	117727	2743	6000	6000	55227	133915	1
21	Collins, Daniel T.	M	3	124800	7200		1320000		1320000		3900	6600	8184	1914	10000	8000	38598	93402	2
3	Porkony, Libena C.	M	2	112000	4200		1162000	1162000			3900	5810	7204	1685	8000	10000	36599	79601	3
																			4
																			5
																			6
																			7

Name _____ Date _____ Class _____

3-2 **APPLICATION PROBLEM (LO5, 6, 7), p. 87**

Journalizing and paying payroll and payroll taxes

1.

Department	Social Security Earnings	Social Security 6.2%	Medicare 1.45%	FUTA Earnings	Federal Unemployment 0.6%	State Unemployment 5.4%	Total Payroll Taxes
Equipment							
Parts							
Administrative							
Total							

2.

CASH PAYMENTS JOURNAL

PAGE

DATE	ACCOUNT TITLE	CK. NO.	POST. REF.	GENERAL DEBIT	GENERAL CREDIT	ACCOUNTS PAYABLE DEBIT	PURCH. DISCOUNT CR. CARPET	PURCH. DISCOUNT CR. TILE	CASH CREDIT
1									
2									
3									
4									
5									
6									
7									
8									
9									
10									
11									
12									
13									
14									
15									

2.

GENERAL JOURNAL

PAGE

	DATE		ACCOUNT TITLE	DOC. NO.	POST. REF.	DEBIT	CREDIT	
1								1
2								2
3								3
4								4
5								5
6								6
7								7
8								8
9								9
10								10
11								11
12								12
13								13
14								14
15								15
16								16
17								17
18								18
19								19
20								20
21								21
22								22
23								23
24								24
25								25
26								26
27								27
28								28
29								29
30								30
31								31
32								32

3-M **MASTERY PROBLEM (LO2, 3, 5, 7), p. 88**

Completing payroll records, journalizing payment of a payroll, and journalizing payroll taxes

1.

COMMISSIONS RECORD

EMPLOYEE NO. _____ EMPLOYEE NAME _____

PAY PERIOD ENDED _____ REGULAR BIWEEKLY SALARY _____

DEPARTMENT _____ POSITION _____

	Carpet	Drapery	
Sales on Account	_____	_____	
Cash and Credit Card Sales	_____	_____	
equals Total Sales for the Month...............................	_____	_____	
Less:			
Sales Discounts	_____	_____	
Sales Returns and Allowances	_____	_____	
equals Total Reductions in Sales	_____	_____	
Equals:			
Net Sales	_____	_____	
times Commission Rate...	_____	_____	_____
equals Commission on Net Sales................................	_____	_____	_____

4.

EARNINGS RECORD FOR QUARTER ENDED _____

EMPLOYEE NO. _____ NAME _____ MARITAL STATUS _____ WITHHOLDING ALLOWANCES _____

HOURLY WAGE _____ SALARY _____ DEPARTMENT _____ POSITION _____

PAY PERIOD NO.	ENDED	1 TOTAL EARNINGS	2 FEDERAL INCOME TAX	3 STATE INCOME TAX	4 SOC. SEC. TAX	DEDUCTIONS 5 MEDICARE TAX	6 HEALTH INSURANCE	7 RETIREMENT PLAN	8 TOTAL	9 NET PAY	10 ACCUMULATED EARNINGS
1											
2											
TOTALS											

2., 3.

PAYROLL REGISTER

SEMIMONTHLY PERIOD ENDED _____ DATE OF PAYMENT _____

EMPL. NO.	EMPLOYEE'S NAME	MARITAL STATUS	NO. OF ALLOWANCES	EARNINGS 1 REGULAR	2 OVERTIME	3 COMMIS-SION	4 TOTAL	DEPARTMENT 5 CARPET	6 DRAPERY	7 ADMINIS-TRATIVE	DEDUCTIONS 8 FEDERAL INCOME TAX	9 STATE INCOME TAX	10 SOCIAL SECURITY TAX	11 MEDICARE TAX	12 HEALTH INSURANCE	13 RETIRE-MENT PLAN	14 TOTAL	15 NET PAY	CHECK NO.
16	Cannon, Ester A.	M	4	1368 00			1368 00	1368 00			29 00	41 04	84 82	19 84	125 00	100 00	399 70	968 30	1
12	Guadalupe, Jorge P.	M	3	1200 00		612 15	1812 15	198 85	1613 30		92 00	54 36	112 35	26 28	100 00	50 00	434 99	1377 16	2
3	Miller, Tina S.	S	2	1280 00	48 00		1328 00			1328 00	97 00	39 84	82 34	19 26	75 00	125 00	438 44	889 56	3
18	Phung, Xuan T.	M	3	952 00	21 00		973 00	973 00			5 00	29 19	60 33	14 11	100 00	120 00	328 63	644 37	4
																			5
																			6
																			7
																			8

3-M MASTERY PROBLEM (continued)

5.

Department	Social Security Earnings	Social Security 6.2%	Medicare 1.45%	FUTA Earnings	Federal Unemployment 0.6%	State Unemployment 5.4%	Total Payroll Taxes
Carpet							
Drapery							
Administrative							
Total							

CASH PAYMENTS JOURNAL

PAGE

	DATE	ACCOUNT TITLE	CK. NO.	POST. REF.	GENERAL DEBIT	GENERAL CREDIT	ACCOUNTS PAYABLE DEBIT	PURCH. DISCOUNT CR. CARPET	PURCH. DISCOUNT CR. TILE	CASH CREDIT	
					1	2	3	4	5	6	
1											1
2											2
3											3
4											4
5											5
6											6
7											7
8											8
9											9
10											10
11											11
12											12
13											13
14											14
15											15

6.

GENERAL JOURNAL

PAGE

	DATE	ACCOUNT TITLE	DOC. NO.	POST. REF.	DEBIT	CREDIT	
1							1
2							2
3							3
4							4
5							5
6							6
7							7
8							8
9							9
10							10
11							11
12							12
13							13
14							14
15							15
16							16
17							17
18							18
19							19
20							20
21							21
22							22
23							23
24							24
25							25
26							26
27							27
28							28
29							29
30							30
31							31
32							32

3-S SOURCE DOCUMENTS PROBLEM (LO2, 3, 5, 7), p. 89

Completing payroll records, journalizing payment of a payroll, and journalizing payroll taxes

Hourly Employee Time Summary

Pay Period: 6/25/20-- to 7/9/20--

Prepared on: 7/11/20--

Name	Department	ID	Week Ended	Regular	Overtime	Totals
Dobbins, Clint A.	Windows	3	6/25/20--	40	3	43
			7/9/20--	36		36
				76	3	79
Godfrey, Betty S.	Doors	2	6/25/20--	40		40
			7/9/20--	40		40
				80		80
Rainwater, Chanta P.	Administrative	12	6/25/20--	40	2	42
			7/9/20--	40	3	43
				80	5	85

COMMISSION SALES REPORT

Month: June

Prepared on: 7/11/20--

Name	Account Title	Doors	Windows
Pizzo, Daniel C.	Sales on Account	5,108.62	2,194.16
	Cash and Credit Card Sales	1,618.31	548.94
	Sales Discounts	99.08	33.37
	Sales Returns and Allowances	219.39	148.34
	Commission Rate	6%	2%
Verdell, May E.	Sales on Account	1,058.38	8,514.16
	Cash and Credit Card Sales	947.11	3,491.36
	Sales Discounts	19.25	124.15
	Sales Returns and Allowances	108.74	615.74
	Commission Rate	6%	8%

Personnel Report

Prepared on: 7/11/20--

ID	Name	Position	Marital Status	Number of Allowances	Hourly Wage Rate	Biweekly Salary	Retirement Contribution
3	Dobbins, Clint A.	Windows Clerk	S	1	$ 16.00	$ —	$ 60.00
2	Godfrey, Betty S.	Doors Clerk	M	1	18.00	—	80.00
8	Pizzo, Daniel C.	Doors Manager	M	2	—	1,200.00	200.00
12	Rainwater, Chanta P.	Accountant	M	4	22.00	—	90.00
10	Verdell, May E.	Windows Manager	S	3	—	900.00	150.00

3-S SOURCE DOCUMENTS PROBLEM (continued)

NO. **905**	$ 5,416.02		
Date: 7/13			20 --
To: First National Bank			
For: July 9 payroll			
BALANCE BROUGHT FORWARD		9,148	15
AMOUNT DEPOSITED			
SUBTOTAL Date		9,148	15
OTHER:			
_____			
_____			
SUBTOTAL		9,148	15
AMOUNT THIS CHECK		5,416	02
BALANCE CARRIED FORWARD		3,732	13

NO. **916**	$ 335.61		
Date: 7/30			20 --
To:			
For: State unemployment taxes for second quarter			
BALANCE BROUGHT FORWARD		10,894	16
AMOUNT DEPOSITED 7 29 --		1,511	15
SUBTOTAL Date		12,405	31
OTHER:			
_____			
SUBTOTAL		12,405	31
AMOUNT THIS CHECK		335	61
BALANCE CARRIED FORWARD		12,069	70

No. 65	Exterior Design
MEMORANDUM	

Employer payroll taxes for the July 9, 20-- pay period.

See attached analysis.

No. 66	Exterior Design
MEMORANDUM	

Made deposit using the EFTPS for employee and employer payroll taxes for the June pay periods: employee federal income tax withholding, $1,098.00; Social Security tax, $2,119.75; and Medicare tax, $495.75.

No. 72	Exterior Design
MEMORANDUM	

Made deposit using the EFTPS for federal unemployment taxes for January to June, $506.61.

3-S   **SOURCE DOCUMENTS PROBLEM (continued)**

1.

COMMISSIONS RECORD

EMPLOYEE NO. _____   EMPLOYEE NAME _____

PAY PERIOD ENDED _____   REGULAR BIWEEKLY SALARY _____

DEPARTMENT _____   POSITION _____

	Doors	Windows	
Sales on Account	_____	_____	
Cash and Credit Card Sales	_____	_____	
equals Total Sales for the Month...........................	_____	_____	
Less:			
Sales Discounts..	_____	_____	
Sales Returns and Allowances	_____	_____	
equals Total Reductions in Sales...........................	_____	_____	
Equals:			
Net Sales..	_____	_____	
times Commission Rate......................................	_____	_____	_____
equals Commission on Net Sales.............................	_____	_____	_____

COMMISSIONS RECORD

EMPLOYEE NO. _____   EMPLOYEE NAME _____

PAY PERIOD ENDED _____   REGULAR BIWEEKLY SALARY _____

DEPARTMENT _____   POSITION _____

	Doors	Windows
Sales on Account	_____	_____
Cash and Credit Card Sales	_____	_____
equals Total Sales for the Month...........................	_____	_____
Less:		
Sales Discounts...	_____	_____
Sales Returns and Allowances	_____	_____
equals Total Reductions in Sales...........................	_____	_____
Equals:		
Net Sales...	_____	_____
times Commission Rate...............................	_____	_____
equals Commission on Net Sales.........................	_____	_____

Name _____ Date _____ Class _____

3-S SOURCE DOCUMENTS PROBLEM (continued)

2.

PAYROLL REGISTER

SEMIMONTHLY PERIOD ENDED _____ DATE OF PAYMENT _____

EMPL. NO.	EMPLOYEE'S NAME	MARITAL STATUS	NO. OF ALLOWANCES	EARNINGS				DEPARTMENT			DEDUCTIONS						TOTAL	NET PAY	CHECK NO.
				REGULAR	OVERTIME	COMMIS- SION	TOTAL	DOORS	WINDOWS	ADMINIS- TRATIVE	FEDERAL INCOME TAX	STATE INCOME TAX	SOCIAL SECURITY TAX	MEDICARE TAX	HEALTH INSURANCE	RETIRE- MENT PLAN			
				1	2	3	4	5	6	7	8	9	10	11	12	13	14	15	
3	Dobbins, Clint A.	S	1																1
2	Godfrey, Betty S.	M	1																2
8	Pizzo, Daniel C.	M	2																3
12	Rainwater, Chanta P.	M	4																4
10	Verdell, May E.	S	3																5
																			6
																			7
																			8
																			9
																			10
																			11
																			12
																			13
																			14
																			15
																			16
																			17

Chapter 3 Calculating and Recording Departmental Payroll Data • 111

3.

EARNINGS RECORD FOR QUARTER ENDED — September 30, 20--

EMPLOYEE NO. 3 NAME Dobbins, Clint A. MARITAL STATUS S WITHHOLDING ALLOWANCES 1

HOURLY WAGE $16.00 SALARY _____ DEPARTMENT Windows POSITION Clerk

| PAY PERIOD | | TOTAL EARNINGS | DEDUCTIONS | | | | | | TOTAL | NET PAY | ACCUMULATED EARNINGS |
NO.	ENDED	1	FEDERAL INCOME TAX 2	STATE INCOME TAX 3	SOC. SEC. TAX 4	MEDICARE TAX 5	HEALTH INSURANCE 6	RETIREMENT PLAN 7	8	9	10
1											2 5 6 0 00
2											
TOTALS											

EARNINGS RECORD FOR QUARTER ENDED — September 30, 20--

EMPLOYEE NO. 2 NAME Godfrey, Betty S. MARITAL STATUS M WITHHOLDING ALLOWANCES 1

HOURLY WAGE $18.00 SALARY _____ DEPARTMENT Doors POSITION Clerk

| PAY PERIOD | | TOTAL EARNINGS | DEDUCTIONS | | | | | | TOTAL | NET PAY | ACCUMULATED EARNINGS |
NO.	ENDED	1	FEDERAL INCOME TAX 2	STATE INCOME TAX 3	SOC. SEC. TAX 4	MEDICARE TAX 5	HEALTH INSURANCE 6	RETIREMENT PLAN 7	8	9	10
1											1 6 0 8 1 00
2											
TOTALS											

EARNINGS RECORD FOR QUARTER ENDED — September 30, 20--

EMPLOYEE NO. 8 NAME Pizzo, Daniel C. MARITAL STATUS M WITHHOLDING ALLOWANCES 2

HOURLY WAGE _____ SALARY $1,200.00 DEPARTMENT Doors POSITION Manager

| PAY PERIOD | | TOTAL EARNINGS | DEDUCTIONS | | | | | | TOTAL | NET PAY | ACCUMULATED EARNINGS |
NO.	ENDED	1	FEDERAL INCOME TAX 2	STATE INCOME TAX 3	SOC. SEC. TAX 4	MEDICARE TAX 5	HEALTH INSURANCE 6	RETIREMENT PLAN 7	8	9	10
1											1 9 6 2 8 88
2											
TOTALS											

3-S SOURCE DOCUMENTS PROBLEM (continued)

EARNINGS RECORD FOR QUARTER ENDED _____

EMPLOYEE NO. _____ NAME _____ MARITAL STATUS _____ WITHHOLDING ALLOWANCES _____

HOURLY WAGE _____ SALARY _____ DEPARTMENT _____ POSITION _____

PAY PERIOD		TOTAL EARNINGS	DEDUCTIONS						NET PAY	ACCUMULATED EARNINGS
NO.	ENDED	1	FEDERAL INCOME TAX 2	STATE INCOME TAX 3	SOC. SEC. TAX 4	MEDICARE TAX 5	HEALTH INSURANCE 6	RETIREMENT PLAN 7	TOTAL 8	9	10
1											1 2 0 0 0 00
2											
TOTALS											

EARNINGS RECORD FOR QUARTER ENDED _____

EMPLOYEE NO. _____ NAME _____ MARITAL STATUS _____ WITHHOLDING ALLOWANCES _____

HOURLY WAGE _____ SALARY _____ DEPARTMENT _____ POSITION _____

PAY PERIOD		TOTAL EARNINGS	DEDUCTIONS						NET PAY	ACCUMULATED EARNINGS
NO.	ENDED	1	FEDERAL INCOME TAX 2	STATE INCOME TAX 3	SOC. SEC. TAX 4	MEDICARE TAX 5	HEALTH INSURANCE 6	RETIREMENT PLAN 7	TOTAL 8	9	10
1											20 1 4 3 50
2											
TOTALS											

4.

Department	Social Security Earnings	Social Security 6.2%	Medicare 1.45%	FUTA Earnings	Federal Unemployment 0.6%	State Unemployment 5.4%	Total Payroll Taxes
Doors							
Windows							
Administrative							
Total							

5.

CASH PAYMENTS JOURNAL

PAGE 12

				1	2	3	4	5	6	
				GENERAL		ACCOUNTS PAYABLE DEBIT	PURCH. DISCOUNT CR.		CASH CREDIT	
DATE	ACCOUNT TITLE	CK. NO.	POST. REF.	DEBIT	CREDIT		WINDOWS	DOORS		
										1
										2
										3
										4
										5
										6
										7
										8
										9
										10
										11
										12
										13
										14
										15

3-S SOURCE DOCUMENTS PROBLEM (concluded)

5.

GENERAL JOURNAL   PAGE 7

	DATE	ACCOUNT TITLE	DOC. NO.	POST. REF.	DEBIT	CREDIT	
1							1
2							2
3							3
4							4
5							5
6							6
7							7
8							8
9							9
10							10
11							11
12							12
13							13
14							14
15							15
16							16
17							17
18							18
19							19
20							20
21							21
22							22
23							23
24							24
25							25
26							26
27							27
28							28
29							29
30							30
31							31
32							32

Calculating federal income tax withholdings using the percentage method

Employee	Earnings	Marital Status	Number of Allowances	Withholding Allowance	Earnings Subject to Withholding	Minimum Tax	Additional Tax	Total Tax
Atkinson	$5,000.00	M	3	$478.80	$4,521.20	$342.58	$242.04	$584.62
Cooper	4,041.00	M	5					
Futral	4,306.00	S	1					
Lowery	3,492.00	M	3					
Pettit	3,383.00	S	2					
Saenz	4,851.00	M	2					

Name	Perfect Score	Your Score
Identifying Accounting Terms	33 Pts.	
Analyzing Departmental Adjusting and Closing Entries	22 Pts.	
Analyzing Financial Reporting Procedures for a Departmentalized Business	10 Pts.	
Total	65 Pts.	

Part One—Identifying Accounting Terms

Directions: Select the one term in Column I that best fits each definition in Column II. Print the letter identifying your choice in the Answers column.

Contains accounting terms for Lesson 4-1.

Column I	Column II	Answers
A. adjusted trial balance	1. The length of time for which a business summarizes its financial information and reports its financial performance. (p. 96)	1._____
B. adjusting entries	2. A fiscal period consisting of 12 consecutive months. (p. 96)	2._____
C. depreciation expense	3. A listing of customer accounts, account balances, and total amount due from all customers. (p. 97)	3._____
D. fiscal period	4. A listing of vendor accounts, account balances, and the total amount due all vendors. (p. 97)	4._____
E. fiscal year	5. A proof of the equality of debits and credits in a general ledger. (p. 98)	5._____
F. plant assets	6. Journal entries recorded to update general ledger accounts at the end of a fiscal period. (p. 98)	6._____
G. schedule of accounts payable	7. A trial balance prepared before adjusting entries are posted. (p. 98)	7._____
H. schedule of accounts receivable	8. Physical assets that will be used for a number of years in the operation of a business. (p. 102)	8._____
I. trial balance	9. The portion of a plant asset's cost that is transferred to an expense account in each fiscal period during that asset's useful life. (p. 102)	9._____
J. unadjusted trial balance	10. A trial balance prepared after adjusting entries are posted. (p. 103)	10._____

Accounting terms for Lessons 4-2 through 4-4 are presented on the following page.

Directions: Select the one term in Column I that best fits each definition in Column II. Print the letter identifying your choice in the Answers column.

Contains accounting terms for Lessons 4-2 through 4-4.

Column I	Column II	Answers
A. accounting cycle	**1.** Assigning control of revenues, costs, and expenses to a specific manager. (p. 108)	1._____
B. balance sheet	**2.** An operating expense identifiable with and chargeable to the operation of a specific department. (p. 108)	2._____
C. capital stock	**3.** An operating expense chargeable to overall business operations and not identifiable with a specific department. (p. 108)	3._____
D. cash flow	**4.** Financial statements reporting revenue, costs, and direct expenses under a specific department's control. (p. 109)	4._____
E. closing entries	**5.** The revenue earned by a department less its cost of merchandise sold and less its direct expenses. (p. 109)	5._____
F. departmental margin	**6.** A statement that reports departmental margin for a specific department. (p. 109)	6._____
G. departmental margin statement	**7.** The operating revenue remaining after cost of merchandise sold has been deducted. (p. 109)	7._____
H. direct expense	**8.** A comparison between two components of financial information. (p. 110)	8._____
I. dividends	**9.** Reporting an amount on a financial statement as a percentage of another item on the same financial statement. (p. 110)	9._____
J. financial ratio	**10.** A financial statement showing the revenue and expenses for a fiscal period. (p. 113)	10._____
K. financing activities	**11.** A financial statement that shows changes in a corporation's ownership for a fiscal period. (p. 113)	11._____
L. gross profit	**12.** Total shares of ownership in a corporation. (p. 113)	12._____
M. income statement	**13.** An amount earned by a corporation and not yet distributed to stockholders. (p. 113)	13._____
N. indirect expense	**14.** Earnings distributed to stockholders. (p. 113)	14._____
O. investing activities	**15.** A financial statement that reports assets, liabilities, and owners' equity on a specific date. (p. 114)	15._____
P. operating activities	**16.** The cash receipts and cash payments of a company. (p. 115)	16._____
Q. post-closing trial balance	**17.** A financial statement that summarizes cash receipts and cash payments resulting from business activities during a fiscal period. (p. 115)	17._____
R. responsibility accounting	**18.** The cash receipts and payments necessary to operate a business on a day-to-day basis. (p. 115)	18._____
S. responsibility statements	**19.** Cash receipts and cash payments involving the sale or purchase of assets used to earn revenue over a period of time. (p. 115)	19._____
T. retained earnings	**20.** Cash receipts and payments involving debt or equity transactions. (p. 115)	20._____
U. statement of cash flows	**21.** Journal entries used to prepare temporary accounts for a new fiscal period. (p. 117)	21._____
V. statement of stockholders' equity	**22.** A trial balance prepared after the closing entries are posted. (p. 120)	22._____
W. vertical analysis	**23.** The series of accounting activities included in recording financial information for a fiscal period. (p. 121)	23._____

Part Two—Analyzing Departmental Adjusting and Closing Entries

Directions: For each transaction below, print in the proper Answers column the identifying letters of the accounts or descriptions of those accounts to be debited and credited.

Account Titles

A. Accum. Depr.—Equipment

B. Allow. for Uncoll. Accounts

C. departmental contra cost accounts

D. departmental contra revenue accounts

E. departmental cost accounts

F. departmental income summary

G. departmental merchandise inventory accounts

H. departmental sales accounts

I. Depr. Expense—Equipment

J. Dividends

K. expense accounts

L. Federal Income Tax Expense

M. Federal Income Tax Payable

N. Income Summary—General

O. Insurance Expense

P. Prepaid Insurance

Q. Retained Earnings

R. Supplies

S. Supplies Expense

T. Uncollectible Accounts Expense

Transactions		Answers Debit	Answers Credit
1-2.	Adjust Allowance for Uncollectible Accounts. (p. 99)	1. _____	2. _____
3-4.	Adjust ending merchandise inventory (increase). (p. 100)	3. _____	4. _____
5-6.	Adjust ending merchandise inventory (decrease). (p. 100)	5. _____	6. _____
7-8.	Adjust Supplies. (p. 101)	7. _____	8. _____
9-10.	Adjust Prepaid Insurance. (p. 101)	9. _____	10. _____
11-12.	Adjust Depr. Expense—Equipment. (p. 102)	11. _____	12. _____
13-14.	Adjust Federal Income Tax Payable. (p. 104)	13. _____	14. _____
15-16.	Close departmental income statement accounts (credit balances), sales, and contra cost accounts. (p. 117)	15. _____	16. _____
17-18.	Close departmental income statement accounts (debit balances), contra revenue, cost, and expense accounts. (p. 118)	17. _____	18. _____
19-20.	Close Income Summary—General account (assume a net income). (p. 119)	19. _____	20. _____
21-22.	Close Dividends. (p. 120)	21. _____	22. _____

Part Three—Analyzing Financial Reporting Procedures for a Departmentalized Business

Directions: Place a *T* for True or an *F* for False in the Answers column to show whether each of the following statements is true or false.

Answers

1. A business should perform bank reconciliations before preparing its financial statements. (p. 96)   1. _____

2. Adjusting entries are posted to the general ledger before an adjusted trial balance is prepared. (p. 103)   2. _____

3. The cost of supplies used by a specific department is an example of a direct expense. (p. 108)   3. _____

4. The cost of electricity used by a business's overall operations is an example of a direct expense. (p. 108)   4. _____

5. A departmental statement of gross profit provides a manager with information about revenue and costs for a specific department. (p. 109)   5. _____

6. Vertical analysis ratios in a departmentalized business are used to analyze the financial results for each department. (p. 110)   6. _____

7. Purchasing merchandise is an example of an operating activity as reported on a statement of cash flows. (p. 115)   7. _____

8. Cash receipts and payments involving debt and equity transactions are examples of investing activities as reported on a statement of cash flows. (p. 115)   8. _____

9. After entries are posted to close income statement accounts, the Income Summary—General account balance should be equal to the net income (or net loss) for the fiscal period. (p. 119)   9. _____

10. A departmentalized business does not need to prepare a post-closing trial balance. (p. 120)   10. _____

4-1 WORK TOGETHER (LO2, 3, 4), p. 107

Preparing an adjusted trial balance

1., 2., 4.

GENERAL JOURNAL

PAGE

	DATE		ACCOUNT TITLE	DOC. NO.	POST. REF.	DEBIT	CREDIT	
1								1
2								2
3								3
4								4
5								5
6								6
7								7
8								8
9								9
10								10
11								11
12								12
13								13
14								14
15								15
16								16
17								17
18								18

4.

Net Income before Federal Income Taxes	×	Tax Rate	=	Federal Income Tax
$	×		=	$

2., 4.   **GENERAL LEDGER**

ACCOUNT Allowance for Uncollectible Accounts   ACCOUNT NO. 1210

DATE	ITEM	POST. REF.	DEBIT	CREDIT	BALANCE DEBIT	BALANCE CREDIT
20-- Dec. 31	Balance	✔				7 7 38

ACCOUNT Merchandise Inventory—Kitchen   ACCOUNT NO. 1305

DATE	ITEM	POST. REF.	DEBIT	CREDIT	BALANCE DEBIT	BALANCE CREDIT
20-- Dec. 31	Balance	✔			140 8 9 0 00	

ACCOUNT Merchandise Inventory—Bath   ACCOUNT NO. 1310

DATE	ITEM	POST. REF.	DEBIT	CREDIT	BALANCE DEBIT	BALANCE CREDIT
20-- Dec. 31	Balance	✔			98 6 2 0 00	

ACCOUNT Supplies   ACCOUNT NO. 1405

DATE	ITEM	POST. REF.	DEBIT	CREDIT	BALANCE DEBIT	BALANCE CREDIT
20-- Dec. 31	Balance	✔			6 0 9 7 89	

ACCOUNT Prepaid Insurance   ACCOUNT NO. 1410

DATE	ITEM	POST. REF.	DEBIT	CREDIT	BALANCE DEBIT	BALANCE CREDIT
20-- Dec. 31	Balance	✔			18 0 0 0 00	

4-1 WORK TOGETHER (continued)

ACCOUNT Accumulated Depreciation—Office Equipment   ACCOUNT NO. 1510

DATE	ITEM	POST. REF.	DEBIT	CREDIT	BALANCE DEBIT	BALANCE CREDIT
20-- Dec. 31	Balance	✔				11 4 2 4 00

ACCOUNT Accumulated Depreciation—Store Equipment   ACCOUNT NO. 1520

DATE	ITEM	POST. REF.	DEBIT	CREDIT	BALANCE DEBIT	BALANCE CREDIT
20-- Dec. 31	Balance	✔				27 7 6 5 00

ACCOUNT Federal Income Tax Payable   ACCOUNT NO. 2305

DATE	ITEM	POST. REF.	DEBIT	CREDIT	BALANCE DEBIT	BALANCE CREDIT

ACCOUNT Income Summary—Kitchen   ACCOUNT NO. 3210

DATE	ITEM	POST. REF.	DEBIT	CREDIT	BALANCE DEBIT	BALANCE CREDIT

ACCOUNT Income Summary—Bath   ACCOUNT NO. 3215

DATE	ITEM	POST. REF.	DEBIT	CREDIT	BALANCE DEBIT	BALANCE CREDIT

ACCOUNT Depreciation Expense—Office Equipment ACCOUNT NO. 7110

DATE	ITEM	POST. REF.	DEBIT	CREDIT	BALANCE DEBIT	BALANCE CREDIT

ACCOUNT Depreciation Expense—Store Equipment ACCOUNT NO. 7115

DATE	ITEM	POST. REF.	DEBIT	CREDIT	BALANCE DEBIT	BALANCE CREDIT

ACCOUNT Insurance Expense ACCOUNT NO. 7120

DATE	ITEM	POST. REF.	DEBIT	CREDIT	BALANCE DEBIT	BALANCE CREDIT

ACCOUNT Supplies Expense ACCOUNT NO. 7150

DATE	ITEM	POST. REF.	DEBIT	CREDIT	BALANCE DEBIT	BALANCE CREDIT

ACCOUNT Uncollectible Accounts Expense ACCOUNT NO. 7155

DATE	ITEM	POST. REF.	DEBIT	CREDIT	BALANCE DEBIT	BALANCE CREDIT

ACCOUNT Federal Income Tax Expense ACCOUNT NO. 8105

DATE	ITEM	POST. REF.	DEBIT	CREDIT	BALANCE DEBIT	BALANCE CREDIT
20-- Dec. 31	Balance	✔			14 0 0 0 00	

4-1 WORK TOGETHER (continued)

3., 5.

Foley's Interiors

Adjusted Trial Balance

December 31, 20--

ACCOUNT TITLE	DEBIT	CREDIT
Cash	34 460 79	
Petty Cash	300 00	
Accounts Receivable	23 018 95	
Allowance for Uncollectible Accounts		
Merchandise Inventory—Kitchen		
Merchandise Inventory—Bath		
Supplies		
Prepaid Insurance		
Office Equipment	26 015 89	
Accumulated Depreciation—Office Equipment		
Store Equipment	51 852 82	
Accumulated Depreciation—Store Equipment		
Accounts Payable		24 116 31
Sales Tax Payable		4 925 59
Employee Income Tax Payable—Federal		1 335 44
Employee Income Tax Payable—State		956 99
Social Security Tax Payable		2 376 90
Medicare Tax Payable		553 24
Medical Insurance Payable		846 42
Retirement Plan Payable		571 94
Unemployment Tax Payable—Federal		16 72
Unemployment Tax Payable—State		112 08
Federal Income Tax Payable		
Dividends Payable		4 000 00
Capital Stock		75 000 00
Retained Earnings		165 073 83
Dividends	16 000 00	
Income Summary—General		
Income Summary—Kitchen		
Income Summary—Bath		

(Note: Trial balance is continued on the next page.)

Foley's Interiors

Adjusted Trial Balance (Concluded)

December 31, 20--

ACCOUNT TITLE	DEBIT	CREDIT
Sales—Kitchen		417 953 07
Sales Discount—Kitchen	6 655 27	
Sales Returns and Allowances—Kitchen	7 634 77	
Sales—Bath		316 014 76
Sales Discount—Bath	4 220 29	
Sales Returns and Allowances—Bath	11 070 52	
Purchases—Kitchen	204 164 91	
Purchases Discount—Kitchen		2 505 71
Purchases Returns and Allowances—Kitchen		4 925 52
Purchases—Bath	128 451 62	
Purchases Discount—Bath		2 157 01
Purchases Returns and Allowances—Bath		6 495 71
Advertising Expense—Kitchen	11 900 00	
Payroll Taxes Expense—Kitchen	5 193 25	
Salary Expense—Kitchen	59 121 95	
Advertising Expense—Bath	4 500 00	
Payroll Taxes Expense—Bath	7 028 66	
Salary Expense—Bath	81 103 91	
Credit Card Fee Expense	4 502 93	
Depreciation Expense—Office Equipment		
Depreciation Expense—Store Equipment		
Insurance Expense		
Miscellaneous Expense	2 813 28	
Payroll Taxes Expense—Administrative	6 149 34	
Rent Expense	18 000 00	
Salary Expense—Administrative	71 001 51	
Supplies Expense		
Uncollectible Accounts Expense		
Utilities Expense	6 435 07	

4-1 ON YOUR OWN (LO2, 3, 4), p. 107

Preparing an adjusted trial balance

1., 2., 4.

GENERAL JOURNAL   PAGE _____

	DATE	ACCOUNT TITLE	DOC. NO.	POST. REF.	DEBIT	CREDIT	
1							1
2							2
3							3
4							4
5							5
6							6
7							7
8							8
9							9
10							10
11							11
12							12
13							13
14							14
15							15
16							16
17							17
18							18

4.

Net Income before Federal Income Taxes	×	Tax Rate	=	Federal Income Tax
$	×		=	$

2., 4.   **GENERAL LEDGER**

ACCOUNT Allowance for Uncollectible Accounts   ACCOUNT NO. 1210

DATE		ITEM	POST. REF.	DEBIT	CREDIT	BALANCE	
						DEBIT	CREDIT
Dec.	31	Balance	✔			1 4 8 36	

ACCOUNT Merchandise Inventory—Parts   ACCOUNT NO. 1305

DATE		ITEM	POST. REF.	DEBIT	CREDIT	BALANCE	
						DEBIT	CREDIT
Dec.	31	Balance	✔			256 4 7 0 00	

ACCOUNT Merchandise Inventory—Accessories   ACCOUNT NO. 1310

DATE		ITEM	POST. REF.	DEBIT	CREDIT	BALANCE	
						DEBIT	CREDIT
Dec.	31	Balance	✔			112 7 4 0 00	

ACCOUNT Supplies   ACCOUNT NO. 1405

DATE		ITEM	POST. REF.	DEBIT	CREDIT	BALANCE	
						DEBIT	CREDIT
Dec.	31	Balance	✔			4 9 3 5 98	

ACCOUNT Prepaid Insurance   ACCOUNT NO. 1410

DATE		ITEM	POST. REF.	DEBIT	CREDIT	BALANCE	
						DEBIT	CREDIT
Dec.	31	Balance	✔			15 0 0 0 00	

4-1 ON YOUR OWN (continued)

ACCOUNT Accumulated Depreciation—Office Equipment   ACCOUNT NO. 1510

DATE		ITEM	POST. REF.	DEBIT	CREDIT	BALANCE	
						DEBIT	CREDIT
Dec.	31	Balance	✔				9 1 4 5 86

ACCOUNT Accumulated Depreciation—Store Equipment   ACCOUNT NO. 1520

DATE		ITEM	POST. REF.	DEBIT	CREDIT	BALANCE	
						DEBIT	CREDIT
Dec.	31	Balance	✔				22 2 9 8 99

ACCOUNT Federal Income Tax Payable   ACCOUNT NO. 2305

DATE	ITEM	POST. REF.	DEBIT	CREDIT	BALANCE	
					DEBIT	CREDIT

ACCOUNT Income Summary—Parts   ACCOUNT NO. 3210

DATE	ITEM	POST. REF.	DEBIT	CREDIT	BALANCE	
					DEBIT	CREDIT

ACCOUNT Income Summary—Accessories   ACCOUNT NO. 3215

DATE	ITEM	POST. REF.	DEBIT	CREDIT	BALANCE	
					DEBIT	CREDIT

ACCOUNT Depreciation Expense—Office Equipment   ACCOUNT NO. 7110

DATE	ITEM	POST. REF.	DEBIT	CREDIT	BALANCE DEBIT	BALANCE CREDIT

ACCOUNT Depreciation Expense—Store Equipment   ACCOUNT NO. 7115

DATE	ITEM	POST. REF.	DEBIT	CREDIT	BALANCE DEBIT	BALANCE CREDIT

ACCOUNT Insurance Expense   ACCOUNT NO. 7120

DATE	ITEM	POST. REF.	DEBIT	CREDIT	BALANCE DEBIT	BALANCE CREDIT

ACCOUNT Supplies Expense   ACCOUNT NO. 7150

DATE	ITEM	POST. REF.	DEBIT	CREDIT	BALANCE DEBIT	BALANCE CREDIT

ACCOUNT Uncollectible Accounts Expense   ACCOUNT NO. 7155

DATE	ITEM	POST. REF.	DEBIT	CREDIT	BALANCE DEBIT	BALANCE CREDIT

ACCOUNT Federal Income Tax Expense   ACCOUNT NO. 8105

DATE	ITEM	POST. REF.	DEBIT	CREDIT	BALANCE DEBIT	BALANCE CREDIT
20-- Dec. 31	Balance	✔			14 0 0 0 00	

4-1 ON YOUR OWN (continued)

3., 5.

Mixon Auto Supplies

Adjusted Trial Balance

December 31, 20--

ACCOUNT TITLE	DEBIT	CREDIT
Cash	57 3 5 4 03	
Petty Cash	2 4 1 66	
Accounts Receivable	18 5 3 3 67	
Allowance for Uncollectible Accounts		
Merchandise Inventory—Parts		
Merchandise Inventory—Accessories		
Supplies		
Prepaid Insurance		
Office Equipment	20 8 2 7 76	
Accumulated Depreciation—Office Equipment		
Store Equipment	41 5 3 1 75	
Accumulated Depreciation—Store Equipment		
Accounts Payable		19 3 0 1 35
Sales Tax Payable		3 9 7 6 77
Employee Income Tax Payable—Federal		1 0 8 0 01
Employee Income Tax Payable—State		7 6 9 94
Social Security Tax Payable		1 9 1 8 06
Medicare Tax Payable		4 4 3 15
Medical Plan Payable		6 8 2 54
Retirement Plan Payable		4 5 8 39
Unemployment Tax Payable—Federal		1 3 52
Unemployment Tax Payable—State		9 0 64
Federal Income Tax Payable		
Dividends Payable		10 0 0 0 00
Capital Stock		200 0 0 0 00
Retained Earnings		204 2 6 5 75
Dividends	37 0 0 0 00	
Income Summary—General		
Income Summary—Parts		
Income Summary—Accessories		

(Note: Trial balance is continued on the next page.)

Mixon Auto Supplies

Adjusted Trial Balance (Concluded)

December 31, 20--

ACCOUNT TITLE	DEBIT	CREDIT
Sales—Parts		442 2 0 8 00
Sales Discount—Parts	5 3 4 6 15	
Sales Returns and Allowances—Parts	6 1 7 1 57	
Sales—Accessories		255 3 8 0 00
Sales Discount—Accessories	3 3 7 8 04	
Sales Returns and Allowances—Accessories	8 9 1 7 49	
Purchases—Parts	201 7 6 5 00	
Purchases Discount—Parts		2 0 1 9 21
Purchases Returns and Allowances—Parts		3 9 6 0 33
Purchases—Accessories	140 4 8 1 19	
Purchases Discount—Accessories		1 7 2 6 79
Purchases Returns and Allowances—Accessories		6 2 1 6 27
Advertising Expense—Parts	6 2 0 0 00	
Payroll Taxes Expense—Parts	4 1 9 2 36	
Salary Expense—Parts	47 6 4 5 19	
Advertising Expense—Accessories	3 8 0 0 00	
Payroll Taxes Expense—Accessories	7 0 7 0 97	
Salary Expense—Accessories	81 5 5 4 20	
Credit Card Fee Expense	4 4 3 0 92	
Depreciation Expense—Office Equipment		
Depreciation Expense—Store Equipment		
Insurance Expense		
Miscellaneous Expense	2 2 5 7 64	
Payroll Taxes Expense—Administrative	4 9 4 5 34	
Rent Expense	16 5 0 0 00	
Salary Expense—Administrative	57 0 5 7 83	
Supplies Expense		
Uncollectible Accounts Expense		
Utilities Expense	5 4 5 8 47	

4-2 WORK TOGETHER (LO6, 7), p. 111

Preparing a departmental margin statement

1., 2.

Foley's Interiors

Departmental Margin Statement—Kitchen

For Year Ended December 31, 20--

						% OF NET SALES*
Operating Revenue:						
Sales						
Less: Sales Discount						
Sales Returns and Allowances						
Net Sales						
Cost of Merchandise Sold:						
Merchandise Inventory, Jan. 1, 20--						
Purchases						
Less: Purchases Discount						
Purchases Returns and Allowances						
Net Purchases						
Total Cost of Merchandise Available for Sale						
Less Merchandise Inventory, Dec. 31, 20--						
Cost of Merchandise Sold						
Gross Profit						
Direct Expenses:						
Advertising Expense						
Payroll Taxes Expense						
Salary Expense						
Total Direct Expenses						
Departmental Margin						
*Rounded to the nearest 0.1%.						

Foley's Interiors

Departmental Margin Statement—Bath

For Year Ended December 31, 20--

					% OF NET SALES*
Operating Revenue:					
Sales					
Less: Sales Discount					
Sales Returns and Allowances					
Net Sales					
Cost of Merchandise Sold:					
Merchandise Inventory, Jan. 1, 20--					
Purchases					
Less: Purchases Discount					
Purchases Returns and Allowances					
Net Purchases					
Total Cost of Merchandise Available for Sale					
Less Merchandise Inventory, Dec. 31, 20--					
Cost of Merchandise Sold					
Gross Profit					
Direct Expenses:					
Advertising Expense					
Payroll Taxes Expense					
Salary Expense					
Total Direct Expenses					
Departmental Margin					
*Rounded to the nearest 0.1%.					

4-2 ON YOUR OWN (LO6, 7), p. 111

Preparing a departmental margin statement

1., 2.

Mixon Auto Supplies

Departmental Margin Statement—Parts

For Year Ended December 31, 20--

		% OF NET SALES*
Operating Revenue:		
Sales		
Less: Sales Discount		
Sales Returns and Allowances		
Net Sales		
Cost of Merchandise Sold:		
Merchandise Inventory, Jan. 1, 20--		
Purchases		
Less: Purchases Discount		
Purchases Returns and Allowances		
Net Purchases		
Total Cost of Merchandise Available for Sale		
Less Merchandise Inventory, Dec. 31, 20--		
Cost of Merchandise Sold		
Gross Profit		
Direct Expenses:		
Advertising Expense		
Payroll Taxes Expense		
Salary Expense		
Total Direct Expenses		
Departmental Margin		
*Rounded to the nearest 0.1%.		

Mixon Auto Supplies

Departmental Margin Statement—Accessories

For Year Ended December 31, 20--

				% OF NET SALES*
Operating Revenue:				
Sales				
Less: Sales Discount				
Sales Returns and Allowances				
Net Sales				
Cost of Merchandise Sold:				
Merchandise Inventory, Jan. 1, 20--				
Purchases				
Less: Purchases Discount				
Purchases Returns and Allowances				
Net Purchases				
Total Cost of Merchandise Available for Sale				
Less Merchandise Inventory, Dec. 31, 20--				
Cost of Merchandise Sold				
Gross Profit				
Direct Expenses:				
Advertising Expense				
Payroll Taxes Expense				
Salary Expense				
Total Direct Expenses				
Departmental Margin				
*Rounded to the nearest 0.1%.				

4-3 WORK TOGETHER (LO8), p. 116

Preparing financial statements

1.

Foley's Interiors

Income Statement

For Year Ended December 31, 20--

	DEPARTMENTAL		COMPANY	% OF NET SALES*
	KITCHEN	BATH		
Net Sales				
Cost of Merchandise Sold				
Gross Profit				
Direct Expenses				
Departmental Margin				
Indirect Expenses:				
Credit Card Fee Expense				
Depreciation Expense—Office Equipment				
Depreciation Expense—Store Equipment				
Insurance Expense				
Miscellaneous Expense				
Payroll Taxes Expense				
Rent Expense				
Salary Expense—Administrative				
Supplies Expense				
Uncollectible Accounts Expense				
Utilities Expense				
Total Indirect Expenses				
Income before Income Tax				
Less Federal Income Tax Expense				
Net Income				
*Rounded to the nearest 0.1%.				

2.

Foley's Interiors

Statement of Stockholders' Equity

For Year Ended December 31, 20--

Capital Stock:							
Retained Earnings:							
Balance, January 1, 20--							
Net Income for 20--							
Less Dividends Declared during 20--							
Net Increase during 20--							
Balance, December 31, 20--							
Total Stockholders' Equity, December 31, 20--							

4-3 WORK TOGETHER (continued)

3.

Foley's Interiors

Balance Sheet

December 31, 20--

							% OF ASSETS*
Assets							
Current Assets:							
Cash							
Petty Cash							
Accounts Receivable							
Less Allowance for Uncollectible Accounts							
Merchandise Inventory—Kitchen							
Merchandise Inventory—Bath							
Supplies							
Prepaid Insurance							
Total Current Assets							
Plant Assets:							
Office Equipment							
Less Accumulated Depreciation—Office Equipment							
Store Equipment							
Less Accumulated Depreciation—Store Equipment							
Total Plant Assets							
Total Assets							
Liabilities							
Current Liabilities:							
Accounts Payable							
Sales Tax Payable							
Employee Income Tax Payable—Federal							
Employee Income Tax Payable—State							
Social Security Tax Payable							
Medicare Tax Payable							
Medical Insurance Payable							
Retirement Plan Payable							
Unemployment Tax Payable—Federal							
Unemployment Tax Payable—State							
Federal Income Tax Payable							
Dividends Payable							
Total Liabilities							
Stockholders' Equity							
Capital Stock							
Retained Earnings							
Total Stockholders' Equity							
Total Liabilities and Stockholders' Equity							
*Rounded to the nearest 0.1%.							

4.

	Foley's Interiors											
	Statement of Cash Flows											
	For Year Ended December 31, 20--											
Cash flows from operating activities:												
Cash receipts from customers												
Cash payments for:												
Total cash payments												
Net cash provided (used) by operating activities												
Cash flows from investing activities:												
Net cash provided (used) by investing activities												
Cash flows from financing activities:												
Net cash provided (used) by financing activities												
Net change in cash												
Cash balance, January 1, 20--												
Cash balance, December 31, 20--												

4-3 ON YOUR OWN (LO8), p. 116

Preparing financial statements

1.

Mixon Auto Supplies

Income Statement

For Year Ended December 31, 20--

	DEPARTMENTAL		COMPANY	% OF NET SALES*
	PARTS	ACCESSORIES		
Net Sales				
Cost of Merchandise Sold				
Gross Profit				
Direct Expenses				
Departmental Margin				
Indirect Expenses:				
Credit Card Fee Expense				
Depreciation Expense—Office Equipment				
Depreciation Expense—Store Equipment				
Insurance Expense				
Miscellaneous Expense				
Payroll Taxes Expense				
Rent Expense				
Salary Expense—Administrative				
Supplies Expense				
Uncollectible Accounts Expense				
Utilities Expense				
Total Indirect Expenses				
Income before Income Tax				
Less Federal Income Tax Expense				
Net Income				
*Rounded to the nearest 0.1%.				

2.

	Mixon Auto Supplies							
	Statement of Stockholders' Equity							
	For Year Ended December 31, 20--							
Capital Stock:								
Retained Earnings:								
Balance, January 1, 20--								
Net Income for 20--								
Less Dividends Declared during 20--								
Net Increase during 20--								
Balance, December 31, 20--								
Total Stockholders' Equity, December 31, 20--								

4-3 ON YOUR OWN (continued)

3.

Mixon Auto Supplies

Balance Sheet

December 31, 20--

								% OF ASSETS*
Assets								
Current Assets:								
Cash								
Petty Cash								
Accounts Receivable								
Less Allowance for Uncollectible Accounts								
Merchandise Inventory—Parts								
Merchandise Inventory—Accessories								
Supplies								
Prepaid Insurance								
Total Current Assets								
Plant Assets:								
Office Equipment								
Less Accumulated Depreciation—Office Equipment								
Store Equipment								
Less Accumulated Depreciation—Store Equipment								
Total Plant Assets								
Total Assets								
Liabilities								
Current Liabilities:								
Accounts Payable								
Sales Tax Payable								
Employee Income Tax Payable—Federal								
Employee Income Tax Payable—State								
Social Security Tax Payable								
Medicare Tax Payable								
Medical Plan Payable								
Retirement Plan Payable								
Unemployment Tax Payable—Federal								
Unemployment Tax Payable—State								
Federal Income Tax Payable								
Dividends Payable								
Total Liabilities								
Stockholders' Equity								
Capital Stock								
Retained Earnings								
Total Stockholders' Equity								
Total Liabilities and Stockholders' Equity								

*Rounded to the nearest 0.1%.

4.

	Mixon Auto Supplies											
	Statement of Cash Flows											
	For Year Ended December 31, 20--											
Cash flows from operating activities:												
Cash receipts from customers												
Cash payments for:												
Total cash payments												
Net cash provided (used) by operating activities												
Cash flows from investing activities:												
Net cash provided (used) by investing activities												
Cash flows from financing activities:												
Net cash provided (used) by financing activities												
Net change in cash												
Cash balance, January 1, 20--												
Cash balance, December 31, 20--												

4-4 WORK TOGETHER (LO9), p. 122

Journalizing closing entries

GENERAL JOURNAL   PAGE

	DATE	ACCOUNT TITLE	DOC. NO.	POST. REF.	DEBIT	CREDIT	
1							1
2							2
3							3
4							4
5							5
6							6
7							7
8							8
9							9
10							10
11							11
12							12
13							13
14							14
15							15
16							16
17							17
18							18
19							19
20							20
21							21
22							22
23							23
24							24
25							25
26							26
27							27
28							28
29							29
30							30
31							31
32							32
33							33
34							34
35							35
36							36
37							37
38							38
39							39
40							40
41							41
42							42

Journalizing closing entries

GENERAL JOURNAL

PAGE

	DATE	ACCOUNT TITLE	DOC. NO.	POST. REF.	DEBIT	CREDIT	
1							1
2							2
3							3
4							4
5							5
6							6
7							7
8							8
9							9
10							10
11							11
12							12
13							13
14							14
15							15
16							16
17							17
18							18
19							19
20							20
21							21
22							22
23							23
24							24
25							25
26							26
27							27
28							28
29							29
30							30
31							31
32							32
33							33
34							34
35							35
36							36
37							37
38							38
39							39
40							40
41							41
42							42

4-1 APPLICATION PROBLEM (LO2, 3, 4), p. 127

Preparing an adjusted trial balance

1., 2., 4.

GENERAL JOURNAL   PAGE _____

	DATE	ACCOUNT TITLE	DOC. NO.	POST. REF.	DEBIT	CREDIT	
1							1
2							2
3							3
4							4
5							5
6							6
7							7
8							8
9							9
10							10
11							11
12							12
13							13
14							14
15							15
16							16
17							17
18							18

4.

Net Income before Federal Income Taxes	×	Tax Rate	=	Federal Income Tax
$	×		=	$

2., 3.   **GENERAL LEDGER**

ACCOUNT Allowance for Uncollectible Accounts   ACCOUNT NO. 1210

DATE		ITEM	POST. REF.	DEBIT	CREDIT	BALANCE	
						DEBIT	CREDIT
Dec. 20--	31	Balance	✔				5 1 6 36

ACCOUNT Merchandise Inventory—Golf   ACCOUNT NO. 1305

DATE		ITEM	POST. REF.	DEBIT	CREDIT	BALANCE	
						DEBIT	CREDIT
Dec. 20--	31	Balance	✔			62 8 4 9 00	

ACCOUNT Merchandise Inventory—Tennis   ACCOUNT NO. 1310

DATE		ITEM	POST. REF.	DEBIT	CREDIT	BALANCE	
						DEBIT	CREDIT
Dec. 20--	31	Balance	✔			49 1 8 3 00	

ACCOUNT Supplies   ACCOUNT NO. 1405

DATE		ITEM	POST. REF.	DEBIT	CREDIT	BALANCE	
						DEBIT	CREDIT
Dec. 20--	31	Balance	✔			3 1 0 5 04	

ACCOUNT Prepaid Insurance   ACCOUNT NO. 1410

DATE		ITEM	POST. REF.	DEBIT	CREDIT	BALANCE	
						DEBIT	CREDIT
Dec. 20--	31	Balance	✔			13 0 0 0 00	

4-1   APPLICATION PROBLEM (continued)

ACCOUNT Accumulated Depreciation—Office Equipment   ACCOUNT NO. 1510

DATE		ITEM	POST. REF.	DEBIT	CREDIT	BALANCE	
						DEBIT	CREDIT
Dec. 20--	31	Balance	✔				9 1 9 5 00

ACCOUNT Accumulated Depreciation—Store Equipment   ACCOUNT NO. 1520

DATE		ITEM	POST. REF.	DEBIT	CREDIT	BALANCE	
						DEBIT	CREDIT
Dec. 20--	31	Balance	✔				22 3 9 0 00

ACCOUNT Federal Income Tax Payable   ACCOUNT NO. 2305

DATE	ITEM	POST. REF.	DEBIT	CREDIT	BALANCE	
					DEBIT	CREDIT

ACCOUNT Income Summary—Golf   ACCOUNT NO. 3210

DATE	ITEM	POST. REF.	DEBIT	CREDIT	BALANCE	
					DEBIT	CREDIT

ACCOUNT Income Summary—Tennis   ACCOUNT NO. 3215

DATE	ITEM	POST. REF.	DEBIT	CREDIT	BALANCE	
					DEBIT	CREDIT

ACCOUNT Depreciation Expense—Office Equipment   ACCOUNT NO. 7110

DATE	ITEM	POST. REF.	DEBIT	CREDIT	BALANCE DEBIT	BALANCE CREDIT

ACCOUNT Depreciation Expense—Store Equipment   ACCOUNT NO. 7115

DATE	ITEM	POST. REF.	DEBIT	CREDIT	BALANCE DEBIT	BALANCE CREDIT

ACCOUNT Insurance Expense   ACCOUNT NO. 7120

DATE	ITEM	POST. REF.	DEBIT	CREDIT	BALANCE DEBIT	BALANCE CREDIT

ACCOUNT Supplies Expense   ACCOUNT NO. 7150

DATE	ITEM	POST. REF.	DEBIT	CREDIT	BALANCE DEBIT	BALANCE CREDIT

ACCOUNT Uncollectible Accounts Expense   ACCOUNT NO. 7155

DATE	ITEM	POST. REF.	DEBIT	CREDIT	BALANCE DEBIT	BALANCE CREDIT

ACCOUNT Federal Income Tax Expense   ACCOUNT NO. 8105

DATE	ITEM	POST. REF.	DEBIT	CREDIT	BALANCE DEBIT	BALANCE CREDIT
20-- Dec. 31	Balance	✔			10 0 0 0 00	

4-1 APPLICATION PROBLEM (continued)

3., 4., 5.

Sunset Sports, Inc.

Adjusted Trial Balance

December 31, 20--

ACCOUNT TITLE	DEBIT	CREDIT
Cash	53 3 1 4 47	
Petty Cash	1 5 0 15	
Accounts Receivable	11 6 7 7 03	
Allowance for Uncollectible Accounts		
Merchandise Inventory—Golf		
Merchandise Inventory—Tennis		
Supplies		
Prepaid Insurance		
Office Equipment	13 1 2 2 52	
Accumulated Depreciation—Office Equipment		
Store Equipment	41 7 1 4 34	
Accumulated Depreciation—Store Equipment		
Accounts Payable		22 4 5 7 79
Sales Tax Payable		2 9 5 9 35
Employee Income Tax Payable—Federal		1 0 7 8 32
Employee Income Tax Payable—State		7 6 8 39
Social Security Tax Payable		1 9 0 5 07
Medicare Tax Payable		4 4 3 83
Medical Plan Payable		6 8 5 15
Retirement Plan Payable		4 5 9 36
Unemployment Tax Payable—Federal		1 3 53
Unemployment Tax Payable—State		9 0 24
Federal Income Tax Payable		
Dividends Payable		5 0 0 0 00
Capital Stock		60 0 0 0 00
Retained Earnings		66 7 6 8 35
Dividends	23 4 0 0 00	
Income Summary—General		
Income Summary—Golf		
Income Summary—Tennis		

(Note: Trial balance is continued on the next page.)

Sunset Sports, Inc.

Adjusted Trial Balance (Concluded)

December 31, 20--

ACCOUNT TITLE	DEBIT	CREDIT
Sales—Golf		362 4 8 3 36
Sales Discount—Golf	5 3 8 5 63	
Sales Returns and Allowances—Golf	6 1 2 6 18	
Sales—Tennis		230 4 9 5 71
Sales Discount—Tennis	3 4 1 6 57	
Sales Returns and Allowances—Tennis	8 8 8 2 27	
Purchases—Golf	154 6 9 4 05	
Purchases Discount—Golf		2 0 2 0 23
Purchases Returns and Allowances—Golf		3 9 6 8 96
Purchases—Tennis	117 4 6 5 31	
Purchases Discount—Tennis		1 7 3 4 91
Purchases Returns and Allowances—Tennis		5 2 3 4 63
Advertising Expense—Golf	4 5 2 0 00	
Payroll Taxes Expense—Golf	4 2 0 2 27	
Salary Expense—Golf	47 6 1 7 46	
Advertising Expense—Tennis	3 8 2 5 00	
Payroll Taxes Expense—Tennis	5 6 8 1 90	
Salary Expense—Tennis	65 5 8 9 31	
Credit Card Fee Expense	3 4 1 5 18	
Depreciation Expense—Office Equipment		
Depreciation Expense—Store Equipment		
Insurance Expense		
Miscellaneous Expense	6 2 1 0 16	
Payroll Taxes Expense—Administrative	4 9 3 2 43	
Rent Expense	14 5 0 0 00	
Salary Expense—Administrative	57 4 6 9 05	
Supplies Expense		
Uncollectible Accounts Expense		
Utilities Expense	5 2 2 0 22	

4-2 APPLICATION PROBLEM (LO6, 7), p. 127

Preparing a departmental margin statement

1., 2.

Sunset Sports, Inc.

Departmental Margin Statement—Golf

For Year Ended December 31, 20--

		% OF NET SALES*
Operating Revenue:		
Sales		
Less: Sales Discount		
Sales Returns and Allowances		
Net Sales		
Cost of Merchandise Sold:		
Merchandise Inventory, Jan. 1, 20--		
Purchases		
Less: Purchases Discount		
Purchases Returns and Allowances		
Net Purchases		
Total Cost of Merchandise Available for Sale		
Less Merchandise Inventory, Dec. 31, 20--		
Cost of Merchandise Sold		
Gross Profit		
Direct Expenses:		
Advertising Expense		
Payroll Taxes Expense		
Salary Expense		
Total Direct Expenses		
Departmental Margin		
*Rounded to the nearest 0.1%.		

Sunset Sports, Inc.

Departmental Margin Statement—Tennis

For Year Ended December 31, 20--

				% OF NET SALES*
Operating Revenue:				
Sales				
Less: Sales Discount				
Sales Returns and Allowances				
Net Sales				
Cost of Merchandise Sold:				
Merchandise Inventory, Jan. 1, 20--				
Purchases				
Less: Purchases Discount				
Purchases Returns and Allowances				
Net Purchases				
Total Cost of Merchandise Available for Sale				
Less Merchandise Inventory, Dec. 31, 20--				
Cost of Merchandise Sold				
Gross Profit				
Direct Expenses:				
Advertising Expense				
Payroll Taxes Expense				
Salary Expense				
Total Direct Expenses				
Departmental Margin				
*Rounded to the nearest 0.1%.				

4-3   APPLICATION PROBLEM (LO8), p. 127

Preparing financial statements

1.

	Sunset Sports, Inc.
	Income Statement
	For Year Ended December 31, 20--

	DEPARTMENTAL		COMPANY	% OF NET SALES*
	GOLF	TENNIS		
Net Sales				
Cost of Merchandise Sold				
Gross Profit				
Direct Expenses				
Departmental Margin				
Indirect Expenses:				
Credit Card Fee Expense				
Depreciation Expense—Office Equipment				
Depreciation Expense—Store Equipment				
Insurance Expense				
Miscellaneous Expense				
Payroll Taxes Expense				
Rent Expense				
Salary Expense—Administrative				
Supplies Expense				
Uncollectible Accounts Expense				
Utilities Expense				
Total Indirect Expenses				
Income before Income Tax				
Less Federal Income Tax Expense				
Net Income				
*Rounded to the nearest 0.1%.				

2.

Sunset Sports, Inc.

Statement of Stockholders' Equity

For Year Ended December 31, 20--

Capital Stock:				
Retained Earnings:				
Balance, January 1, 20--				
Net Income for 20--				
Less Dividends Declared during 20--				
Net Increase during 20--				
Balance, December 31, 20--				
Total Stockholders' Equity, December 31, 20--				

4-3 **APPLICATION PROBLEM (continued)**

3.

Sunset Sports, Inc.

Balance Sheet

December 31, 20--

						% OF ASSETS*
Assets						
Current Assets:						
Cash						
Petty Cash						
Accounts Receivable						
Less Allowance for Uncollectible Accounts						
Merchandise Inventory—Golf						
Merchandise Inventory—Tennis						
Supplies						
Prepaid Insurance						
Total Current Assets						
Plant Assets:						
Office Equipment						
Less Accumulated Depreciation—Office Equipment						
Store Equipment						
Less Accumulated Depreciation—Store Equipment						
Total Plant Assets						
Total Assets						
Liabilities						
Current Liabilities:						
Accounts Payable						
Sales Tax Payable						
Employee Income Tax Payable—Federal						
Employee Income Tax Payable—State						
Social Security Tax Payable						
Medicare Tax Payable						
Medical Plan Payable						
Retirement Plan Payable						
Unemployment Tax Payable—Federal						
Unemployment Tax Payable—State						
Federal Income Tax Payable						
Dividends Payable						
Total Liabilities						
Stockholders' Equity						
Capital Stock						
Retained Earnings						
Total Stockholders' Equity						
Total Liabilities and Stockholders' Equity						
*Rounded to the nearest 0.1%.						

4.

Sunset Sports, Inc.

Statement of Cash Flows

For Year Ended December 31, 20--

Cash flows from operating activities:					
Cash receipts from customers					
Cash payments for:					
Total cash payments					
Net cash provided (used) by operating activities					
Cash flows from investing activities:					
Net cash provided (used) by investing activities					
Cash flows from financing activities:					
Net cash provided (used) by financing activities					
Net change in cash					
Cash balance, January 1, 20--					
Cash balance, December 31, 20--					

4-4 APPLICATION PROBLEM (LO9), p. 128

Journalizing closing entries

GENERAL JOURNAL   PAGE _____

	DATE	ACCOUNT TITLE	DOC. NO.	POST. REF.	DEBIT	CREDIT	
1							1
2							2
3							3
4							4
5							5
6							6
7							7
8							8
9							9
10							10
11							11
12							12
13							13
14							14
15							15
16							16
17							17
18							18
19							19
20							20
21							21
22							22
23							23
24							24
25							25
26							26
27							27
28							28
29							29
30							30
31							31
32							32
33							33
34							34
35							35
36							36
37							37
38							38
39							39
40							40
41							41
42							42

Completing end-of-fiscal-period work for a departmentalized merchandising business

1., 2., 4.

GENERAL JOURNAL   PAGE

	DATE	ACCOUNT TITLE	DOC. NO.	POST. REF.	DEBIT	CREDIT	
1							1
2							2
3							3
4							4
5							5
6							6
7							7
8							8
9							9
10							10
11							11
12							12
13							13
14							14
15							15
16							16
17							17
18							18

4.

Net Income before Federal Income Taxes	×	Tax Rate	=	Federal Income Tax
$	×		=	$

4-M MASTERY PROBLEM (continued)

2., 4.   **GENERAL LEDGER**

ACCOUNT Allowance for Uncollectible Accounts   ACCOUNT NO. 1210

DATE	ITEM	POST. REF.	DEBIT	CREDIT	BALANCE DEBIT	BALANCE CREDIT
20-- Dec. 31	Balance	✔			2 4 8 3 55	

ACCOUNT Merchandise Inventory—Antiques   ACCOUNT NO. 1305

DATE	ITEM	POST. REF.	DEBIT	CREDIT	BALANCE DEBIT	BALANCE CREDIT
20-- Dec. 31	Balance	✔			246 1 2 9 27	

ACCOUNT Merchandise Inventory—Modern   ACCOUNT NO. 1310

DATE	ITEM	POST. REF.	DEBIT	CREDIT	BALANCE DEBIT	BALANCE CREDIT
20-- Dec. 31	Balance	✔			223 0 5 4 45	

ACCOUNT Supplies   ACCOUNT NO. 1405

DATE	ITEM	POST. REF.	DEBIT	CREDIT	BALANCE DEBIT	BALANCE CREDIT
20-- Dec. 31	Balance	✔			6 7 2 5 58	

ACCOUNT Prepaid Insurance   ACCOUNT NO. 1410

DATE	ITEM	POST. REF.	DEBIT	CREDIT	BALANCE DEBIT	BALANCE CREDIT
20-- Dec. 31	Balance	✔			16 0 0 0 00	

ACCOUNT Accumulated Depreciation—Office Equipment ACCOUNT NO. 1510

DATE	ITEM	POST. REF.	DEBIT	CREDIT	BALANCE DEBIT	BALANCE CREDIT
20-- Dec. 31	Balance	✔				10 9 8 8 99

ACCOUNT Accumulated Depreciation—Store Equipment ACCOUNT NO. 1520

DATE	ITEM	POST. REF.	DEBIT	CREDIT	BALANCE DEBIT	BALANCE CREDIT
20-- Dec. 31	Balance	✔				14 0 9 0 41

ACCOUNT Federal Income Tax Payable ACCOUNT NO. 2305

DATE	ITEM	POST. REF.	DEBIT	CREDIT	BALANCE DEBIT	BALANCE CREDIT

ACCOUNT Income Summary—General ACCOUNT NO. 3205

DATE	ITEM	POST. REF.	DEBIT	CREDIT	BALANCE DEBIT	BALANCE CREDIT

ACCOUNT Income Summary—Antiques ACCOUNT NO. 3210

DATE	ITEM	POST. REF.	DEBIT	CREDIT	BALANCE DEBIT	BALANCE CREDIT

ACCOUNT Income Summary—Modern ACCOUNT NO. 3215

DATE	ITEM	POST. REF.	DEBIT	CREDIT	BALANCE DEBIT	BALANCE CREDIT

4-M MASTERY PROBLEM (continued)

ACCOUNT Depreciation Expense—Office Equipment ACCOUNT NO. 7110

DATE	ITEM	POST. REF.	DEBIT	CREDIT	BALANCE DEBIT	BALANCE CREDIT

ACCOUNT Depreciation Expense—Store Equipment ACCOUNT NO. 7115

DATE	ITEM	POST. REF.	DEBIT	CREDIT	BALANCE DEBIT	BALANCE CREDIT

ACCOUNT Insurance Expense ACCOUNT NO. 7120

DATE	ITEM	POST. REF.	DEBIT	CREDIT	BALANCE DEBIT	BALANCE CREDIT

ACCOUNT Supplies Expense ACCOUNT NO. 7150

DATE	ITEM	POST. REF.	DEBIT	CREDIT	BALANCE DEBIT	BALANCE CREDIT

ACCOUNT Uncollectible Accounts Expense ACCOUNT NO. 7155

DATE	ITEM	POST. REF.	DEBIT	CREDIT	BALANCE DEBIT	BALANCE CREDIT

ACCOUNT Federal Income Tax Expense ACCOUNT NO. 8105

DATE	ITEM	POST. REF.	DEBIT	CREDIT	BALANCE DEBIT	BALANCE CREDIT
Dec. 31	Balance	✔			36 0 0 0 00	

3., 5.

Forde Furniture Gallery

Adjusted Trial Balance

December 31, 20--

ACCOUNT TITLE	DEBIT	CREDIT
Cash	74 0 4 8 36	
Petty Cash	4 7 8 24	
Accounts Receivable	36 6 3 8 89	
Allowance for Uncollectible Accounts		
Merchandise Inventory—Antiques		
Merchandise Inventory—Modern		
Supplies		
Prepaid Insurance		
Office Equipment	51 3 0 9 14	
Accumulated Depreciation—Office Equipment		
Store Equipment	62 2 6 3 88	
Accumulated Depreciation—Store Equipment		
Accounts Payable		38 2 1 6 85
Sales Tax Payable		7 8 2 5 99
Employee Income Tax Payable—Federal		2 1 2 6 15
Employee Income Tax Payable—State		1 5 1 9 03
Social Security Tax Payable		3 7 7 5 91
Medicare Tax Payable		8 7 9 96
Medical Insurance Payable		1 3 5 1 24
Retirement Plan Payable		9 0 5 60
Unemployment Tax Payable—Federal		2 6 75
Unemployment Tax Payable—State		1 7 9 56
Federal Income Tax Payable		
Dividends Payable		15 0 0 0 00
Capital Stock		300 0 0 0 00
Retained Earnings		214 2 1 1 56
Dividends	60 0 0 0 00	
Income Summary—General		
Income Summary—Antiques		
Income Summary—Modern		

(Note: Trial balance is continued on the next page.)

4-M MASTERY PROBLEM (continued)

Forde Furniture Gallery

Adjusted Trial Balance (Concluded)

December 31, 20--

ACCOUNT TITLE	DEBIT	CREDIT
Sales—Antiques		870 0 5 2 67
Sales Discount—Antiques	10 5 8 7 38	
Sales Returns and Allowances—Antiques	12 2 0 1 54	
Sales—Modern		505 6 3 3 93
Sales Discount—Modern	6 6 9 3 73	
Sales Returns and Allowances—Modern	17 6 6 6 89	
Purchases—Antiques	399 4 7 2 04	
Purchases Discount—Antiques		3 9 8 3 45
Purchases Returns and Allowances—Antiques		7 8 5 6 02
Purchases—Modern	275 9 6 8 46	
Purchases Discount—Modern		3 4 2 4 51
Purchases Returns and Allowances—Modern		12 2 8 1 20
Advertising Expense—Antiques	16 2 0 0 00	
Payroll Taxes Expense—Antiques	8 3 0 2 37	
Salary Expense—Antiques	94 0 2 3 44	
Advertising Expense—Modern	12 6 0 0 00	
Payroll Taxes Expense—Modern	13 9 9 5 63	
Salary Expense—Modern	161 1 0 6 96	
Credit Card Fee Expense	8 7 4 6 70	
Depreciation Expense—Office Equipment		
Depreciation Expense—Store Equipment		
Insurance Expense		
Miscellaneous Expense	4 4 4 7 60	
Payroll Taxes Expense—Administrative	9 7 3 8 93	
Rent Expense	24 0 0 0 00	
Salary Expense—Administrative	112 7 2 8 83	
Supplies Expense		
Uncollectible Accounts Expense		
Utilities Expense	10 7 1 7 92	

Total of income statement credit accounts .... $ _____

Less total of income statement debit accounts

    excluding federal income tax expense .... _____

Equals net income before federal income tax expense ..... $ _____

6.

	Forde Furniture Gallery													% OF NET SALES*
	Departmental Margin Statement—Antiques													
	For Year Ended December 31, 20--													

*Rounded to the nearest 0.1%.

4-M   MASTERY PROBLEM (continued)

Forde Furniture Gallery

Departmental Margin Statement—Modern

For Year Ended December 31, 20--

			% OF NET SALES*
*Rounded to the nearest 0.1%.			

7.

Forde Furniture Gallery					
Income Statement					
For Year Ended December 31, 20--					
	DEPARTMENTAL		COMPANY		% OF NET SALES*
	ANTIQUES	MODERN			
*Rounded to the nearest 0.1%.					

4-M MASTERY PROBLEM (continued)

7.

Forde Furniture Gallery

Statement of Stockholders' Equity

For Year Ended December 31, 20--

7.

Forde Furniture Gallery

Balance Sheet

December 31, 20--

					% OF ASSETS*

*Rounded to the nearest 0.1%.

4-M **MASTERY PROBLEM (continued)**

8.

Forde Furniture Gallery

Statement of Cash Flows

For Year Ended December 31, 20--

9.

GENERAL JOURNAL

PAGE

	DATE	ACCOUNT TITLE	DOC. NO.	POST. REF.	DEBIT	CREDIT	
1							1
2							2
3							3
4							4
5							5
6							6
7							7
8							8
9							9
10							10
11							11
12							12
13							13
14							14
15							15
16							16
17							17
18							18
19							19
20							20
21							21
22							22
23							23
24							24
25							25
26							26
27							27
28							28
29							29
30							30
31							31
32							32
33							33
34							34
35							35
36							36
37							37
38							38
39							39
40							40
41							41
42							42

4-C CHALLENGE PROBLEM (LO6, 7), p. 129

Analyzing a departmental margin statement

1.

Crystal Pools
Departmental Margin Statement—Chemicals Department
For Years Ended December 31, 20X7 and 20X6

	20X7		20X6	
	AMOUNTS	% OF NET SALES	AMOUNTS	% OF NET SALES
Operating Revenue:				
Net Sales	514 85 1 36		480 1 6 4 68	100.0
Cost of Merchandise Sold:				
Merchandise Inventory, Jan. 1, 20--	61 8 4 8 08		58 1 4 8 61	
Purchases	302 1 8 4 61		274 0 1 8 61	
Total Cost of Merchandise Available for Sale	364 0 3 2 69		332 1 6 7 22	
Less Merchandise Inventory, Dec. 31, 20--	65 1 0 8 47		61 8 4 8 08	
Cost of Merchandise Sold	298 9 2 4 22		270 3 1 9 14	56.3
Gross Profit	215 9 2 7 14		209 8 4 5 54	43.7
Direct Expenses:				
Advertising Expense	16 5 0 0 00		16 1 0 0 00	3.4
Delivery Expense	8 1 4 8 36		8 1 6 8 15	1.7
Depreciation Expense—Store Equipment	6 2 5 0 00		5 9 5 0 00	1.2
Payroll Taxes Expense	5 2 6 5 30		5 1 0 2 79	1.1
Salary Expense	50 2 4 3 70		48 6 8 6 15	10.1
Supplies Expense	4 9 1 6 68		3 8 3 1 14	0.8
Total Direct Expenses	91 3 2 4 04		87 8 3 8 23	18.3
Departmental Margin	124 6 0 3 10		122 0 0 7 31	25.4

2.

Change in % of Net Sales	
a. Cost of Merchandise Sold	
b. Gross Profit	
c. Total Direct Expenses	
d. Departmental Margin	

3.

a.

_____

_____

_____

_____

_____

_____

b.

_____

_____

_____

_____

_____

_____

c.

_____

_____

_____

_____

_____

APPENDIX PROBLEM 4-1, p. 134

Preparing a work sheet

1., 2., 3.

Foley's Interiors

Adjusted Trial Balance

December 31, 20--

| | | TRIAL BALANCE | | ADJUSTMENTS | |
	ACCOUNT TITLE	DEBIT	CREDIT	DEBIT	CREDIT
1	Cash	34 4 6 0 79			
2	Petty Cash	3 0 0 00			
3	Accounts Receivable	23 0 1 8 95			
4	Allowance for Uncollectible Accounts		7 7 38		
5	Merchandise Inventory—Kitchen	140 8 9 0 00			
6	Merchandise Inventory—Bath	98 6 2 0 00			
7	Supplies	6 0 9 7 89			
8	Prepaid Insurance	18 0 0 0 00			
9	Office Equipment	26 0 1 5 89			
10	Accumulated Depreciation—Office Equipment		11 4 2 4 00		
11	Store Equipment	51 8 5 2 82			
12	Accumulated Depreciation—Store Equipment		27 7 6 5 00		
13	Accounts Payable		24 1 1 6 31		
14	Sales Tax Payable		4 9 2 5 59		
15	Employee Income Tax Payable—Federal		1 3 3 5 44		
16	Employee Income Tax Payable—State		9 5 6 99		
17	Social Security Tax Payable		2 3 7 6 90		
18	Medicare Tax Payable		5 5 3 24		
19	Medical Insurance Payable		8 4 6 42		
20	Retirement Plan Payable		5 7 1 94		
21	Unemployment Tax Payable—Federal		1 6 72		
22	Unemployment Tax Payable—State		1 1 2 08		
23	Federal Income Tax Payable				
24	Dividends Payable		4 0 0 0 00		
25	Capital Stock		75 0 0 0 00		
26	Retained Earnings		165 0 7 3 83		
27	Dividends	16 0 0 0 00			
28	Income Summary—Kitchen				
29	Income Summary—Bath				
30	Sales—Kitchen		417 9 5 3 07		
31	Sales Discount—Kitchen	6 6 5 5 27			
32	Sales Returns and Allowances—Kitchen	7 6 3 4 77			
33	Sales—Bath		316 0 1 4 76		
34	Sales Discount—Bath	4 2 2 0 29			

(Note: Work Sheet continues on p. 177.)

	5	6	7	8	9	10	11	12	
	DEPARTMENTAL STATEMENTS				INCOME STATEMENT		BALANCE SHEET		
	KITCHEN		BATH						
	DEBIT	CREDIT	DEBIT	CREDIT	DEBIT	CREDIT	DEBIT	CREDIT	
									1
									2
									3
									4
									5
									6
									7
									8
									9
									10
									11
									12
									13
									14
									15
									16
									17
									18
									19
									20
									21
									22
									23
									24
									25
									26
									27
									28
									29
									30
									31
									32
									33
									34

(Note: Work Sheet continues on p. 178.)

APPENDIX PROBLEM 4-1 (continued)

	ACCOUNT TITLE	TRIAL BALANCE		ADJUSTMENTS	
		DEBIT	CREDIT	DEBIT	CREDIT
35	Sales Returns and Allowances—Bath	11 0 7 0 52			
36	Purchases—Kitchen	204 1 6 4 91			
37	Purchases Discount—Kitchen		2 5 0 5 71		
38	Purchases Returns and Allowances—Kitchen		4 9 2 5 52		
39	Purchases—Bath	128 4 5 1 62			
40	Purchases Discount—Bath		2 1 5 7 01		
41	Purchases Returns and Allowances—Bath		6 4 9 5 71		
42	Advertising Expense—Kitchen	11 9 0 0 00			
43	Payroll Taxes Expense—Kitchen	5 1 9 3 25			
44	Salary Expense—Kitchen	59 1 2 1 95			
45	Advertising Expense—Bath	4 5 0 0 00			
46	Payroll Taxes Expense—Bath	7 0 2 8 66			
47	Salary Expense—Bath	81 1 0 3 91			
48	Credit Card Fee Expense	4 5 0 2 93			
49	Depreciation Expense—Office Equipment				
50	Depreciation Expense—Store Equipment				
51	Insurance Expense				
52	Miscellaneous Expense	2 8 1 3 28			
53	Payroll Taxes Expense—Administrative	6 1 4 9 34			
54	Rent Expense	18 0 0 0 00			
55	Salary Expense—Administrative	71 0 0 1 51			
56	Supplies Expense				
57	Uncollectible Accounts Expense				
58	Utilities Expense	6 4 3 5 07			
59					
60	Department Margin—Kitchen				
61	Department Margin—Bath				
62					
63	Federal Income Tax Expense	14 0 0 0 00			
64		1069 2 0 3 62	1069 2 0 3 62		
65	Net Income				
66					
67					
68					

APPENDIX PROBLEM 4-1 (concluded)

	5		6		7		8		9		10		11		12	
	DEPARTMENTAL STATEMENTS							INCOME STATEMENT				BALANCE SHEET			
	KITCHEN				BATH										
	DEBIT		CREDIT		DEBIT		CREDIT		DEBIT		CREDIT		DEBIT		CREDIT	

(empty worksheet, rows 35–68)

APPENDIX PROBLEM 4-2, p. 134

Preparing a work sheet

1., 2., 3.

Mixon Auto Supplies

Adjusted Trial Balance

December 31, 20--

	ACCOUNT TITLE	TRIAL BALANCE		ADJUSTMENTS	
		DEBIT	CREDIT	DEBIT	CREDIT
1	Cash	57 3 5 4 03			
2	Petty Cash	2 4 1 66			
3	Accounts Receivable	18 5 3 3 67			
4	Allowance for Uncollectible Accounts		1 4 8 36		
5	Merchandise Inventory—Parts	256 4 7 0 00			
6	Merchandise Inventory—Accessories	112 7 4 0 00			
7	Supplies	4 9 3 5 98			
8	Prepaid Insurance	15 0 0 0 00			
9	Office Equipment	20 8 2 7 76			
10	Accumulated Depreciation—Office Equipment		9 1 4 5 86		
11	Store Equipment	41 5 3 1 75			
12	Accumulated Depreciation—Store Equipment		22 2 9 8 99		
13	Accounts Payable		19 3 0 1 35		
14	Sales Tax Payable		3 9 7 6 77		
15	Employee Income Tax Payable—Federal		1 0 8 0 01		
16	Employee Income Tax Payable—State		7 6 9 94		
17	Social Security Tax Payable		1 9 1 8 06		
18	Medicare Tax Payable		4 4 3 15		
19	Medical Plan Payable		6 8 2 54		
20	Retirement Plan Payable		4 5 8 39		
21	Unemployment Tax Payable—Federal		1 3 52		
22	Unemployment Tax Payable—State		9 0 64		
23	Federal Income Tax Payable				
24	Dividends Payable		10 0 0 0 00		
25	Capital Stock		200 0 0 0 00		
26	Retained Earnings		204 2 6 5 75		
27	Dividends	37 0 0 0 00			
28	Income Summary—General				
29	Income Summary—Parts				
30	Income Summary—Accessories				
31	Sales—Parts		442 2 0 8 00		
32	Sales Discount—Parts	5 3 4 6 15			
33	Sales Returns and Allowances—Parts	6 1 7 1 57			
34	Sales—Accessories		255 3 8 0 00		

(Note: Work Sheet continues on p. 181.)

	5	6	7	8	9	10	11	12	
	DEPARTMENTAL STATEMENTS				**INCOME STATEMENT**		**BALANCE SHEET**		
	PARTS		**ACCESSORIES**						
	DEBIT	CREDIT	DEBIT	CREDIT	DEBIT	CREDIT	DEBIT	CREDIT	
									1
									2
									3
									4
									5
									6
									7
									8
									9
									10
									11
									12
									13
									14
									15
									16
									17
									18
									19
									20
									21
									22
									23
									24
									25
									26
									27
									28
									29
									30
									31
									32
									33
									34

(Note: Work Sheet continues on p. 182.)

APPENDIX PROBLEM 4-2 (continued)

	ACCOUNT TITLE	TRIAL BALANCE		ADJUSTMENTS	
		DEBIT	CREDIT	DEBIT	CREDIT
35	Sales Discount—Accessories	3 3 7 8 04			
36	Sales Returns and Allowances—Accessories	8 9 1 7 49			
37	Purchases—Parts	201 7 6 5 00			
38	Purchases Discount—Parts		2 0 1 9 21		
39	Purchases Returns and Allowances—Parts		3 9 6 0 33		
40	Purchases—Accessories	140 4 8 1 19			
41	Purchases Discount—Accessories		1 7 2 6 79		
42	Purchases Returns and Allowances—Accessories		6 2 1 6 27		
43	Advertising Expense—Parts	6 2 0 0 00			
44	Payroll Taxes Expense—Parts	4 1 9 2 36			
45	Salary Expense—Parts	47 6 4 5 19			
46	Advertising Expense—Accessories	3 8 0 0 00			
47	Payroll Taxes Expense—Accessories	7 0 7 0 97			
48	Salary Expense—Accessories	81 5 5 4 20			
49	Credit Card Fee Expense	4 4 3 0 92			
50	Depreciation Expense—Office Equipment				
51	Depreciation Expense—Store Equipment				
52	Insurance Expense				
53	Miscellaneous Expense	2 2 5 7 64			
54	Payroll Taxes Expense—Administrative	4 9 4 5 34			
55	Rent Expense	16 5 0 0 00			
56	Salary Expense—Administrative	57 0 5 7 83			
57	Supplies Expense				
58	Uncollectible Accounts Expense				
59	Utilities Expense	5 4 5 8 47			
60					
61	Department Margin—Parts				
62	Department Margin—Accessories				
63					
64	Federal Income Tax Expense	14 0 0 0 00			
65	Totals	1185 9 5 5 57	1185 9 5 5 57		
66					
67					
68					

	5	6	7	8	9	10	11	12	
	DEPARTMENTAL STATEMENTS				INCOME STATEMENT		BALANCE SHEET		
	PARTS		ACCESSORIES						
	DEBIT	CREDIT	DEBIT	CREDIT	DEBIT	CREDIT	DEBIT	CREDIT	
									35
									36
									37
									38
									39
									40
									41
									42
									43
									44
									45
									46
									47
									48
									49
									50
									51
									52
									53
									54
									55
									56
									57
									58
									59
									60
									61
									62
									63
									64
									65
									66
									67
									68

APPENDIX PROBLEM 4-3, p. 134

Preparing a work sheet

1., 2., 3.

Sunset Sports, Inc.

Work Sheet

December 31, 20--

		ACCOUNT TITLE	TRIAL BALANCE DEBIT	TRIAL BALANCE CREDIT	ADJUSTMENTS DEBIT	ADJUSTMENTS CREDIT
1		Cash	53314 47			
2		Petty Cash	150 15			
3		Accounts Receivable	11677 03			
4		Allowance for Uncollectible Accounts		516 36		
5		Merchandise Inventory—Golf	62849 00			
6		Merchandise Inventory—Tennis	49183 00			
7		Supplies	3105 04			
8		Prepaid Insurance	13000 00			
9		Office Equipment	13122 52			
10		Accumulated Depreciation—Office Equipment		9195 00		
11		Store Equipment	41714 34			
12		Accumulated Depreciation—Store Equipment		22390 00		
13		Accounts Payable		22457 79		
14		Sales Tax Payable		2959 35		
15		Employee Income Tax Payable—Federal		1078 32		
16		Employee Income Tax Payable—State		768 39		
17		Social Security Tax Payable		1905 07		
18		Medicare Tax Payable		443 83		
19		Medical Plan Payable		685 15		
20		Retirement Plan Payable		459 36		
21		Unemployment Tax Payable—Federal		13 53		
22		Unemployment Tax Payable—State		90 24		
23		Federal Income Tax Payable				
24		Dividends Payable		5000 00		
25		Capital Stock		60000 00		
26		Retained Earnings		66768 35		
27		Dividends	23400 00			
28		Income Summary—General				
29		Income Summary—Golf				
30		Income Summary—Tennis				
31		Sales—Golf		362483 36		
32		Sales Discount—Golf	5385 63			
33		Sales Returns and Allowances—Golf	6126 18			
34		Sales—Tennis		230495 71		

(Note: Work Sheet continues on p. 185.)

	5		6		7		8		9		10		11		12	
	DEPARTMENTAL STATEMENTS							INCOME STATEMENT			BALANCE SHEET				
	GOLF				TENNIS										
	DEBIT		CREDIT		DEBIT		CREDIT		DEBIT		CREDIT		DEBIT		CREDIT	

DEPARTMENTAL STATEMENTS				INCOME STATEMENT		BALANCE SHEET		
GOLF		TENNIS						
DEBIT	CREDIT	DEBIT	CREDIT	DEBIT	CREDIT	DEBIT	CREDIT	
								1
								2
								3
								4
								5
								6
								7
								8
								9
								10
								11
								12
								13
								14
								15
								16
								17
								18
								19
								20
								21
								22
								23
								24
								25
								26
								27
								28
								29
								30
								31
								32
								33
								34

(Note: Work Sheet continues on p. 186.)

APPENDIX PROBLEM 4-3 (continued)

	ACCOUNT TITLE	TRIAL BALANCE DEBIT	TRIAL BALANCE CREDIT	ADJUSTMENTS DEBIT	ADJUSTMENTS CREDIT
35	Sales Discount—Tennis	3 4 1 6 57			
36	Sales Returns and Allowances—Tennis	8 8 8 2 27			
37	Purchases—Golf	154 6 9 4 05			
38	Purchases Discount—Golf		2 0 2 0 23		
39	Purchases Returns and Allowances—Golf		3 9 6 8 96		
40	Purchases—Tennis	117 4 6 5 31			
41	Purchases Discount—Tennis		1 7 3 4 91		
42	Purchases Returns and Allowances—Tennis		5 2 3 4 63		
43	Advertising Expense—Golf	4 5 2 0 00			
44	Payroll Taxes Expense—Golf	4 2 0 2 27			
45	Salary Expense—Golf	47 6 1 7 46			
46	Advertising Expense—Tennis	3 8 2 5 00			
47	Payroll Taxes Expense—Tennis	5 6 8 1 90			
48	Salary Expense—Tennis	65 5 8 9 31			
49	Credit Card Fee Expense	3 4 1 5 18			
50	Depreciation Expense—Office Equipment				
51	Depreciation Expense—Store Equipment				
52	Insurance Expense				
53	Miscellaneous Expense	6 2 1 0 16			
54	Payroll Taxes Expense—Administrative	4 9 3 2 43			
55	Rent Expense	14 5 0 0 00			
56	Salary Expense—Administrative	57 4 6 9 05			
57	Supplies Expense				
58	Uncollectible Accounts Expense				
59	Utilities Expense	5 2 2 0 22			
60					
61	Department Margin—Golf				
62	Department Margin—Tennis				
63					
64	Federal Income Tax Expense	10 0 0 0 00			
65	Totals	800 6 6 8 54	800 6 6 8 54		
66					
67					
68					

5	6	7	8	9	10	11	12	
DEPARTMENTAL STATEMENTS				INCOME STATEMENT		BALANCE SHEET		
GOLF		TENNIS						
DEBIT	CREDIT	DEBIT	CREDIT	DEBIT	CREDIT	DEBIT	CREDIT	
								35
								36
								37
								38
								39
								40
								41
								42
								43
								44
								45
								46
								47
								48
								49
								50
								51
								52
								53
								54
								55
								56
								57
								58
								59
								60
								61
								62
								63
								64
								65
								66
								67
								68

REINFORCEMENT ACTIVITY 1, p. 135

Processing and Reporting Departmentalized Accounting Data

1., 2., 4., 5., 8., 9., 12., 14., 21.

GENERAL LEDGER

ACCOUNT Cash   ACCOUNT NO. 1105

DATE		ITEM	POST. REF.	DEBIT	CREDIT	BALANCE DEBIT	BALANCE CREDIT
20-- Dec.	1	Balance	✔			34 1 4 2 62	

ACCOUNT Petty Cash   ACCOUNT NO. 1110

DATE		ITEM	POST. REF.	DEBIT	CREDIT	BALANCE DEBIT	BALANCE CREDIT
20-- Dec.	1	Balance	✔			5 0 0 00	

ACCOUNT Accounts Receivable   ACCOUNT NO. 1205

DATE		ITEM	POST. REF.	DEBIT	CREDIT	BALANCE DEBIT	BALANCE CREDIT
20-- Dec.	1	Balance	✔			12 3 5 6 74	

ACCOUNT Allowance for Uncollectible Accounts   ACCOUNT NO. 1210

DATE		ITEM	POST. REF.	DEBIT	CREDIT	BALANCE DEBIT	BALANCE CREDIT
20-- Dec.	1	Balance	✔				5 1 7 43

ACCOUNT Merchandise Inventory—Equipment   ACCOUNT NO. 1305

DATE		ITEM	POST. REF.	DEBIT	CREDIT	BALANCE DEBIT	BALANCE CREDIT
20-- Dec.	1	Balance	✔			81 4 8 3 61	

REINFORCEMENT ACTIVITY 1 (continued)

ACCOUNT Merchandise Inventory—Accessories   ACCOUNT NO. 1310

DATE		ITEM	POST. REF.	DEBIT	CREDIT	BALANCE DEBIT	BALANCE CREDIT
20-- Dec.	1	Balance	✔			157 4 1 4 10	

ACCOUNT Supplies   ACCOUNT NO. 1405

DATE		ITEM	POST. REF.	DEBIT	CREDIT	BALANCE DEBIT	BALANCE CREDIT
20-- Dec.	1	Balance	✔			8 1 4 3 04	

ACCOUNT Prepaid Insurance   ACCOUNT NO. 1410

DATE		ITEM	POST. REF.	DEBIT	CREDIT	BALANCE DEBIT	BALANCE CREDIT
20-- Dec.	1	Balance	✔			16 2 0 0 00	

ACCOUNT Office Equipment   ACCOUNT NO. 1505

DATE		ITEM	POST. REF.	DEBIT	CREDIT	BALANCE DEBIT	BALANCE CREDIT
20-- Dec.	1	Balance	✔			29 1 4 0 61	

ACCOUNT Accumulated Depreciation—Office Equipment   ACCOUNT NO. 1510

DATE		ITEM	POST. REF.	DEBIT	CREDIT	BALANCE DEBIT	BALANCE CREDIT
20-- Dec.	1	Balance	✔				13 0 5 0 00

REINFORCEMENT ACTIVITY 1 (continued)

ACCOUNT Store Equipment   ACCOUNT NO. 1515

DATE	ITEM	POST. REF.	DEBIT	CREDIT	BALANCE DEBIT	BALANCE CREDIT
20-- Dec. 1	Balance	✔			38 1 6 7 51	

ACCOUNT Accumulated Depreciation—Store Equipment   ACCOUNT NO. 1520

DATE	ITEM	POST. REF.	DEBIT	CREDIT	BALANCE DEBIT	BALANCE CREDIT
20-- Dec. 1	Balance	✔				15 3 6 0 00

ACCOUNT Accounts Payable   ACCOUNT NO. 2105

DATE	ITEM	POST. REF.	DEBIT	CREDIT	BALANCE DEBIT	BALANCE CREDIT
20-- Dec. 1	Balance	✔				20 3 7 6 63

ACCOUNT Sales Tax Payable   ACCOUNT NO. 2110

DATE	ITEM	POST. REF.	DEBIT	CREDIT	BALANCE DEBIT	BALANCE CREDIT
20-- Dec. 1	Balance	✔				2 6 4 1 62

ACCOUNT Employee Income Tax Payable—Federal   ACCOUNT NO. 2115

DATE	ITEM	POST. REF.	DEBIT	CREDIT	BALANCE DEBIT	BALANCE CREDIT
20-- Dec. 1	Balance	✔				5 2 4 00

ACCOUNT Employee Income Tax Payable—State — ACCOUNT NO. 2120

DATE		ITEM	POST. REF.	DEBIT	CREDIT	BALANCE	
						DEBIT	CREDIT
20-- Dec.	1	Balance	✔				4 2 9 00

ACCOUNT Social Security Tax Payable — ACCOUNT NO. 2125

DATE		ITEM	POST. REF.	DEBIT	CREDIT	BALANCE	
						DEBIT	CREDIT
20-- Dec.	1	Balance	✔				9 6 1 85

ACCOUNT Medicare Tax Payable — ACCOUNT NO. 2130

DATE		ITEM	POST. REF.	DEBIT	CREDIT	BALANCE	
						DEBIT	CREDIT
20-- Dec.	1	Balance	✔				2 2 4 95

ACCOUNT Medical Insurance Payable — ACCOUNT NO. 2135

DATE		ITEM	POST. REF.	DEBIT	CREDIT	BALANCE	
						DEBIT	CREDIT
20-- Dec.	1	Balance	✔				4 5 0 00

ACCOUNT Retirement Plan Payable — ACCOUNT NO. 2140

DATE		ITEM	POST. REF.	DEBIT	CREDIT	BALANCE	
						DEBIT	CREDIT
20-- Dec.	1	Balance	✔				5 2 0 00

REINFORCEMENT ACTIVITY 1 (continued)

ACCOUNT Unemployment Tax Payable—Federal   ACCOUNT NO. 2145

DATE	ITEM	POST. REF.	DEBIT	CREDIT	BALANCE DEBIT	BALANCE CREDIT
20-- Dec. 1	Balance	✔				2 1 0 60

ACCOUNT Unemployment Tax Payable—State   ACCOUNT NO. 2150

DATE	ITEM	POST. REF.	DEBIT	CREDIT	BALANCE DEBIT	BALANCE CREDIT
20-- Dec. 1	Balance	✔				4 2 4 62

ACCOUNT Federal Income Tax Payable   ACCOUNT NO. 2155

DATE	ITEM	POST. REF.	DEBIT	CREDIT	BALANCE DEBIT	BALANCE CREDIT

ACCOUNT Dividends Payable   ACCOUNT NO. 2160

DATE	ITEM	POST. REF.	DEBIT	CREDIT	BALANCE DEBIT	BALANCE CREDIT

ACCOUNT Capital Stock   ACCOUNT NO. 3105

DATE	ITEM	POST. REF.	DEBIT	CREDIT	BALANCE DEBIT	BALANCE CREDIT
20-- Dec. 1	Balance	✔				150 0 0 0 00

ACCOUNT Retained Earnings   ACCOUNT NO. 3110

DATE		ITEM	POST. REF.	DEBIT	CREDIT	BALANCE DEBIT	BALANCE CREDIT
Dec.	1	Balance	✔				114 80 3 91

ACCOUNT Dividends   ACCOUNT NO. 3115

DATE		ITEM	POST. REF.	DEBIT	CREDIT	BALANCE DEBIT	BALANCE CREDIT
Dec.	1	Balance	✔			21 5 0 0 00	

ACCOUNT Income Summary—General   ACCOUNT NO. 3205

DATE		ITEM	POST. REF.	DEBIT	CREDIT	BALANCE DEBIT	BALANCE CREDIT

ACCOUNT Income Summary—Equipment   ACCOUNT NO. 3210

DATE		ITEM	POST. REF.	DEBIT	CREDIT	BALANCE DEBIT	BALANCE CREDIT

ACCOUNT Income Summary—Accessories   ACCOUNT NO. 3215

DATE		ITEM	POST. REF.	DEBIT	CREDIT	BALANCE DEBIT	BALANCE CREDIT

REINFORCEMENT ACTIVITY 1 (continued)

ACCOUNT Sales—Equipment   ACCOUNT NO. 4105

DATE	ITEM	POST. REF.	DEBIT	CREDIT	BALANCE DEBIT	BALANCE CREDIT
20-- Dec. 1	Balance	✔				203 0 1 8 62

ACCOUNT Sales Discount—Equipment   ACCOUNT NO. 4110

DATE	ITEM	POST. REF.	DEBIT	CREDIT	BALANCE DEBIT	BALANCE CREDIT
20-- Dec. 1	Balance	✔			2 1 4 62	

ACCOUNT Sales Returns and Allowances—Equipment   ACCOUNT NO. 4115

DATE	ITEM	POST. REF.	DEBIT	CREDIT	BALANCE DEBIT	BALANCE CREDIT
20-- Dec. 1	Balance	✔			2 4 8 6 68	

ACCOUNT Sales—Accessories   ACCOUNT NO. 4205

DATE	ITEM	POST. REF.	DEBIT	CREDIT	BALANCE DEBIT	BALANCE CREDIT
20-- Dec. 1	Balance	✔				394 5 4 8 62

ACCOUNT Sales Discount—Accessories   ACCOUNT NO. 4210

DATE	ITEM	POST. REF.	DEBIT	CREDIT	BALANCE DEBIT	BALANCE CREDIT
20-- Dec. 1	Balance	✔			2 8 4 6 62	

ACCOUNT Sales Returns and Allowances—Accessories   ACCOUNT NO. 4215

DATE		ITEM	POST. REF.	DEBIT	CREDIT	BALANCE DEBIT	BALANCE CREDIT
20-- Dec.	1	Balance	✔			6 1 1 4 15	

ACCOUNT Purchases—Equipment   ACCOUNT NO. 5105

DATE		ITEM	POST. REF.	DEBIT	CREDIT	BALANCE DEBIT	BALANCE CREDIT
20-- Dec.	1	Balance	✔			102 4 8 3 31	

ACCOUNT Purchases Discount—Equipment   ACCOUNT NO. 5110

DATE		ITEM	POST. REF.	DEBIT	CREDIT	BALANCE DEBIT	BALANCE CREDIT
20-- Dec.	1	Balance	✔				1 1 8 4 14

ACCOUNT Purchases Returns and Allowances—Equipment   ACCOUNT NO. 5115

DATE		ITEM	POST. REF.	DEBIT	CREDIT	BALANCE DEBIT	BALANCE CREDIT
20-- Dec.	1	Balance	✔				4 1 1 7 61

ACCOUNT Purchases—Accessories   ACCOUNT NO. 5205

DATE		ITEM	POST. REF.	DEBIT	CREDIT	BALANCE DEBIT	BALANCE CREDIT
20-- Dec.	1	Balance	✔			221 4 9 3 61	

REINFORCEMENT ACTIVITY 1 (continued)

ACCOUNT Purchases Discount—Accessories   ACCOUNT NO. 5210

DATE	ITEM	POST. REF.	DEBIT	CREDIT	BALANCE DEBIT	BALANCE CREDIT
20-- Dec. 1	Balance	✔				4 1 6 2 04

ACCOUNT Purchases Returns and Allowances—Accessories   ACCOUNT NO. 5215

DATE	ITEM	POST. REF.	DEBIT	CREDIT	BALANCE DEBIT	BALANCE CREDIT
20-- Dec. 1	Balance	✔				12 9 1 4 62

ACCOUNT Advertising Expense—Equipment   ACCOUNT NO. 6105

DATE	ITEM	POST. REF.	DEBIT	CREDIT	BALANCE DEBIT	BALANCE CREDIT
20-- Dec. 1	Balance	✔			16 2 0 0 00	

ACCOUNT Payroll Taxes Expense—Equipment   ACCOUNT NO. 6110

DATE	ITEM	POST. REF.	DEBIT	CREDIT	BALANCE DEBIT	BALANCE CREDIT
20-- Dec. 1	Balance	✔			3 6 5 4 08	

ACCOUNT Salary Expense—Equipment   ACCOUNT NO. 6115

DATE	ITEM	POST. REF.	DEBIT	CREDIT	BALANCE DEBIT	BALANCE CREDIT
20-- Dec. 1	Balance	✔			36 4 1 9 57	

ACCOUNT Advertising Expense—Accessories — ACCOUNT NO. 6205

DATE		ITEM	POST. REF.	DEBIT	CREDIT	BALANCE DEBIT	BALANCE CREDIT
20-- Dec.	1	Balance	✔			6 3 5 0 00	

ACCOUNT Payroll Taxes Expense—Accessories — ACCOUNT NO. 6210

DATE		ITEM	POST. REF.	DEBIT	CREDIT	BALANCE DEBIT	BALANCE CREDIT
20-- Dec.	1	Balance	✔			3 8 8 3 11	

ACCOUNT Salary Expense—Accessories — ACCOUNT NO. 6215

DATE		ITEM	POST. REF.	DEBIT	CREDIT	BALANCE DEBIT	BALANCE CREDIT
20-- Dec.	1	Balance	✔			39 4 1 3 25	

ACCOUNT Credit Card Fee Expense — ACCOUNT NO. 7105

DATE		ITEM	POST. REF.	DEBIT	CREDIT	BALANCE DEBIT	BALANCE CREDIT
20-- Dec.	1	Balance	✔			5 1 2 1 64	

ACCOUNT Depreciation Expense—Office Equipment — ACCOUNT NO. 7110

DATE		ITEM	POST. REF.	DEBIT	CREDIT	BALANCE DEBIT	BALANCE CREDIT
20-- Dec.	1	Balance	✔			10 4 8 0 00	

REINFORCEMENT ACTIVITY 1 (continued)

ACCOUNT Depreciation Expense—Store Equipment   ACCOUNT NO. 7115

DATE		ITEM	POST. REF.	DEBIT	CREDIT	BALANCE DEBIT	BALANCE CREDIT
20-- Dec.	1	Balance	✔			16 1 8 0 00	

ACCOUNT Insurance Expense   ACCOUNT NO. 7120

DATE		ITEM	POST. REF.	DEBIT	CREDIT	BALANCE DEBIT	BALANCE CREDIT

ACCOUNT Miscellaneous Expense   ACCOUNT NO. 7125

DATE		ITEM	POST. REF.	DEBIT	CREDIT	BALANCE DEBIT	BALANCE CREDIT
20-- Dec.	1	Balance	✔			6 4 1 8 22	

ACCOUNT Payroll Taxes Expense—Administrative   ACCOUNT NO. 7130

DATE		ITEM	POST. REF.	DEBIT	CREDIT	BALANCE DEBIT	BALANCE CREDIT
20-- Dec.	1	Balance	✔			2 0 4 9 28	

ACCOUNT Rent Expense   ACCOUNT NO. 7135

DATE		ITEM	POST. REF.	DEBIT	CREDIT	BALANCE DEBIT	BALANCE CREDIT
20-- Dec.	1	Balance	✔			25 3 0 0 00	

REINFORCEMENT ACTIVITY 1 (continued)

ACCOUNT Salary Expense—Administrative   ACCOUNT NO. 7140

DATE	ITEM	POST. REF.	DEBIT	CREDIT	BALANCE DEBIT	BALANCE CREDIT
20-- Dec. 1	Balance	✔			15 4 4 1 63	

ACCOUNT Supplies Expense   ACCOUNT NO. 7145

DATE	ITEM	POST. REF.	DEBIT	CREDIT	BALANCE DEBIT	BALANCE CREDIT

ACCOUNT Uncollectible Accounts Expense   ACCOUNT NO. 7150

DATE	ITEM	POST. REF.	DEBIT	CREDIT	BALANCE DEBIT	BALANCE CREDIT

ACCOUNT Utilities Expense   ACCOUNT NO. 7155

DATE	ITEM	POST. REF.	DEBIT	CREDIT	BALANCE DEBIT	BALANCE CREDIT
20-- Dec. 1	Balance	✔			6 8 4 2 26	

ACCOUNT Federal Income Tax Expense   ACCOUNT NO. 8105

DATE	ITEM	POST. REF.	DEBIT	CREDIT	BALANCE DEBIT	BALANCE CREDIT
20-- Dec. 1	Balance	✔			12 0 0 0 00	

REINFORCEMENT ACTIVITY 1 (continued)

1., 5.

		PURCHASES JOURNAL				PAGE 12	

	DATE		ACCOUNT CREDITED	PURCH. NO.	POST. REF.	ACCOUNTS PAYABLE CREDIT	PURCHASES DEBIT EQUIPMENT	PURCHASES DEBIT ACCESSORIES	
1									1
2									2
3									3
4									4
5									5
6									6
7									7
8									8
9									9
10									10
11									11
12									12
13									13
14									14
15									15
16									16
17									17
18									18
19									19
20									20
21									21
22									22
23									23
24									24
25									25
26									26
27									27
28									28
29									29
30									30
31									31

REINFORCEMENT ACTIVITY 1 (continued)

1., 2.

CASH PAYMENTS JOURNAL

DATE	ACCOUNT TITLE	CK. NO.	POST. REF.	GENERAL DEBIT	GENERAL CREDIT	ACCOUNTS PAYABLE DEBIT	PURCH. DISCOUNT CR. EQUIPMENT	PURCH. DISCOUNT CR. ACCESSORIES	CASH CREDIT
				1	2	3	4	5	6
1									
2									
3									
4									
5									
6									
7									
8									
9									
10									
11									
12									
13									
14									
15									
16									
17									
18									
19									
20									
21									
22									
23									
24									
25									
26									
27									

REINFORCEMENT ACTIVITY 1 (continued)

3., 6., 9.

CASH PAYMENTS JOURNAL

DATE	ACCOUNT TITLE	CK. NO.	POST. REF.	GENERAL DEBIT	GENERAL CREDIT	ACCOUNTS PAYABLE DEBIT	PURCH. DISCOUNT CR. EQUIPMENT	PURCH. DISCOUNT CR. ACCESSORIES	CASH CREDIT
				1	2	3	4	5	6

REINFORCEMENT ACTIVITY 1 (continued)

1., 4.

SALES JOURNAL

	DATE		ACCOUNT DEBITED	SALE. NO.	POST. REF.	ACCOUNTS RECEIVABLE DEBIT	SALES TAX PAYABLE CREDIT	SALES CREDIT	
						1	2	EQUIPMENT 3	ACCESSORIES 4
1									
2									
3									
4									
5									
6									
7									
8									
9									
10									
11									
12									
13									
14									
15									
16									
17									
18									
19									
20									
21									
22									
23									
24									
25									
26									
27									
28									
29									
30									
31									

REINFORCEMENT ACTIVITY 1 (continued)

1., 6.

CASH RECEIPTS JOURNAL

PAGE 12

				GENERAL		ACCOUNTS RECEIVABLE CREDIT	SALES TAX PAYABLE CREDIT	SALES CREDIT		SALES DISCOUNT DEBIT		CASH DEBIT
DATE	ACCOUNT TITLE	DOC. NO.	POST. REF.	DEBIT	CREDIT			EQUIPMENT	ACCESSORIES	EQUIPMENT	ACCESSORIES	
				1	2	3	4	5	6	7	8	9
1												
2												
3												
4												
5												
6												
7												
8												
9												
10												
11												
12												
13												

Prove Cash:

Cash on hand at the beginning of the month............ $ _____

Plus total cash received during the month

Equals total.. $ _____

Less total cash paid during the month.....................

Equals total cash on hand at the end of the month...... $ _____

REINFORCEMENT ACTIVITY 1 (continued)

1.

GENERAL JOURNAL

PAGE 16

	DATE		ACCOUNT TITLE	DOC. NO.	POST. REF.	DEBIT	CREDIT	
1								1
2								2
3								3
4								4
5								5
6								6
7								7
8								8
9								9
10								10
11								11
12								12
13								13
14								14
15								15
16								16
17								17
18								18

Net Income before Federal Income Taxes	×	Tax Rate	=	Federal Income Tax
$	×		=	$

REINFORCEMENT ACTIVITY 1 (continued)

1.   **ACCOUNTS PAYABLE LEDGER**

VENDOR Burkes Industries   VENDOR NO. 210

DATE	ITEM	POST. REF.	DEBIT	CREDIT	CREDIT BALANCE

VENDOR Central Kitchen Supply   VENDOR NO. 220

DATE	ITEM	POST. REF.	DEBIT	CREDIT	CREDIT BALANCE

VENDOR Fulgham Pottery   VENDOR NO. 230

DATE	ITEM	POST. REF.	DEBIT	CREDIT	CREDIT BALANCE
Dec. 1	Balance	✔			3 1 4 8 04

VENDOR Hunley Equipment Co.   VENDOR NO. 240

DATE	ITEM	POST. REF.	DEBIT	CREDIT	CREDIT BALANCE
Dec. 1	Balance	✔			5 9 5 8 94

VENDOR Kitchen Concepts   VENDOR NO. 250

DATE	ITEM	POST. REF.	DEBIT	CREDIT	CREDIT BALANCE
Dec. 1	Balance	✔			5 1 4 8 57

VENDOR Specialty Supply   VENDOR NO. 260

DATE	ITEM	POST. REF.	DEBIT	CREDIT	CREDIT BALANCE
20-- Dec. 1	Balance	✔			6 1 2 1 08

VENDOR Triangle Manufacturing   VENDOR NO. 270

DATE	ITEM	POST. REF.	DEBIT	CREDIT	CREDIT BALANCE

10.

Jewel's Kitchen, Inc.

Schedule of Accounts Payable

December 31, 20--

REINFORCEMENT ACTIVITY 1 (continued)

1.   **ACCOUNTS RECEIVABLE LEDGER**

CUSTOMER Virgie Berger   CUSTOMER NO. 110

DATE	ITEM	POST. REF.	DEBIT	CREDIT	DEBIT BALANCE

CUSTOMER Carlisle Steakhouse   CUSTOMER NO. 120

DATE	ITEM	POST. REF.	DEBIT	CREDIT	DEBIT BALANCE

CUSTOMER Denton Seafood   CUSTOMER NO. 130

DATE	ITEM	POST. REF.	DEBIT	CREDIT	DEBIT BALANCE
20-- Dec. 1	Balance	✔			4 1 0 8 62

CUSTOMER Hamilton Group   CUSTOMER NO. 140

DATE	ITEM	POST. REF.	DEBIT	CREDIT	DEBIT BALANCE
20-- Dec. 1	Balance	✔			3 6 1 8 29

CUSTOMER LaFlore Café   CUSTOMER NO. 150

DATE	ITEM	POST. REF.	DEBIT	CREDIT	DEBIT BALANCE

CUSTOMER Mary McCrory   CUSTOMER NO. 160

DATE		ITEM	POST. REF.	DEBIT	CREDIT	DEBIT BALANCE

CUSTOMER Polk County Schools   CUSTOMER NO. 170

DATE		ITEM	POST. REF.	DEBIT	CREDIT	DEBIT BALANCE
20-- Dec.	1	Balance	✔			2 4 8 1 14

CUSTOMER Waukawy Country Club   CUSTOMER NO. 180

DATE		ITEM	POST. REF.	DEBIT	CREDIT	DEBIT BALANCE
20-- Dec.	1	Balance	✔			2 1 4 8 69

10.

Jewel's Kitchen, Inc.

Schedule of Accounts Receivable

December 31, 20--

REINFORCEMENT ACTIVITY 1 (continued)

11., 12., 14.

GENERAL JOURNAL   PAGE

	DATE		ACCOUNT TITLE	DOC. NO.	POST. REF.	DEBIT	CREDIT	
1								1
2								2
3								3
4								4
5								5
6								6
7								7
8								8
9								9
10								10
11								11
12								12
13								13
14								14
15								15
16								16
17								17
18								18
19								19
20								20
21								21
22								22
23								23
24								24
25								25
26								26
27								27
28								28
29								29
30								30
31								31

Jewel's Kitchen, Inc.

Adjusted Trial Balance

December 31, 20--

ACCOUNT TITLE	DEBIT	CREDIT
Cash		
Petty Cash		
Accounts Receivable		
Allowance for Uncollectible Accounts		
Merchandise Inventory—Equipment		
Merchandise Inventory—Accessories		
Supplies		
Prepaid Insurance		
Office Equipment		
Accumulated Depreciation—Office Equipment		
Store Equipment		
Accumulated Depreciation—Store Equipment		
Accounts Payable		
Sales Tax Payable		
Employee Income Tax Payable—Federal		
Employee Income Tax Payable—State		
Social Security Tax Payable		
Medicare Tax Payable		
Medical Insurance Payable		
Retirement Plan Payable		
Unemployment Tax Payable—Federal		
Unemployment Tax Payable—State		
Federal Income Tax Payable		
Dividends Payable		
Capital Stock		
Retained Earnings		
Dividends		
Income Summary—General		
Income Summary—Equipment		
Income Summary—Accessories		

(Note: Trial balance is continued on the next page.)

REINFORCEMENT ACTIVITY 1 (continued)

Jewel's Kitchen, Inc.

Adjusted Trial Balance (Concluded)

December 31, 20--

ACCOUNT TITLE	DEBIT	CREDIT
Sales—Equipment		
Sales Discount—Equipment		
Sales Returns and Allowances—Equipment		
Sales—Accessories		
Sales Discount—Accessories		
Sales Returns and Allowances—Accessories		
Purchases—Equipment		
Purchases Discount—Equipment		
Purchases Returns and Allowances—Equipment		
Purchases—Accessories		
Purchases Discount—Accessories		
Purchases Returns and Allowances—Accessories		
Advertising Expense—Equipment		
Payroll Taxes Expense—Equipment		
Salary Expense—Equipment		
Advertising Expense—Accessories		
Payroll Taxes Expense—Accessories		
Salary Expense—Accessories		
Credit Card Fee Expense		
Depreciation Expense—Office Equipment		
Depreciation Expense—Store Equipment		
Insurance Expense		
Miscellaneous Expense		
Payroll Taxes Expense—Administrative		
Rent Expense		
Salary Expense—Administrative		
Supplies Expense		
Uncollectible Accounts Expense		
Utilities Expense		

16.

Jewel's Kitchen, Inc.

Departmental Margin Statement—Equipment

For Year Ended December 31, 20--

		% OF NET SALES*

*Rounded to the nearest 0.1%.

REINFORCEMENT ACTIVITY 1 (continued)

Jewel's Kitchen, Inc.

Departmental Margin Statement—Accessories

For Year Ended December 31, 20--

		% OF NET SALES*

*Rounded to the nearest 0.1%.

17.

	DEPARTMENTAL		COMPANY	% OF NET SALES*
	EQUIPMENT	ACCESSORIES		

Jewel's Kitchen, Inc.

Income Statement

For Year Ended December 31, 20--

*Rounded to the nearest 0.1%.

REINFORCEMENT ACTIVITY 1 (continued)

18.

Jewel's Kitchen, Inc.

Statement of Stockholders' Equity

For Year Ended December 31, 20--

19.

Jewel's Kitchen, Inc.

Balance Sheet

December 31, 20--

			% OF ASSETS*

*Rounded to the nearest 0.1%.

REINFORCEMENT ACTIVITY 1 (continued)

20.

Jewel's Kitchen, Inc.

Statement of Cash Flows

For Year Ended December 31, 20--

REINFORCEMENT ACTIVITY 1 (continued)

21.

GENERAL JOURNAL

PAGE

	DATE	ACCOUNT TITLE	DOC. NO.	POST. REF.	DEBIT	CREDIT	
1							1
2							2
3							3
4							4
5							5
6							6
7							7
8							8
9							9
10							10
11							11
12							12
13							13
14							14
15							15
16							16
17							17
18							18
19							19
20							20
21							21
22							22
23							23
24							24
25							25
26							26
27							27
28							28
29							29
30							30
31							31
32							32
33							33
34							34
35							35
36							36
37							37
38							38
39							39
40							40
41							41
42							42

REINFORCEMENT ACTIVITY 1 (concluded)

22.

	Jewel's Kitchen, Inc.	
	Post-Closing Trial Balance	
	December 31, 20--	

ACCOUNT TITLE	DEBIT	CREDIT

Part One—Identifying Accounting Terms

Directions: Select the one term in Column I that best fits each definition in Column II. Print the letter identifying your choice in the Answers column.

Column I	Column II	Answers
A. consignee	**1.** Goods that are given to a business to sell but for which title remains with the vendor. (p. 146)	1._____
B. consignment	**2.** The person or business that receives goods on consignment. (p. 146)	2._____
C. consignor	**3.** The person or business that gives goods on consignment. (p. 146)	3._____
D. days' sales in inventory	**4.** A form used to show the type of merchandise, quantity received, quantity sold, and balance on hand. (p. 147)	4._____
E. deflation	**5.** A file of stock records for all merchandise on hand. (p. 147)	5._____
F. first-in, first-out inventory costing method	**6.** A form used during a physical inventory to record information about each item of merchandise on hand. (p. 148)	6._____
G. generally accepted accounting principles	**7.** The standards and rules that accountants follow while recording and reporting financial activities. (p. 151)	7._____
H. gross profit method of estimating inventory	**8.** Using the price of merchandise purchased first to calculate the cost of merchandise sold first. (p. 151)	8._____
I. inflation	**9.** Using the price of merchandise purchased last to calculate the cost of merchandise sold first. (p. 152)	9._____
J. international financial reporting standards	**10.** Using the average cost of the beginning inventory plus merchandise purchased during a fiscal period to calculate the cost of merchandise sold. (p. 153)	10._____
K. inventory record	**11.** The rate at which the price for goods and services increases over time. (p. 154)	11._____
L. inventory turnover ratio	**12.** The rate at which the price for goods and services decreases over time. (p. 155)	12._____
M. last-in, first-out inventory costing method	**13.** A set of accounting standards being adopted across the world. (p. 156)	13._____
N. lower of cost or market inventory costing method	**14.** Using the lower of cost or market price to calculate the cost of the ending merchandise inventory. (p. 157)	14._____
O. retail method of estimating inventory	**15.** Estimating inventory by using the previous year's percentage of gross profit on operations. (p. 159)	15._____
P. stock ledger	**16.** Estimating inventory by using a percentage based on both cost and retail prices. (p. 160)	16._____
Q. stock record	**17.** The number of times the average amount of merchandise inventory is sold during a specific period of time. (p. 161)	17._____
R. weighted-average inventory costing method	**18.** The time needed to sell an average amount of merchandise inventory. (p. 161)	18._____

Part Two—Analyzing Concepts and Practices Related to Inventory Control

Directions: Place a *T* for True or an *F* for False in the Answers column to show whether each of the following statements is true or false.

Answers

1. The cost of merchandise available for sale consists of the cost of the beginning inventory and the purchases added to inventory during the fiscal period. (p. 145)

1. _____

2. Calculating an accurate merchandise inventory cost in order to adequately report a business's financial progress and condition is an application of the accounting concept Full Disclosure. (p. 145)

2. _____

3. If the cost of the ending merchandise inventory is overstated, the net income will be understated. (p. 145)

3. _____

4. If the cost of the ending merchandise inventory is understated, the total stockholders' equity will be overstated. (p. 145)

4. _____

5. When the terms of sale for goods in transit are FOB shipping point, the title to the goods passes to the buyer when the goods are received by the buyer. (p. 146)

5. _____

6. When goods are sent to a business on consignment, title to the goods passes to the business accepting the consignment when the consignor delivers the goods to a transportation business. (p. 146)

6. _____

7. A continuous record of merchandise inventory increases and decreases and the balance on hand is known as a *perpetual inventory*. (p. 147)

7. _____

8. A periodic inventory provides day-to-day records about the quantity of merchandise on hand. (p. 147)

8. _____

9. An inventory determined periodically by counting, weighing, or measuring items of merchandise on hand is known as a *physical inventory*. (p. 148)

9. _____

10. Because of the expense, many businesses take a physical inventory only once a year. (p. 148)

10. _____

11. Businesses using a perpetual inventory method never need to take a physical inventory. (p. 148)

11. _____

12. The weighted-average inventory costing method is based on the assumption that each item in the ending inventory has a cost equal to the average price paid for similar items. (p. 153)

12. _____

13. During a period of increasing prices, the weighted-average inventory costing method usually will give the lowest cost of ending inventory. (p. 154)

13. _____

14. A business that uses the LIFO method for tax reporting must also using the LIFO method for financial reporting. (p. 154)

14. _____

15. During a period of decreasing prices, the FIFO inventory costing method usually will give the lowest cost of ending inventory. (p. 155)

15. _____

16. International financial reporting standards only allow inventory to be costed using the LIFO and weighted-average methods. (p. 156)

16. _____

17. Taking a physical inventory once a month for interim monthly financial statements is usually too expensive to be worthwhile. (p. 159)

17. _____

18. Using the retail method of estimating inventory is more expensive than the gross profit method because more records must be kept. (p. 160)

18. _____

19. An inventory turnover ratio expresses a relationship between an average inventory and the cost of merchandise sold. (p. 161)

19. _____

20. An inventory turnover ratio of 4.5 means that, on average, each item of inventory is sold 81 days after it is purchased. (p. 161)

20. _____

5-1 WORK TOGETHER (LO2), p. 150

5-1 ON YOUR OWN (LO2), p. 150

Completing a stock record for a perpetual inventory system

1., 2.

STOCK RECORD

Description _____   Stock No. _____

Reorder _____   Minimum _____   Location _____

1	2	3	4	5	6	7
	INCREASES			DECREASES		BALANCE
DATE	PURCHASE INVOICE NO.	QUANTITY	DATE	SALES INVOICE NO.	QUANTITY	QUANTITY

2.

INVENTORY RECORD

DATE October 31, 20--   ITEM Security Cameras

1	2	3	4	5
STOCK NUMBER	DESCRIPTIONS	NO. OF UNITS ON HAND	UNIT PRICE	TOTAL COST
C-0264	Monitoring station	16	231.25	3,700.00
D-3543	Ceiling mount stationary camera	52	30 @ 89.25	4,630.00
			22 @ 88.75	
D-3643	Ceiling mount 360-degree camera	33	94.69	3,124.77
C-2755	Wireless Internet video camera	25	214.75	5,368.75
C-4264	Wireless monitoring camera	88	69.95	6,155.60
C-7543	Outdoor stationary camera	62	89.25	5,533.50
C-6275	Outdoor night camera	25	94.45	2,361.25
A-253	Mounting bracket	124	21.58	2,675.92
C-7542	Rotating ceiling mount camera	49	251.63	12,329.87
C-7245	Color wireless monitoring camera	68	215.66	14,664.88
	Total			60,544.54

5-2 WORK TOGETHER (LO3, 5), p. 158

Costing ending inventory using FIFO, LIFO, and weighted-average

FIFO Inventory Costing Method

Purchase Dates	Units Purchased	Unit Price	Total Cost	FIFO Units on Hand	FIFO Cost
Beginning inventory					
February					
May					
August					
November					
Totals					

LIFO Inventory Costing Method

Purchase Dates	Units Purchased	Unit Price	Total Cost	LIFO Units on Hand	LIFO Cost
Beginning inventory					
February					
May					
August					
November					
Totals					

Weighted-Average Inventory Costing Method

Purchase Dates	Units Purchased	Unit Price	Total Cost
Beginning inventory			
February			
May			
August			
November			
Totals			

Costing ending inventory using FIFO, LIFO, and weighted-average

FIFO Inventory Costing Method					
Purchase Dates	Units Purchased	Unit Price	Total Cost	FIFO Units on Hand	FIFO Cost
Beginning inventory					
February					
May					
August					
November					
Totals					

LIFO Inventory Costing Method					
Purchase Dates	Units Purchased	Unit Price	Total Cost	LIFO Units on Hand	LIFO Cost
Beginning inventory					
February					
May					
August					
November					
Totals					

Weighted-Average Inventory Costing Method			
Purchase Dates	Units Purchased	Unit Price	Total Cost
Beginning inventory			
February			
May			
August			
November			
Totals			

5-3 WORK TOGETHER (LO6, 7), p. 162

Estimating inventory using the gross profit and retail methods; financial anlysis of merchandise inventory

1.

ESTIMATED MERCHANDISE INVENTORY SHEET
Gross Profit Method

DEPARTMENT _____ DATE _____

1	Beginning inventory...		$ _____
2	Net purchases to date..		_____
3	Merchandise available for sale		$ _____
4	Net sales to date..	$ _____	
5	Less estimated gross profit...................................	_____	
	(Net sales × Estimated gross profit percentage ____ %)		
6	Estimated cost of merchandise sold......................		_____
7	Estimated ending inventory		$ _____

2.

ESTIMATED MERCHANDISE INVENTORY SHEET
Retail Method

COMPANY _____ DATE _____

		Cost	Retail
1	Beginning inventory..	$ _____	$ _____
2	Net purchases to date..	_____	_____
3	Merchandise available for sale	$ _____	$ _____
4	Net sales to date..		_____
5	Estimated ending inventory at retail		$ _____
6	Estimated ending inventory	$ _____	
	(Inventory at retail × Percentage ____ %)		

3.

$$\left(\begin{array}{c} \text{January 1} \\ \text{Merchandise} \\ \text{Inventory} \end{array} \quad + \quad \begin{array}{c} \text{December 31} \\ \text{Merchandise} \\ \text{Inventory} \end{array} \right) \quad \div \quad 2 \quad = \quad \begin{array}{c} \text{Average} \\ \text{Merchandise} \\ \text{Inventory} \end{array}$$

$$+ \qquad\qquad \div \quad 2 \quad =$$

$$\begin{array}{c} \text{Cost of} \\ \text{Merchandise} \\ \text{Sold} \end{array} \quad \div \quad \begin{array}{c} \text{Average} \\ \text{Merchandise} \\ \text{Inventory} \end{array} \quad = \quad \begin{array}{c} \text{Inventory} \\ \text{Turnover} \\ \text{Ratio} \end{array}$$

$$\div \qquad\qquad =$$

$$\text{Days in Year} \quad \div \quad \begin{array}{c} \text{Inventory Turnover} \\ \text{Ratio} \end{array} \quad = \quad \begin{array}{c} \text{Days' Sales in} \\ \text{Inventory} \end{array}$$

$$\div \qquad\qquad =$$

5-3 ON YOUR OWN (LO6, 7), p. 162

Estimating inventory using the gross profit and retail methods; financial analysis of merchandise inventory

1.

<table>
<tr><td colspan="3" align="center">ESTIMATED MERCHANDISE INVENTORY SHEET
Gross Profit Method</td></tr>
<tr><td colspan="2">DEPARTMENT _____</td><td>DATE _____</td></tr>
<tr><td>1</td><td>Beginning inventory..</td><td>$ _____</td></tr>
<tr><td>2</td><td>Net purchases to date..</td><td>_____</td></tr>
<tr><td>3</td><td>Merchandise available for sale ....</td><td>$ _____</td></tr>
<tr><td>4</td><td>Net sales to date.. $ _____</td><td></td></tr>
<tr><td>5</td><td>Less estimated gross profit.. _____</td><td></td></tr>
<tr><td></td><td>(Net sales × Estimated gross profit percentage ____ %)</td><td></td></tr>
<tr><td>6</td><td>Estimated cost of merchandise sold..</td><td>_____</td></tr>
<tr><td>7</td><td>Estimated ending inventory ....</td><td>$ _____</td></tr>
</table>

2.

<table>
<tr><td colspan="3" align="center">ESTIMATED MERCHANDISE INVENTORY SHEET
Retail Method</td></tr>
<tr><td colspan="3">COMPANY _____   DATE _____</td></tr>
<tr><td></td><td>Cost</td><td>Retail</td></tr>
<tr><td>1   Beginning inventory...</td><td>$ _____</td><td>$ _____</td></tr>
<tr><td>2   Net purchases to date..</td><td>_____</td><td>_____</td></tr>
<tr><td>3   Merchandise available for sale ....</td><td>$ _____</td><td>$ _____</td></tr>
<tr><td>4   Net sales to date..</td><td></td><td>_____</td></tr>
<tr><td>5   Estimated ending inventory at retail ....</td><td></td><td>$ _____</td></tr>
<tr><td>6   Estimated ending inventory ....</td><td>$ _____</td><td></td></tr>
<tr><td>   (Inventory at retail × Percentage ____ %)</td><td></td><td></td></tr>
</table>

3.

$$\left(\begin{array}{c}\text{January 1}\\\text{Merchandise}\\\text{Inventory}\end{array} + \begin{array}{c}\text{December 31}\\\text{Merchandise}\\\text{Inventory}\end{array}\right) \div 2 = \begin{array}{c}\text{Average}\\\text{Merchandise}\\\text{Inventory}\end{array}$$

$$+ \qquad\qquad \div\ 2\ =$$

$$\begin{array}{c}\text{Cost of}\\\text{Merchandise}\\\text{Sold}\end{array} \div \begin{array}{c}\text{Average}\\\text{Merchandise}\\\text{Inventory}\end{array} = \begin{array}{c}\text{Inventory}\\\text{Turnover}\\\text{Ratio}\end{array}$$

$$\div \qquad\qquad =$$

$$\text{Days in Year} \div \begin{array}{c}\text{Inventory Turnover}\\\text{Ratio}\end{array} = \begin{array}{c}\text{Days' Sales in}\\\text{Inventory}\end{array}$$

$$\div \qquad\qquad =$$

5-1 APPLICATION PROBLEM (LO2), p. 167

Keeping perpetual inventory records

1., 2.

STOCK RECORD

Description _____   Stock No. _____
Reorder _____ Minimum _____ Location _____

1	2	3	4	5	6	7
INCREASES			DECREASES			BALANCE
DATE	PURCHASE INVOICE NO.	QUANTITY	DATE	SALES INVOICE NO.	QUANTITY	QUANTITY

APPLICATION PROBLEM (LO3, 5), p. 167

Determining inventory cost using FIFO, LIFO, weighted-average, and lower of cost or market

1.

Stock Item: B26

Purchases				FIFO Method		LIFO Method		Weighted-Average Method
Date	Units Purchased	Unit Price	Total Cost	Units	Cost	Units	Cost	
Beginning inventory	6	$6.50						
January	15	6.60						
March	18	6.60						
July	15	6.80						
October	20	6.80						
Totals								
Prices are _____								
Ending inventory								
Cost of merchandise sold								
Reported net income								

Stock Item: C45

Purchases				FIFO Method		LIFO Method		Weighted-Average Method
Date	Units Purchased	Unit Price	Total Cost	Units	Cost	Units	Cost	
Beginning inventory	72	$8.50						
March	90	8.60						
June	80	8.62						
August	90	8.68						
December	90	8.72						
Totals								
Prices are _____								
Ending inventory								
Cost of merchandise sold								
Reported net income								

5-2 APPLICATION PROBLEM (concluded)

Stock Item: D55									
Purchases				**FIFO Method**		**LIFO Method**		**Weighted-Average Method**
Date	Units Purchased	Unit Price	Total Cost	Units	Cost	Units	Cost	
Beginning inventory	3	$12.62						
February	9	12.60						
May	12	12.60						
September	9	12.50						
November	15	11.95						
Totals								
Prices are _____								
Ending inventory								
Cost of merchandise sold								
Reported net income								

2.

Stock Item	Quantity of Units on Hand	Market Price	Total Market Price	FIFO Cost	Lower of Cost of Market
B26	24	$ 6.90			
C45	80	8.80			
D55	18	11.75			
Reported cost of merchandise inventory					

APPLICATION PROBLEM (LO6, 7), p. 168

Estimating cost of merchandise inventory; financial analysis of merchandise inventory

1.

	ESTIMATED MERCHANDISE INVENTORY SHEET	
	Gross Profit Method	

DEPARTMENT _____ DATE _____

1	Beginning inventory...		$ _____
2	Net purchases to date...		_____
3	Merchandise available for sale		$ _____
4	Net sales to date..	$ _____	
5	Less estimated gross profit...	_____	
	(Net sales × Estimated gross profit percentage ____ %)		
6	Estimated cost of merchandise sold....................................		_____
7	Estimated ending inventory		$ _____

2.

	ESTIMATED MERCHANDISE INVENTORY SHEET	
	Retail Method	

COMPANY _____ DATE _____

		Cost	Retail
1	Beginning inventory...	$ _____	$ _____
2	Net purchases to date...	_____	_____
3	Merchandise available for sale	$ _____	$ _____
4	Net sales to date..		_____
5	Estimated ending inventory at retail		$ _____
6	Estimated ending inventory	$ _____	
	(Inventory at retail × Percentage ____ %)		

5-3 **APPLICATION PROBLEM (concluded)**

3.

$\left(\begin{array}{c}\text{January 1}\\\text{Merchandise}\\\text{Inventory}\end{array}\right.$ + $\left.\begin{array}{c}\text{December 31}\\\text{Merchandise}\\\text{Inventory}\end{array}\right)$ ÷ 2 = $\begin{array}{c}\text{Average}\\\text{Merchandise}\\\text{Inventory}\end{array}$

+ ÷ 2 =

$\begin{array}{c}\text{Cost of}\\\text{Merchandise}\\\text{Sold}\end{array}$ ÷ $\begin{array}{c}\text{Average}\\\text{Merchandise}\\\text{Inventory}\end{array}$ = $\begin{array}{c}\text{Inventory}\\\text{Turnover}\\\text{Ratio}\end{array}$

÷ =

Days in Year ÷ $\begin{array}{c}\text{Inventory Turnover}\\\text{Ratio}\end{array}$ = $\begin{array}{c}\text{Days' Sales in}\\\text{Inventory}\end{array}$

÷ =

5-M MASTERY PROBLEM (LO3, 5, 6, 7), p. 168

Costing and financial analysis of merchandise inventory

1.

Stock Item: 1548-C

Purchases				FIFO Method		LIFO Method		Weighted-Average Method
Date	Units Purchased	Unit Price	Total Cost	Units	Cost	Units	Cost	
Beginning inventory	12	$9.40						
February	20	9.82						
May	25	9.75						
July	20	9.80						
August	15	9.85						
December	16	9.95						
Totals								

Stock Item: 5324-B

Purchases				FIFO Method		LIFO Method		Weighted-Average Method
Date	Units Purchased	Unit Price	Total Cost	Units	Cost	Units	Cost	
Beginning inventory	56	$8.90						
May	50	6.80						
August	45	6.85						
October	50	6.85						
Totals								

Stock Item: 0234-H

Purchases				FIFO Method		LIFO Method		Weighted-Average Method
Date	Units Purchased	Unit Price	Total Cost	Units	Cost	Units	Cost	
Beginning inventory	3	$6.45						
January	9	8.40						
March	12	8.42						
June	12	8.45						
August	9	8.45						
October	10	8.50						
Totals								

2.

Stock Item	Quantity of Units on Hand	Market Price	Total Market Price	LIFO Cost	Lower of Cost of Market
1548-C					
5324-B					
0234-H					
			Reported cost of merchandise inventory		

5-M **MASTERY PROBLEM (continued)**

3.

	ESTIMATED MERCHANDISE INVENTORY SHEET

ESTIMATED MERCHANDISE INVENTORY SHEET
Gross Profit Method

DEPARTMENT _____ DATE _____

1	Beginning inventory..		$ _____
2	Net purchases to date..		_____
3	Merchandise available for sale		$ _____
4	Net sales to date...	$ _____	
5	Less estimated gross profit..	_____	
	(Net sales × Estimated gross profit percentage ____ %)		
6	Estimated cost of merchandise sold...........................		_____
7	Estimated ending inventory		$ _____

4.

ESTIMATED MERCHANDISE INVENTORY SHEET
Retail Method

COMPANY _____ DATE _____

		Cost	Retail
1	Beginning inventory..	$ _____	$ _____
2	Net purchases to date..	_____	_____
3	Merchandise available for sale	$ _____	$ _____
4	Net sales to date...		_____
5	Estimated ending inventory at retail		$ _____
6	Estimated ending inventory	$ _____	
	(Inventory at retail × Percentage ____ %)		

5., 6.

$$\left(\begin{array}{c} \text{January 1} \\ \text{Merchandise} \\ \text{Inventory} \end{array} \; + \; \begin{array}{c} \text{December 31} \\ \text{Merchandise} \\ \text{Inventory} \end{array} \right) \; \div \; 2 \; = \; \begin{array}{c} \text{Average} \\ \text{Merchandise} \\ \text{Inventory} \end{array}$$

$$ + \div \; 2 \; =$$

$$\begin{array}{c} \text{Cost of} \\ \text{Merchandise} \\ \text{Sold} \end{array} \; \div \; \begin{array}{c} \text{Average} \\ \text{Merchandise} \\ \text{Inventory} \end{array} \; = \; \begin{array}{c} \text{Inventory} \\ \text{Turnover} \\ \text{Ratio} \end{array}$$

$$\div =$$

$$\text{Days in Year} \; \div \; \begin{array}{c} \text{Inventory Turnover} \\ \text{Ratio} \end{array} \; = \; \begin{array}{c} \text{Days' Sales in} \\ \text{Inventory} \end{array}$$

$$\div =$$

5-C CHALLENGE PROBLEM (LO7), p. 169

Financial analysis of merchandise inventory

1.

Corporation A

$$
\left(\begin{array}{c} \text{January 1} \\ \text{Merchandise} \\ \text{Inventory} \end{array} \quad + \quad \begin{array}{c} \text{December 31} \\ \text{Merchandise} \\ \text{Inventory} \end{array} \right) \quad \div \quad 2 \quad = \quad \begin{array}{c} \text{Average} \\ \text{Merchandise} \\ \text{Inventory} \end{array}
$$

$$
+ \qquad\qquad\qquad \div \quad 2 \quad =
$$

$$
\begin{array}{c} \text{Cost of} \\ \text{Merchandise} \\ \text{Sold} \end{array} \quad \div \quad \begin{array}{c} \text{Average} \\ \text{Merchandise} \\ \text{Inventory} \end{array} \quad = \quad \begin{array}{c} \text{Inventory} \\ \text{Turnover} \\ \text{Ratio} \end{array}
$$

$$
\div \qquad\qquad\qquad =
$$

Corporation B

$$
\left(\begin{array}{c} \text{January 1} \\ \text{Merchandise} \\ \text{Inventory} \end{array} \quad + \quad \begin{array}{c} \text{December 31} \\ \text{Merchandise} \\ \text{Inventory} \end{array} \right) \quad \div \quad 2 \quad = \quad \begin{array}{c} \text{Average} \\ \text{Merchandise} \\ \text{Inventory} \end{array}
$$

$$
+ \qquad\qquad\qquad \div \quad 2 \quad =
$$

$$
\begin{array}{c} \text{Cost of} \\ \text{Merchandise} \\ \text{Sold} \end{array} \quad \div \quad \begin{array}{c} \text{Average} \\ \text{Merchandise} \\ \text{Inventory} \end{array} \quad = \quad \begin{array}{c} \text{Inventory} \\ \text{Turnover} \\ \text{Ratio} \end{array}
$$

$$
\div \qquad\qquad\qquad =
$$

Corporation C

$$
\left(\begin{array}{c} \text{January 1} \\ \text{Merchandise} \\ \text{Inventory} \end{array} \quad + \quad \begin{array}{c} \text{December 31} \\ \text{Merchandise} \\ \text{Inventory} \end{array} \right) \quad \div \quad 2 \quad = \quad \begin{array}{c} \text{Average} \\ \text{Merchandise} \\ \text{Inventory} \end{array}
$$

$$
+ \qquad\qquad\qquad \div \quad 2 \quad =
$$

$$
\begin{array}{c} \text{Cost of} \\ \text{Merchandise} \\ \text{Sold} \end{array} \quad \div \quad \begin{array}{c} \text{Average} \\ \text{Merchandise} \\ \text{Inventory} \end{array} \quad = \quad \begin{array}{c} \text{Inventory} \\ \text{Turnover} \\ \text{Ratio} \end{array}
$$

$$
\div \qquad\qquad\qquad =
$$

2.

Corporation A

Days in Year	÷	Inventory Turnover Ratio	=	Days' Sales in Inventory
	÷		=	

Corporation B

Days in Year	÷	Inventory Turnover Ratio	=	Days' Sales in Inventory
	÷		=	

Corporation C

Days in Year	÷	Inventory Turnover Ratio	=	Days' Sales in Inventory
	÷		=	

Corporation A _____

Corporation B _____

Corporation C _____

Study Guide 6

Name	Perfect Score	Your Score
Identifying Accounting Terms	8 Pts.	
Analyzing Transactions Recorded in Special Journals	14 Pts.	
Analyzing Practices Involved in Journalizing Uncollectible Accounts Expense	20 Pts.	
Total	42 Pts.	

Part One—Identifying Accounting Terms

Directions: Select the one term in Column I that best fits each definition in Column II. Print the letter identifying your choice in the Answers column.

Column I	Column II	Answers
A. accounts receivable turnover ratio	**1.** Accounts receivable that cannot be collected. (p. 174)	1._____
B. aging accounts receivable	**2.** Canceling the balance of a customer account because the customer is not expected to pay. (p. 174)	2._____
C. allowance method	**3.** Recording uncollectible accounts expense only when an amount is actually known to be uncollectible. (p. 175)	3._____
D. book value	**4.** Crediting the estimated value of uncollectible accounts to a contra account. (p. 178)	4._____
E. days' sales in accounts receivable	**5.** The difference between an asset's account balance and its related contra account balance. (p. 178)	5._____
F. direct write-off method	**6.** Analyzing accounts receivable according to when they are due. (p. 180)	6._____
G. uncollectible accounts	**7.** The number of times the average amount of accounts receivable is collected during a specified period. (p. 186)	7._____
H. writing off an account	**8.** The average period of time to collect an account receivable. (p. 186)	8._____

Part Two—Analyzing Transactions Recorded in Special Journals

Directions: For each entry below, print in the proper Answers column the letters identifying which accounts are to be debited and credited.

Account Titles	Transactions	Answers Debit	Credit
A. Accounts Receivable	*(a) Direct write-off method:*		
B. Allowance for Uncollectible Accounts	**1-2.** Wrote off customer's account as uncollectible. (p. 175)	**1.** _____	**2.** _____
C. Cash	**3-4.** Reopened customer account previously written off as uncollectible. (p. 176)	**3.** _____	**4.** _____
D. Uncollectible Accounts Expense	**5-6.** Received cash in full payment of customer account, described in question 2. (p. 176)	**5.** _____	**6.** _____
	(b) Allowance method:		
	7-8. Recorded adjustment for uncollectible accounts expense when using the percentage of accounts receivable account balance to calculate the amount. (pp. 179)	**7.** _____	**8.** _____
	9-10. Recorded adjustment for uncollectible accounts expense when using aging accounts receivable method to calculate the amount. (p. 181)	**9.** _____	**10.** _____
	11-12. Wrote off customer account as uncollectible. (p. 182)	**11.** _____	**12.** _____
	13-14. Reopened customer account previously written off as uncollectible. (p. 183)	**13.** _____	**14.** _____

Part Three—Analyzing Practices Involved in Journalizing Uncollectible Accounts Expense

Directions: Place a *T* for True or an *F* for False in the Answers column to show whether each of the following statements is true or false.

Answers

1. Uncollectible accounts are sometimes referred to as bad debts. (p. 174)

    1. _____

2. Until a specific amount is actually known to be uncollectible, the amount remains recorded in Accounts Receivable. (p. 174)

    2. _____

3. When a customer account is known to be uncollectible, the account becomes a liability. (p. 174)

    3. _____

4. Using the direct write-off method, collecting a previously written off account results in a credit to an expense account. (p. 176)

    4. _____

5. The direct write-off method is more difficult to apply than the allowance method. (p. 178)

    5. _____

6. A business can use the direct write-off method if accounts receivable are reported on the balance sheet at net realizable value. (p. 178)

    6. _____

7. A disadvantage of the direct write-off method of recording uncollectible accounts expense is that the expense may not be recorded in the same fiscal period as the revenue for the sale. (p. 178)

    7. _____

8. Recording uncollectible accounts expense in the same fiscal period in which the original sale on account was made is an application of the Matching Expenses with Revenue accounting concept. (p. 178)

    8. _____

9. Because there is no way of knowing for sure which customer accounts will become uncollectible, the allowance method uses an estimate based on past history to determine uncollectible accounts expense. (p. 178)

    9. _____

10. The book value of accounts receivable represents the total amount owed to the business from sales on account. (p. 178)

    10. _____

11. The book value of accounts receivable is often referred to as the net realizable value. (p. 178)

    11. _____

12. The formula for calculating the amount of uncollectible accounts expense based on a percentage of net sales is: Net sales *times* percentage *equals* estimated uncollectible accounts expense. (p. 179)

    12. _____

13. An aging of accounts receivable analyzes accounts receivable by age categories according to when payments are due. (p. 180)

    13. _____

14. A company that estimates its uncollectible accounts receivable are $5,000.00 and a $200.00 credit balance in Allowances for Uncollectible Accounts will increase the allowance account by $5,200.00. (p. 181)

    14. _____

15. The journal entry used to write off an uncollectible account is the same, regardless of the method used to calculate the estimate of Allowance for Uncollectible Accounts. (p. 182)

    15. _____

16. A company may continue its attempts to collect an account even after the account has been written off. (p. 182)

    16. _____

17. Using the allowance method, writing off an uncollectible accounts receivable reduces the net realizable value of accounts receivable. (p. 182)

    17. _____

18. Using the allowance method, writing off an account increases Uncollectible Accounts Expense. (p. 182)

    18. _____

19. The accounts receivable turnover ratio is calculated by dividing net sales by the average book value of accounts receivable. (p. 186)

    19. _____

20. A company whose accounts receivable turnover ratio declines from 9.3 to 8.7 is doing a better job in collecting its accounts receivable. (p. 187)

    20. _____

6-1 WORK TOGETHER (LO1), p. 177

Journalizing entries to write off uncollectible accounts—direct write-off method

GENERAL JOURNAL   PAGE _____

	DATE		ACCOUNT TITLE	DOC. NO.	POST. REF.	DEBIT	CREDIT	
1								1
2								2
3								3
4								4
5								5
6								6
7								7
8								8
9								9
10								10
11								11
12								12
13								13
14								14
15								15
16								16
17								17
18								18
19								19
20								20
21								21
22								22
23								23
24								24
25								25
26								26
27								27
28								28
29								29

CASH RECEIPTS JOURNAL

DATE	ACCOUNT TITLE	DOC. NO.	POST. REF.	GENERAL DEBIT	GENERAL CREDIT	ACCOUNTS RECEIVABLE CREDIT	SALES CREDIT	SALES TAX PAYABLE CREDIT	SALES DISCOUNT DEBIT	CASH DEBIT

6-1 ON YOUR OWN (LO1), p. 177

Journalizing entries to write off uncollectible accounts—direct write-off method

GENERAL JOURNAL

PAGE _____

	DATE	ACCOUNT TITLE	DOC. NO.	POST. REF.	DEBIT	CREDIT	
1							1
2							2
3							3
4							4
5							5
6							6
7							7
8							8
9							9
10							10
11							11
12							12
13							13
14							14
15							15
16							16
17							17
18							18
19							19
20							20
21							21
22							22
23							23
24							24
25							25
26							26
27							27
28							28
29							29

CASH RECEIPTS JOURNAL

	DATE	ACCOUNT TITLE	DOC. NO.	POST. REF.	GENERAL DEBIT	GENERAL CREDIT	ACCOUNTS RECEIVABLE CREDIT	SALES CREDIT	SALES TAX PAYABLE CREDIT	SALES DISCOUNT DEBIT	CASH DEBIT	
					1	2	3	4	5	6	7	
1												1
2												2
3												3
4												4
5												5
6												6
7												7
8												8
9												9
10												10
11												11
12												12
13												13
14												14
15												15
16												16
17												17
18												18
19												19
20												20
21												21
22												22

6-2 WORK TOGETHER (LO3), p. 185

Estimating amount of uncollectible accounts expense; journalizing the adjusting entry

1.

GENERAL JOURNAL   PAGE 13

	DATE		ACCOUNT TITLE	DOC. NO.	POST. REF.	DEBIT	CREDIT	
1								1
2								2
3								3
4								4

2.

Age Group	Amount	Percentage	Uncollectible
Current	$32,154.62	3.0%	
1–30	14,178.96	6.0%	
31–60	5,148.61	10.0%	
61–90	3,215.11	20.0%	
Over 90	1,842.05	50.0%	
	$56,539.35		
Current Balance of Allowance for Uncollectible Accounts			
Estimated Addition to Allowance for Uncollectible Accounts			

GENERAL JOURNAL   PAGE 18

	DATE		ACCOUNT TITLE	DOC. NO.	POST. REF.	DEBIT	CREDIT	
1								1
2								2
3								3
4								4

3.

GENERAL JOURNAL   PAGE 1

	DATE		ACCOUNT TITLE	DOC. NO.	POST. REF.	DEBIT	CREDIT	
1								1
2								2
3								3
4								4
5								5

PAGE 4

CASH RECEIPTS JOURNAL

	DATE	ACCOUNT TITLE	DOC. NO.	POST. REF.	GENERAL DEBIT	GENERAL CREDIT	ACCOUNTS RECEIVABLE CREDIT	SALES CREDIT	SALES TAX PAYABLE CREDIT	SALES DISCOUNT DEBIT	CASH DEBIT	
					1	2	3	4	5	6	7	
1												1
2												2
3												3
4												4
5												5
6												6
7												7
8												8
9												9
10												10
11												11
12												12
13												13
14												14
15												15
16												16
17												17
18												18
19												19
20												20
21												21
22												22

6-2 ON YOUR OWN (LO3), p. 185

Estimating amount of uncollectible accounts expense; journalizing the adjusting entry

1.

GENERAL JOURNAL   PAGE 16

	DATE	ACCOUNT TITLE	DOC. NO.	POST. REF.	DEBIT	CREDIT	
1							1
2							2
3							3
4							4

2.

Age Group	Amount	Percentage	Uncollectible
Current	$28,106.64	2.0%	
1–30	10,418.65	5.0%	
31–60	6,109.46	12.0%	
61–90	4,118.30	25.0%	
Over 90	2,219.36	60.0%	
	$50,972.41		
Current Balance of Allowance for Uncollectible Accounts			
Estimated Addition to Allowance for Uncollectible Accounts			

GENERAL JOURNAL   PAGE 18

	DATE	ACCOUNT TITLE	DOC. NO.	POST. REF.	DEBIT	CREDIT	
1							1
2							2
3							3
4							4

3.

GENERAL JOURNAL   PAGE 1

	DATE	ACCOUNT TITLE	DOC. NO.	POST. REF.	DEBIT	CREDIT	
1							1
2							2
3							3
4							4
5							5

CASH RECEIPTS JOURNAL

PAGE 3

DATE	ACCOUNT TITLE	DOC. NO.	POST. REF.	GENERAL DEBIT	GENERAL CREDIT	ACCOUNTS RECEIVABLE CREDIT	SALES CREDIT	SALES TAX PAYABLE CREDIT	SALES DISCOUNT DEBIT	CASH DEBIT
				1	2	3	4	5	6	7

6-3 WORK TOGETHER (LO4, 5), p. 188

Financial analysis of accounts receivable

1. Accounts receivable turnover ratio:

2. Days' sales in accounts receivable:

3.

_____
_____
_____
_____
_____
_____
_____

Financial analysis of accounts receivable

1. Accounts receivable turnover ratio:

2. Days' sales in accounts receivable:

3.

_____

_____

_____

_____

_____

_____

_____

6-1 APPLICATION PROBLEM (LO1), p. 192

Journalizing entries to write off uncollectible accounts—direct write-off method

GENERAL JOURNAL   PAGE _____

	DATE	ACCOUNT TITLE	DOC. NO.	POST. REF.	DEBIT	CREDIT	
1							1
2							2
3							3
4							4
5							5
6							6
7							7
8							8
9							9
10							10
11							11
12							12
13							13
14							14
15							15
16							16
17							17
18							18
19							19
20							20
21							21
22							22
23							23
24							24
25							25
26							26
27							27
28							28
29							29

CASH RECEIPTS JOURNAL

DATE	ACCOUNT TITLE	DOC. NO.	POST. REF.	GENERAL DEBIT	GENERAL CREDIT	ACCOUNTS RECEIVABLE CREDIT	SALES CREDIT	SALES TAX PAYABLE CREDIT	SALES DISCOUNT DEBIT	CASH DEBIT	
											1
											2
											3
											4
											5
											6
											7
											8
											9
											10
											11
											12
											13
											14
											15
											16
											17
											18
											19
											20
											21
											22

Name _____ Date _____ Class _____

6-2 APPLICATION PROBLEM (LO3), p. 192

Estimating amount of uncollectible accounts expense; journalizing the adjusting entry

1.

GENERAL JOURNAL PAGE

	DATE	ACCOUNT TITLE	DOC. NO.	POST. REF.	DEBIT	CREDIT	
1							1
2							2
3							3
4							4

2.

Age Group	Amount	Percentage	Uncollectible
Current	$22,108.95	2.0%	
1–30	13,048.62	5.0%	
31–60	3,108.14	12.0%	
61–90	4,094.46	30.0%	
Over 90	2,795.60	80.0%	
	$45,155.77		
Current Balance of Allowance for Uncollectible Accounts			
Estimated Addition to Allowance for Uncollectible Accounts			

GENERAL JOURNAL PAGE

	DATE	ACCOUNT TITLE	DOC. NO.	POST. REF.	DEBIT	CREDIT	
1							1
2							2
3							3
4							4
5							5
6							6
7							7
8							8
9							9
10							10
11							11

3.

GENERAL JOURNAL

PAGE

	DATE		ACCOUNT TITLE	DOC. NO.	POST. REF.	DEBIT	CREDIT	
1								1
2								2
3								3
4								4
5								5
6								6
7								7
8								8
9								9
10								10
11								11
12								12
13								13
14								14
15								15
16								16
17								17
18								18
19								19
20								20
21								21
22								22
23								23
24								24
25								25
26								26
27								27
28								28
29								29
30								30

6-2 APPLICATION PROBLEM (concluded)

CASH RECEIPTS JOURNAL

PAGE

DATE	ACCOUNT TITLE	DOC. NO.	POST. REF.	GENERAL DEBIT	GENERAL CREDIT	ACCOUNTS RECEIVABLE CREDIT	SALES CREDIT	SALES TAX PAYABLE CREDIT	SALES DISCOUNT DEBIT	CASH DEBIT
				1	2	3	4	5	6	7

APPLICATION PROBLEM (LO4, 5), p. 193

Financial analysis of accounts receivable

1. Accounts receivable turnover ratio:

2. Days' sales in accounts receivable:

3.

_____
_____
_____
_____
_____
_____
_____

6-M MASTERY PROBLEM (LO3, 4, 5), p. 193

Journalizing entries for uncollectible accounts—allowance method; calculating and journalizing the adjusting entry for uncollectible accounts expense

1., 2.

GENERAL JOURNAL   PAGE

	DATE	ACCOUNT TITLE	DOC. NO.	POST. REF.	DEBIT	CREDIT	
1							1
2							2
3							3
4							4
5							5
6							6
7							7
8							8
9							9
10							10
11							11
12							12
13							13
14							14
15							15
16							16
17							17
18							18
19							19
20							20
21							21
22							22
23							23
24							24
25							25
26							26
27							27
28							28
29							29

1.

CASH RECEIPTS JOURNAL

	DATE	ACCOUNT TITLE	DOC. NO.	POST. REF.	GENERAL DEBIT 1	GENERAL CREDIT 2	ACCOUNTS RECEIVABLE CREDIT 3	SALES CREDIT 4	SALES TAX PAYABLE CREDIT 5	SALES DISCOUNT DEBIT 6	CASH DEBIT 7	
1												1
2												2
3												3
4												4
5												5
6												6
7												7
8												8
9												9
10												10
11												11
12												12
13												13
14												14
15												15
16												16
17												17
18												18
19												19
20												20
21												21
22												22

6-M MASTERY PROBLEM (concluded)

3. Accounts receivable turnover ratio:

Days' sales in accounts receivable:

Estimating amount of uncollectible accounts expense; journalizing the adjusting entry

1.

Customer	Account Balance	Not Yet Due	Days Account Balance Past Due			
			1–30	31–60	61–90	Over 90
Ballard Corporation	$ 2,383.70					
Colister Company	3,874.80					
Eads & Godfrey	1,260.30					
Garrett, Inc.	2,031.00					
Jeffries Distributors	1,406.50					
McEwen Industries	2,722.10					
Perryman Company	2,047.20					
Ruffin Associates	3,615.20					
Turnage Supply	5,664.80					
Totals	$25,005.60					

2.

Age Group	Amount	Percentage	Uncollectible
Current 1–30 31–60 61–90 Over 90			
Current Balance of Allowance for Uncollectible Accounts			
Estimated Addition to Allowance for Uncollectible Accounts			

3.

GENERAL JOURNAL   PAGE

	DATE	ACCOUNT TITLE	DOC. NO.	POST. REF.	DEBIT	CREDIT	
1							1
2							2
3							3
4							4

Study Guide 7

Name	Perfect Score	Your Score
Analyzing Concepts and Practices Related to Depreciation and Plant Assets	22 Pts.	
Identifying Accounting Terms	10 Pts.	
Analyzing Plant Asset Transactions	16 Pts.	
Total	48 Pts.	

Part One—Analyzing Concepts and Practices Related to Depreciation and Plant Assets

Directions: Place a *T* for True or an *F* for False in the Answers column to show whether each of the following statements is true or false.

Answers

1. Plant assets are sometimes referred to as fixed assets. (p. 198)

1. _____

2. A company purchases a building and land for $400,000. The building is appraised for $300,000 and the land for $150,000. The cost assigned to the land should be $150,000. (p. 201)

2. _____

3. An accounting form on which a business records information about each plant asset is called a plant asset record. (p. 202)

3. _____

4. The value of an asset determined by tax authorities for the purpose of calculating taxes is called the millage rate. (p. 202)

4. _____

5. International financial reporting standards require that significant components of a plant asset be recorded individually in different plant asset accounts. (p. 203)

5. _____

6. Salvage value is also referred to as residual value, scrap value, or trade-in value. (p. 205)

6. _____

7. Because of land's permanent nature, it is not subject to depreciation. (p. 205)

7. _____

8. Original cost, estimated useful life, and miles driven in a year are the three factors considered when calculating annual depreciation expense. (p. 205)

8. _____

9. The formula for calculating a plant asset's annual straight-line depreciation expense is: Original cost minus estimated salvage value divided by years of estimated useful life equals annual depreciation expense. (p. 206)

9. _____

10. Whatever method a business selects to calculate depreciation expense for a portion of a year, that method should be used consistently from year to year. (p. 207)

10. _____

11. A business installs a new roof on a warehouse in the 10th year of its 30-year useful life. The cost of replacing the roof should be added to the cost of the plant asset. (p. 209)

11. _____

12. Three common ways of disposing of plant assets are discarding, selling, and trading. (p. 211)

12. _____

13. When a plant asset is discarded, no notation needs to be made on the plant asset record. (p. 211)

13. _____

14. If a plant asset is disposed of during a fiscal year, depreciation expense for part of a year is recorded. (p. 212)

14. _____

15. A gain or loss on plant assets is not recorded when one plant asset is traded for a similar plant asset. (p. 214)

15. _____

16. The double declining-balance rate of depreciation for a plant asset with a 4-year useful life is 25%. (p. 218)

16. _____

17. Calculating the estimated annual depreciation expense based on the amount of production expected from a plant asset is called the units-of-production method of deprecation. (p. 219)

17. _____

18. The two most commonly-used MACRS classes, for plant assets other than real estate, are the three- and five-year property classes. (p. 220)

18. _____

19. MACRS depreciation is an acceptable depreciation method for financial reporting. (p. 221)

19. _____

20. MACRS depreciation rates are based on the straight-line method using the modified half-year convention. (p. 221)

20. _____

21. The double-declining balance depreciation method ignores the salvage value. (p. 221)

21. _____

22. The estimated value of land after natural resources are removed should be considered in calculating a depletion rate. (p. 222)

22. _____

Part Two—Identifying Accounting Terms

Directions: Select the one term in Column I that best fits each definition in Column II. Print the letter identifying your choice in the Answers column.

Column I	**Column II**	**Answers**
A. book value of a plant asset	1. Cash and other assets expected to be exchanged for cash or consumed within a year. (p. 198)	1. _____
B. current assets	2. Land and anything attached to it. (p. 202)	2. _____
C. declining-balance method of depreciation	3. All property not classified as real property. (p. 202)	3. _____
	4. The amount that will be received for an asset at the time of its disposal. (p. 205)	4. _____
D. depletion		
E. half-year convention	5. Recording an equal amount of depreciation expense for a plant asset in each year of its useful life. (p. 206)	5. _____
F. modified half-year convention	6. The original cost of a plant asset minus accumulated depreciation. (p. 206)	6. _____
G. personal property		
H. real property	7. A method that recognizes one half of a year's depreciation in the year of acquisition. (p. 207)	7. _____
I. salvage value	8. A method that recognizes a full year's depreciation if the asset is acquired in the first half of the year. (p. 207)	8. _____
J. straight-line method of depreciation	9. A type of accelerated depreciation that multiplies the book value of an asset by a constant depreciation rate to determine annual depreciation. (p. 218)	9. _____
	10. The decrease in the value of a plant asset because of the removal of a natural resource. (p. 222)	10. _____

Part Three—Analyzing Plant Asset Transactions

Directions: For each transaction below, print in the proper Answers columns the identifying letter of the accounts to be debited and credited.

Account Titles	Transactions	Answers Debit	Credit
A. Accumulated Depreciation—Equipment.	**1-2.** Paid cash for new equipment. (p. 199)	1. _____	2. _____
B. Cash	**3-4.** Recorded annual depreciation on equipment. (p. 209)	3. _____	4. _____
C. Depreciation Expense—Equipment.	**5-6.** Discarded equipment with no book value. (p. 211)	5. _____	6. _____
D. Gain on Plant Assets	**7-8.** Recorded depreciation for part of year. (p. 212)	7. _____	8. _____
E. Equipment	**9-10.** Discarded equipment with a book value, all depreciation recorded. (p. 212)	9. _____	10. _____
F. Loss on Plant Assets	**11-12.** Received cash for the sale of equipment for less than book value, all depreciation recorded. (p. 213)	11. _____	12. _____
	13-14. Received cash for the sale of equipment for more than book value, all depreciation recorded. (p. 213)	13. _____	14. _____
	15-16. Paid cash plus old equipment for new equipment with a list price of $4,500.00; original cost of old equipment, $3,500.00; total accumulated depreciation recorded to date of trade, $500.00. (p. 214)	15. _____	16. _____

7-1   WORK TOGETHER (LO1), p. 204

Journalizing asset purchase transactions

1.

CASH PAYMENTS JOURNAL

PAGE 1

| | | | | | | | 1 GENERAL | | 3 | 4 | 5 | |
DATE	ACCOUNT TITLE	CK. NO.	POST. REF.	DEBIT	CREDIT	ACCOUNTS PAYABLE DEBIT	PURCHASES DISCOUNT CREDIT	CASH CREDIT	
									1
									2
									3
									4
									5
									6
									7
									8
									9

1.

GENERAL JOURNAL

PAGE 4

DATE	ACCOUNT TITLE	DOC. NO.	POST. REF.	DEBIT	CREDIT	
						1
						2
						3
						4
						5
						6
						7
						8
						9

2.

PLANT ASSET RECORD No. _____   General Ledger Account No. _____

Description _____   General Ledger Account _____

Date
Bought _____   Serial
                            Number _____   Original Cost _____

Estimated
Useful Life _____   Estimated
                              Salvage
                              Value _____   Depreciation
                                                          Method _____

Disposed of: Discarded _____   Sold _____   Traded _____
Date _____   Disposal Amount _____

Year	Annual Depreciation Expense	Accumulated Depreciation	Ending Book Value

PLANT ASSET RECORD No. _____   General Ledger Account No. _____

Description _____   General Ledger Account _____

Date
Bought _____   Serial
                            Number _____   Original Cost _____

Estimated
Useful Life _____   Estimated
                              Salvage
                              Value _____   Depreciation
                                                          Method _____

Disposed of: Discarded _____   Sold _____   Traded _____
Date _____   Disposal Amount _____

Year	Annual Depreciation Expense	Accumulated Depreciation	Ending Book Value

7-1 WORK TOGETHER (continued)

PLANT ASSET RECORD No. _____   General Ledger Account No. _____

Description _____   General Ledger Account _____

Date
Bought _____   Serial
Number _____   Original Cost _____

Estimated
Useful Life _____   Estimated
Salvage
Value _____   Depreciation
Method _____

Disposed of: Discarded _____   Sold _____   Traded _____
Date _____   Disposal Amount _____

Year	Annual Depreciation Expense	Accumulated Depreciation	Ending Book Value

PLANT ASSET RECORD No. _____   General Ledger Account No. _____

Description _____   General Ledger Account _____

| Date Bought | _____ | Serial Number | _____ | Original Cost | _____ |

Estimated Useful Life _____   Estimated Salvage Value _____   Depreciation Method _____

Disposed of: Discarded _____   Sold _____   Traded _____

Date _____   Disposal Amount _____

Year	Annual Depreciation Expense	Accumulated Depreciation	Ending Book Value

	Appraised Value	Percentage of Total Appraised Value	Assigned Cost
Building			
Land	_____		_____
Total	_____		_____

7-1 ON YOUR OWN (LO1), p. 204

Journalizing asset purchase transactions

1.

CASH PAYMENTS JOURNAL

PAGE 2

| | | CK. NO. | POST. REF. | GENERAL | | ACCOUNTS PAYABLE DEBIT | PURCHASES DISCOUNT CREDIT | CASH CREDIT |
| | | | | DEBIT | CREDIT | | | |
DATE	ACCOUNT TITLE			1	2	3	4	5
									1
									2
									3
									4
									5
									6
									7
									8
									9

1.

GENERAL JOURNAL

PAGE 1

DATE	ACCOUNT TITLE	DOC. NO.	POST. REF.	DEBIT	CREDIT
						1
						2
						3
						4
						5
						6
						7
						8
						9

2.

PLANT ASSET RECORD No. _____   General Ledger Account No. _____

Description _____   General Ledger Account _____

Date   Serial
Bought   _____   Number _____   Original Cost   _____

                              Estimated
Estimated   Salvage   Depreciation
Useful Life _____   Value   _____   Method   _____

Disposed of: Discarded _____   Sold _____   Traded _____

Date _____   Disposal Amount _____

Year	Annual Depreciation Expense	Accumulated Depreciation	Ending Book Value

PLANT ASSET RECORD No. _____   General Ledger Account No. _____

Description _____   General Ledger Account _____

Date   Serial
Bought   _____   Number _____   Original Cost   _____

                              Estimated
Estimated   Salvage   Depreciation
Useful Life _____   Value   _____   Method   _____

Disposed of: Discarded _____   Sold _____   Traded _____

Date _____   Disposal Amount _____

Year	Annual Depreciation Expense	Accumulated Depreciation	Ending Book Value

PLANT ASSET RECORD No. _____   General Ledger Account No. _____

Description _____   General Ledger Account _____

Date   Serial
Bought _____   Number _____ Original Cost _____

                        Estimated
Estimated   Salvage   Depreciation
Useful Life _____ Value _____   Method   _____

Disposed of: Discarded _____ Sold _____ Traded _____
Date _____   Disposal Amount _____

Year	Annual Depreciation Expense	Accumulated Depreciation	Ending Book Value

PLANT ASSET RECORD No. _____   General Ledger Account No. _____

Description _____   General Ledger Account _____

Date   Serial
Bought   _____   Number _____   Original Cost   _____

                                  Estimated
Estimated   Salvage   Depreciation
Useful Life _____   Value _____   Method _____

Disposed of: Discarded _____   Sold _____   Traded _____
Date _____   Disposal Amount _____

Year	Annual Depreciation Expense	Accumulated Depreciation	Ending Book Value

	Appraised Value	Percentage of Total Appraised Value	Assigned Cost
Building			
Land	_____		_____
Total	_____		_____

7-2 WORK TOGETHER (LO4, 5), p. 210

Calculating and journalizing depreciation

1.

Plant asset:	Printer	Original cost:	$840.00
Depreciation method:	Straight-line	Estimated salvage value:	$0.00
		Estimated useful life:	3 years

Year	Beginning Book Value	Annual Depreciation	Accumulated Depreciation	Ending Book Value

Plant asset:	Conveyor table	Original cost:	$1,800.00
Depreciation method:	Straight-line	Estimated salvage value:	$200.00
		Estimated useful life:	5 years

Year	Beginning Book Value	Annual Depreciation	Accumulated Depreciation	Ending Book Value

Plant asset:	Warehouse	Original cost:	$225,000.00
Depreciation method:	Straight-line	Estimated salvage value:	$25,000.00
		Estimated useful life:	25 years

Year	Beginning Book Value	Annual Depreciation	Accumulated Depreciation	Ending Book Value

3.

GENERAL JOURNAL

	DATE		ACCOUNT TITLE	DOC. NO.	POST. REF.	DEBIT	CREDIT	
1								1
2								2
3								3
4								4
5								5
6								6
7								7
8								8
9								9
10								10
11								11
12								12
13								13
14								14
15								15
16								16
17								17
18								18
19								19
20								20
21								21
22								22
23								23
24								24
25								25
26								26
27								27
28								28
29								29
30								30
31								31
32								32

7-2 ON YOUR OWN (LO4, 5), p. 210

Calculating and journalizing depreciation

1.

Plant asset:	Tablet	Original cost:	$650.00
Depreciation method:	Straight-line	Estimated salvage value:	$0.00
		Estimated useful life:	5 years

Year	Beginning Book Value	Annual Depreciation	Accumulated Depreciation	Ending Book Value

Plant asset:	Point-of-sale system	Original cost:	$2,500.00
Depreciation method:	Straight-line	Estimated salvage value:	$500.00
		Estimated useful life:	5 years

Year	Beginning Book Value	Annual Depreciation	Accumulated Depreciation	Ending Book Value

Plant asset:	Store	Original cost:	$120,000.00
Depreciation method:	Straight-line	Estimated salvage value:	$20,000.00
		Estimated useful life:	25 years

Year	Beginning Book Value	Annual Depreciation	Accumulated Depreciation	Ending Book Value

3.

GENERAL JOURNAL

PAGE 15

	DATE		ACCOUNT TITLE	DOC. NO.	POST. REF.	DEBIT	CREDIT	
1								1
2								2
3								3
4								4
5								5
6								6
7								7
8								8
9								9
10								10
11								11
12								12
13								13
14								14
15								15
16								16
17								17
18								18
19								19
20								20
21								21
22								22
23								23
24								24
25								25
26								26
27								27
28								28
29								29
30								30
31								31
32								32

Name _____ Date _____ Class _____

Recording the disposal of plant assets

1.

CASH RECEIPTS JOURNAL

PAGE 1

	DATE	ACCOUNT TITLE	DOC. NO.	POST. REF.	GENERAL DEBIT 1	GENERAL CREDIT 2	ACCOUNTS RECEIVABLE CREDIT 3	SALES CREDIT 4	SALES TAX PAYABLE CREDIT 5	SALES DISCOUNT DEBIT 6	CASH DEBIT 7	
1												1
2												2
3												3
4												4
5												5
6												6
7												7
8												8
9												9
10												10
11												11
12												12
13												13
14												14

1.

CASH PAYMENTS JOURNAL

PAGE 18

	DATE	ACCOUNT TITLE	CK. NO.	POST. REF.	GENERAL DEBIT 1	GENERAL CREDIT 2	ACCOUNTS PAYABLE DEBIT 3	PURCHASES DISCOUNT CREDIT 4	CASH CREDIT 5	
1										1
2										2
3										3
4										4

1.

GENERAL JOURNAL

	DATE	ACCOUNT TITLE	DOC. NO.	POST. REF.	DEBIT	CREDIT	
1							1
2							2
3							3
4							4
5							5
6							6
7							7
8							8
9							9
10							10
11							11
12							12
13							13
14							14
15							15
16							16
17							17
18							18
19							19
20							20
21							21
22							22
23							23
24							24
25							25
26							26
27							27
28							28
29							29
30							30
31							31
32							32

7-3 **WORK TOGETHER (concluded)**

2.

PLANT ASSET RECORD No. __289__   General Ledger Account No. __1230__

Description __Desk__   General Ledger Account __Office Equipment__

| Date Bought | January 14, 20X0 | Serial Number | 6-33264-36 | Original Cost | $1,500.00 |

| Estimated Useful Life | 7 years | Estimated Salvage Value | $100.00 | Depreciation Method | Straight-line |

Disposed of: Discarded _____   Sold _____   Traded _____

Date _____   Disposal Amount _____

Year	Annual Depreciation Expense	Accumulated Depreciation	Ending Book Value
20X0	$200.00	$ 200.00	$1,300.00
20X1	200.00	400.00	1,100.00
20X2	200.00	600.00	900.00
20X3	200.00	800.00	700.00
20X4	200.00	1,000.00	500.00

PLANT ASSET RECORD No. __332__   General Ledger Account No. __1240__

Description __Truck__   General Ledger Account __Warehouse Equipment__

| Date Bought | July 8, 20X2 | Serial Number | 02-63232-6432 | Original Cost | $32,000.00 |

| Estimated Useful Life | 5 years | Estimated Salvage Value | $5,000.00 | Depreciation Method | Straight-line |

Disposed of: Discarded _____   Sold _____   Traded _____

Date _____   Disposal Amount _____

Year	Annual Depreciation Expense	Accumulated Depreciation	Ending Book Value
20X2	$2,700.00	$ 2,700.00	$29,300.00
20X3	5,400.00	8,100.00	23,900.00
20X4	5,400.00	13,500.00	18,500.00

Recording the disposal of plant assets

1.

CASH RECEIPTS JOURNAL

PAGE 3

DATE	ACCOUNT TITLE	DOC. NO.	POST. REF.	GENERAL DEBIT	GENERAL CREDIT	ACCOUNTS RECEIVABLE CREDIT	SALES CREDIT	SALES TAX PAYABLE CREDIT	SALES DISCOUNT DEBIT	CASH DEBIT

1.

CASH PAYMENTS JOURNAL

PAGE 18

DATE	ACCOUNT TITLE	CK. NO.	POST. REF.	GENERAL DEBIT	GENERAL CREDIT	ACCOUNTS PAYABLE DEBIT	PURCHASES DISCOUNT CREDIT	CASH CREDIT

7-3 **ON YOUR OWN (continued)**

1.

GENERAL JOURNAL

PAGE 3

	DATE	ACCOUNT TITLE	DOC. NO.	POST. REF.	DEBIT	CREDIT	
1							1
2							2
3							3
4							4
5							5
6							6
7							7
8							8
9							9
10							10
11							11
12							12
13							13
14							14
15							15
16							16
17							17
18							18
19							19
20							20
21							21
22							22
23							23
24							24
25							25
26							26
27							27
28							28
29							29
30							30
31							31
32							32

2.

PLANT ASSET RECORD No. __233__   General Ledger Account No. __1240__

Description __Display case__   General Ledger Account __Store Equipment__

Date Bought __March 20, 20X0__   Serial Number __9198-9CG__   Original Cost __$6,750.00__

Estimated Useful Life __7 years__   Estimated Salvage Value __$1,500.00__   Depreciation Method __Straight-line__

Disposed of: Discarded _____   Sold _____   Traded _____

Date _____   Disposal Amount _____

Year	Annual Depreciation Expense	Accumulated Depreciation	Ending Book Value
20X0	$562.50	$ 562.50	$6,187.50
20X1	750.00	1,312.50	5,437.50
20X2	750.00	2,062.50	4,687.50
20X3	750.00	2,812.50	3,937.50
20X4	750.00	3,562.50	3,187.50

PLANT ASSET RECORD No. __460__   General Ledger Account No. __1230__

Description __Chair__   General Ledger Account __Office Eqiupment__

Date Bought __July 8, 20X2__   Serial Number __02-63232-6432__   Original Cost __$800.00__

Estimated Useful Life __7 years__   Estimated Salvage Value __$100.00__   Depreciation Method __Straight-line__

Disposed of: Discarded _____   Sold _____   Traded _____

Date _____   Disposal Amount _____

Year	Annual Depreciation Expense	Accumulated Depreciation	Ending Book Value
20X2	$ 50.00	$ 50.00	$750.00
20X3	100.00	150.00	650.00
20X4	100.00	250.00	550.00

7-4 WORK TOGETHER (LO8, 9, 10, 12), p. 223

Computing depreciation using various depreciation methods and calculating depletion

1.

Plant asset:	Machine	Original cost:	$24,000.00
Depreciation method:	Double-declining balance	Estimated salvage value:	$3,000.00
		Estimated useful life:	5 years

Year	Beginning Book Value	Declining-Balance Rate	Annual Depreciation	Ending Book Value
1				
2				
3				
4				
5				
6				
7				
8				
9				

Plant asset:	Machine	Estimated salvage value:	$3,000.00
Depreciation method:	Units-of-production	Estimated total depreciation:	
Original cost:	$24,000.00	Estimated useful life:	16,000 hours
		Depreciation rate:	

Year	Beginning Book Value	Production Hours	Annual Depreciation	Ending Book Value
1				
2				
3				
4				
5				

Computing depreciation using various depreciation methods and calculating depletion

Plant asset:	Machine	Original cost:	$24,000.00
Depreciation method:	MACRS	Property Class:	5-year

Year	Beginning Book Value	Depreciation Rate	Annual Depreciation	Ending Book Value
1				
2				
3				
4				
5				
6				
7				
8				
9				

2.

Plant asset:	Gas well	Estimated salvage value:	$60,000.00
Depreciation method:	Units-of-production	Estimated total depletion:	
Original cost:	$840,000.00	Estimated useful life:	800,000 MCF
		Depletion rate:	

Year	Beginning Book Value	MCF Recovered	Annual Depreciation	Ending Book Value
1				
2				
3				
4				

7-4 ON YOUR OWN (LO8, 9, 10, 12), p. 224

Computing depreciation using various depreciation methods and calculating depletion

1.

Plant asset:	Truck	Original cost:	$38,000.00
Depreciation method:	Double-declining balance	Estimated salvage value:	$2,500.00
		Estimated useful life:	3 years

Year	Beginning Book Value	Declining-Balance Rate	Annual Depreciation	Ending Book Value
1				
2				
3				
4				
5				
6				
7				
8				
9				

Plant asset:	Truck	Estimated salvage value:	$2,500.00
Depreciation method:	Units-of-production	Estimated total depreciation:	
Original cost:	$38,000.00	Estimated useful life:	300,000 miles
		Depreciation rate:	

Year	Beginning Book Value	Miles Driven	Annual Depreciation	Ending Book Value
1				
2				
3				
4				
5				

| | | | Plant asset: Truck | | Original cost: | $38,000.00 |
| | | | Depreciation method: MACRS | | Property class: | 5-year |

Year	Beginning Book Value	Depreciation Rate	Annual Depreciation	Ending Book Value
1				
2				
3				
4				
5				
6				
7				
8				
9				

2.

Plant asset: Mineral mine Original cost: $420,000.00
Depreciation method: Units-of-production Estimated salvage value: $80,000.00
Estimated total depletion: _____
Estimated useful life: 120,000 tons
Depletion rate: _____

Year	Beginning Book Value	Tons Mined	Annual Depletion	Ending Book Value
1				
2				
3				
4				
5				

7-1 APPLICATION PROBLEM (LO1, 2), p. 228

Journalizing asset purchase transactions

1.

CASH PAYMENTS JOURNAL

PAGE 1

| | | | | GENERAL | | ACCOUNTS PAYABLE DEBIT | PURCHASES DISCOUNT CREDIT | CASH CREDIT | |
DATE	ACCOUNT TITLE	CK. NO.	POST. REF.	DEBIT	CREDIT				
					1				1
					2				2
					3				3
					4				4
					5				5
					6				6
					7				7
					8				8
					9				9

1.

GENERAL JOURNAL

PAGE 8

DATE	ACCOUNT TITLE	DOC. NO.	POST. REF.	DEBIT	CREDIT	
						1
						2
						3
						4
						5
						6
						7
						8
						9

2.

PLANT ASSET RECORD No. _____   General Ledger Account No. _____

Description _____   General Ledger Account _____

Date
Bought _____   Serial Number _____   Original Cost _____

Estimated
Useful Life _____   Estimated Salvage Value _____   Depreciation Method _____

Disposed of: Discarded _____   Sold _____   Traded _____

Date _____   Disposal Amount _____

Year	Annual Depreciation Expense	Accumulated Depreciation	Ending Book Value

PLANT ASSET RECORD No. _____   General Ledger Account No. _____

Description _____   General Ledger Account _____

Date
Bought _____   Serial Number _____   Original Cost _____

Estimated
Useful Life _____   Estimated Salvage Value _____   Depreciation Method _____

Disposed of: Discarded _____   Sold _____   Traded _____

Date _____   Disposal Amount _____

Year	Annual Depreciation Expense	Accumulated Depreciation	Ending Book Value

7-1 **APPLICATION PROBLEM (continued)**

PLANT ASSET RECORD No. _____   General Ledger Account No. _____

Description _____   General Ledger Account _____

Date
Bought _____   Serial
Number _____   Original Cost _____

Estimated
Useful Life _____   Estimated
Salvage
Value _____   Depreciation
Method _____

Disposed of: Discarded _____   Sold _____   Traded _____

Date _____   Disposal Amount _____

Year	Annual Depreciation Expense	Accumulated Depreciation	Ending Book Value

PLANT ASSET RECORD No. _____   General Ledger Account No. _____

Description _____   General Ledger Account _____

Date
Bought _____   Serial
Number _____ Original Cost _____

Estimated
Useful Life _____
Estimated
Salvage
Value _____
Depreciation
Method _____

Disposed of: Discarded _____   Sold _____ Traded _____
Date _____   Disposal Amount _____

Year	Annual Depreciation Expense	Accumulated Depreciation	Ending Book Value

	Appraised Value	Percentage of Total Appraised Value	Assigned Cost
Building			
Land			
Total......................	_____		_____

3.

	Appraised Value	Percentage of Total Appraised Value	Assigned Cost
Engine			
Transmission			
Tires			
Frame			
Total......................	_____		_____

7-2 APPLICATION PROBLEM (LO4, 5), p. 228

Calculating and journalizing depreciation

1.

Plant asset:	Copy machine	Original cost:	$2,400.00
Depreciation method:	Straight-line	Estimated salvage value:	$200.00
		Estimated useful life:	5 years
		Date purchased:	January 12

Year	Beginning Book Value	Annual Depreciation	Accumulated Depreciation	Ending Book Value

Plant asset:	Shelving unit	Original cost:	$4,800.00
Depreciation method:	Straight-line	Estimated salvage value:	$1,000.00
		Estimated useful life:	5 years
		Date purchased:	August 22

Year	Beginning Book Value	Annual Depreciation	Accumulated Depreciation	Ending Book Value

Plant asset:	Warehouse	Original cost:	$180,000.00
Depreciation method:	Straight-line	Estimated salvage value:	$60,000.00
		Estimated useful life:	25 years
		Date purchased:	September 27

Year	Beginning Book Value	Annual Depreciation	Accumulated Depreciation	Ending Book Value

3.

GENERAL JOURNAL

PAGE 15

	DATE	ACCOUNT TITLE	DOC. NO.	POST. REF.	DEBIT	CREDIT	
1							1
2							2
3							3
4							4
5							5
6							6
7							7
8							8
9							9
10							10
11							11
12							12
13							13
14							14
15							15
16							16
17							17
18							18
19							19
20							20
21							21
22							22
23							23
24							24
25							25
26							26
27							27
28							28
29							29
30							30
31							31
32							32

7-3 **APPLICATION PROBLEM (LO7), p. 229**

Recording the disposal of plant assets

1.

CASH RECEIPTS JOURNAL

PAGE 1

DATE	ACCOUNT TITLE	DOC. NO.	POST. REF.	GENERAL DEBIT	GENERAL CREDIT	ACCOUNTS RECEIVABLE CREDIT	SALES CREDIT	SALES TAX PAYABLE CREDIT	SALES DISCOUNT DEBIT	CASH DEBIT
				1	2	3	4	5	6	7

CASH PAYMENTS JOURNAL

PAGE 18

DATE	ACCOUNT TITLE	CK. NO.	POST. REF.	GENERAL DEBIT	GENERAL CREDIT	ACCOUNTS PAYABLE DEBIT	PURCHASES DISCOUNT CREDIT	CASH CREDIT
				1	2	3	4	5

1.

1.

GENERAL JOURNAL

PAGE 2

	DATE		ACCOUNT TITLE	DOC. NO.	POST. REF.	DEBIT	CREDIT	
1								1
2								2
3								3
4								4
5								5
6								6
7								7
8								8
9								9
10								10
11								11
12								12
13								13
14								14
15								15
16								16
17								17
18								18
19								19
20								20
21								21
22								22
23								23
24								24
25								25
26								26
27								27
28								28
29								29
30								30
31								31
32								32

7-3   APPLICATION PROBLEM (concluded)

2.

PLANT ASSET RECORD No. __289__   General Ledger Account No. __1230__

Description __Desk__   General Ledger Account __Office Equipment__

| Date Bought | January 14, 20X0 | Serial Number | 6-33264-36 | Original Cost | $1,500.00 |

| Estimated Useful Life | 7 years | Estimated Salvage Value | $100.00 | Depreciation Method | Straight-line |

Disposed of: Discarded _____   Sold _____   Traded _____

Date _____   Disposal Amount _____

Year	Annual Depreciation Expense	Accumulated Depreciation	Ending Book Value
20X0	$200.00	$ 200.00	$1,300.00
20X1	200.00	400.00	1,100.00
20X2	200.00	600.00	900.00
20X3	200.00	800.00	700.00
20X4	200.00	1,000.00	500.00

PLANT ASSET RECORD No. __332__   General Ledger Account No. __1250__

Description __Truck__   General Ledger Account __Transportation Equipment__

| Date Bought | July 8, 20X2 | Serial Number | 02-63232-6432 | Original Cost | $32,000.00 |

| Estimated Useful Life | 5 years | Estimated Salvage Value | $5,000.00 | Depreciation Method | Straight-line |

Disposed of: Discarded _____   Sold _____   Traded _____

Date _____   Disposal Amount _____

Year	Annual Depreciation Expense	Accumulated Depreciation	Ending Book Value
20X2	$2,700.00	$ 2,700.00	$29,300.00
20X3	5,400.00	8,100.00	23,900.00
20X4	5,400.00	13,500.00	18,500.00

Computing depreciation using various depreciation methods and calculating depletion

1.

Plant asset:	Car		Original cost:	$40,000.00
Depreciation method:	Double-declining balance		Estimated salvage value:	$5,000.00
			Estimated useful life:	5 years

Year	Beginning Book Value	Declining-Balance Rate	Annual Depreciation	Ending Book Value
1				
2				
3				
4				
5				
6				
7				
8				
9				

Plant asset:	Car		Original cost:	$40,000.00
Depreciation method:	Units-of-production		Estimated salvage value:	$5,000.00
			Estimated total depreciation	
			Estimated useful life:	100,000 miles
			Depreciation rate:	

Year	Beginning Book Value	Miles Driven	Annual Depreciation	Ending Book Value
1				
2				
3				
4				
5				
6				
7				
8				
9				

7-4 **APPLICATION PROBLEM (concluded)**

Plant asset:	Car		Original cost:	$40,000.00
Depreciation method:	MACRS		Property class:	5-year

Year	Beginning Book Value	Depreciation Rate	Annual Depreciation	Ending Book Value
1				
2				
3				
4				
5				
6				
7				
8				
9				

2.

Plant asset:	Coal mine	Original cost:	$825,000.00
Depreciation method:	Units-of-production	Estimated salvage value:	$100,000.00
		Estimated total depletion:	
		Estimated useful life:	700,000 tons
		Depletion rate:	

Year	Beginning Book Value	Tons Mined	Annual Depletion	Ending Book Value
1				
2				
3				
4				
5				
6				
7				
8				
9				

Recording entries for plant assets

1.

CASH RECEIPTS JOURNAL

PAGE 9

	DATE	ACCOUNT TITLE	DOC. NO.	POST. REF.	GENERAL DEBIT	GENERAL CREDIT	ACCOUNTS RECEIVABLE CREDIT	SALES CREDIT	SALES TAX PAYABLE CREDIT	SALES DISCOUNT DEBIT	CASH DEBIT
					1	2	3	4	5	6	7
1											
2											
3											
4											
5											
6											
7											
8											
9											
10											
11											

1.

CASH PAYMENTS JOURNAL

PAGE 3

	DATE	ACCOUNT TITLE	CK. NO.	POST. REF.	GENERAL DEBIT	GENERAL CREDIT	ACCOUNTS PAYABLE DEBIT	PURCHASES DISCOUNT CREDIT	CASH CREDIT
					1	2	3	4	5
1									
2									
3									
4									
5									
6									
7									

7-M   MASTERY PROBLEM (continued)

1.

GENERAL JOURNAL   PAGE 3

	DATE		ACCOUNT TITLE	DOC. NO.	POST. REF.	DEBIT	CREDIT	
1								1
2								2
3								3
4								4
5								5
6								6
7								7
8								8
9								9
10								10
11								11
12								12
13								13
14								14
15								15
16								16
17								17
18								18
19								19
20								20
21								21
22								22
23								23
24								24
25								25
26								26
27								27
28								28
29								29
30								30
31								31
32								32

1., 2.

PLANT ASSET RECORD No. __233__   General Ledger Account No. __1230__

Description __Computer__   General Ledger Account __Office Equipment__

Date Bought __June 23, 19X9__   Serial Number __C16443P__   Original Cost __$2,300.00__

Estimated Useful Life __3 years__   Estimated Salvage Value __$500.00__   Depreciation Method __Straight-line__

Disposed of: Discarded _____   Sold _____   Traded _____
Date _____   Disposal Amount _____

Year	Annual Depreciation Expense	Accumulated Depreciation	Ending Book Value
19X9	$300.00	$ 300.00	$2,000.00
20X0	600.00	900.00	1,400.00
20X1			

PLANT ASSET RECORD No. _____   General Ledger Account No. _____

Description _____   General Ledger Account _____

Date Bought _____   Serial Number _____   Original Cost _____

Estimated Useful Life _____   Estimated Salvage Value _____   Depreciation Method _____

Disposed of: Discarded _____   Sold _____   Traded _____
Date _____   Disposal Amount _____

Year	Annual Depreciation Expense	Accumulated Depreciation	Ending Book Value

7-M MASTERY PROBLEM (concluded)

3.

Plant asset:	Office desk	Original cost:	$2,900.00
Depreciation method:	Double declining-balance	Estimated salvage value:	$300.00
		Estimated useful life:	7 years

Year	Beginning Book Value	Declining-Balance Rate	Annual Depreciation	Ending Book Value
1				
2				
3				
4				
5				
6				
7				
8				

| Plant asset: | Office desk | Original cost: | $2,900.00 |
| Depreciation method: | MACRS | Property class: | 7-year |

Year	Beginning Book Value	Depreciation Rate	Annual Depreciation	Ending Book Value
1				
2				
3				
4				
5				
6				
7				
8				
9				

4.

	Percentage of Total Appraised Value	Assigned Cost
Land	45%	
Warehouse		
Structure	35%	
Electrical systems	12%	
Roof	5%	
Landscaping	3%	
Total Cost		

Calculating depletion with a change in estimates

1., 2.

Plant asset:	Coal mine	Original cost:	$720,000.00
Depreciation method:	Units-of-production	Estimated salvage value:	$50,000.00
		Estimated total depletion:	
		Estimated tons:	326,000 tons

Year	Beginning Book Value	Tons Mined	Depletion Rate	Annual Depletion	Ending Book Value
1					
2					
3					
4					
5					
6					
7					
8					
9					

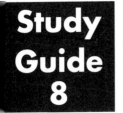

Name		Perfect Score	Your Score
	Identifying Accounting Terms	19 Pts.	
Analyzing Procedures for Notes Payable, Prepaid Expenses, and Accrued Expenses		12 Pts.	
Analyzing Entries for Notes Payable, Prepaid Expenses, and Accrued Expenses		22 Pts.	
	Total	53 Pts.	

Part One—Identifying Accounting Terms

Directions: Select the one term in Column I that best fits each definition in Column II. Print the letter identifying your choice in the Answers column.

Column I	Column II	Answers
A. accrued expenses	**1.** Obtaining capital by borrowing money for a period of time. (p. 236)	1._____
B. current liabilities	**2.** A written and signed promise to pay a sum of money at a specified time. (p. 236)	2._____
C. date of a note	**3.** Promissory notes signed by a business and given to a creditor. (p. 236)	3._____
D. debt financing		
E. interest	**4.** The day a note is issued. (p. 236)	4._____
F. interest expense	**5.** The original amount of a note. (p. 236)	5._____
G. interest rate	**6.** The date on which the principal of a note is due to be repaid. (p. 236)	6._____
H. interest-bearing note	**7.** A note paid in full with a single payment at the end of the maturity date. (p. 236)	7._____
I. line of credit	**8.** An amount paid for the use of money for a period of time. (p. 236)	8._____
J. lump-sum payment		
K. maturity date	**9.** The percentage of the principal that is due for the use of the funds secured by a note. (p. 236)	9._____
L. maturity value	**10.** Liabilities due within a short time, usually within a year. (p. 237)	10._____
M. noninterest-bearing note		
N. notes payable	**11.** Interest accrued on borrowed funds. (p. 239)	11._____
O. prepaid expense	**12.** The amount that is due on the maturity date of a note. (p. 239)	12._____
P. prime interest rate	**13.** A note having a stated interest rate. (p. 239)	13._____
Q. principal	**14.** A note that deducts interest from the face value of the note. (p. 239)	14._____
R. promissory note		
S. reversing entry	**15.** A bank loan agreement that provides immediate short-term access to cash. (p. 241)	15._____
	16. The interest rate charged to a bank's most creditworthy customers. (p. 241)	16._____
	17. Cash paid for an expense in one fiscal period that is not used until a later period. (p. 243)	17._____
	18. An entry made at the beginning of one fiscal period to reverse an adjusting entry made in the previous fiscal period. (p. 245)	18._____
	19. Expenses incurred in one fiscal period but not paid until a later fiscal period. (p. 249)	19._____

Part Two—Analyzing Procedures for Notes Payable, Prepaid Expenses, and Accrued Expenses

Directions: Place a *T* for True or an *F* for False in the Answers column to show whether each of the following statements is true or false.

Answers

1. The amount of note interest is slightly higher using a 360-day year compared to a 365-day year. (p. 238)

1. _____

2. Interest expense is reported as an operating expense. (p. 239)

2. _____

3. The proceeds of a noninterest-bearing note are less than its maturity value. (p. 239)

3. _____

4. The interest rate on a credit line can change, based on market interest rates. (p. 240)

4. _____

5. When prepaid expenses are initially recorded as expenses, no adjusting entry is required prior to preparing financial statements. (p. 244)

5. _____

6. If an adjusting entry creates a balance in an asset or a liability account, the adjusting entry is reversed. (p. 245)

6. _____

7. A reversing entry is usually the opposite of the adjusting entry made to the same accounts. (p. 245)

7. _____

8. Generally accepted accounting principles require that expenditures for future advertising expenses be recorded in a prepaid asset account. (p. 247)

8. _____

9. The reversing entry for an accrued expense results in a temporary credit balance in the expense account. (p. 250)

9. _____

10. Recording repair costs during a warranty period as an expense in the same period the merchandise is sold is an application of the accounting concept Matching Expenses with Revenue. (p. 253)

10. _____

11. Accrued Warranty Liability and Allowance for Uncollectible Accounts each have natural credit balances. (p. 254)

11. _____

12. The accounting for warranties and uncollectible accounts differ only in that Accrued Warranty Liability has a contra asset account. (p. 254)

12. _____

Part Three—Analyzing Entries for Notes Payable, Prepaid Expenses, and Accrued Expenses

Directions: For each transaction below, print in the proper Answers columns the identifying letter of the accounts to be debited and credited. The company initially records prepaid expenses as expenses.

Account Titles		Transactions	Answers	
			Debit	**Credit**
A. Accrued Warranty Liability	**1-2.**	Issued a 90-day note to the bank. (p. 237)	1._____	2._____
B. Cash	**3-4.**	Paid cash for the maturity value of a note payable. (p. 239)	3._____	4._____
C. Insurance Expense				
D. Interest Expense	**5-6.**	Drew from a line of credit. (p. 241)	5._____	6._____
E. Interest Payable	**7-8.**	Paid a line of credit. (p. 241)	7._____	8._____
F. Line of Credit	**9-10.**	Adjusting entry for prepaid insurance initially recorded as an expense. (p. 244)	9._____	10._____
G. Notes Payable				
H. Prepaid Insurance	**11-12.**	Reversing entry for supplies expense. (p. 245)	11._____	12._____
I. Supplies	**13-14.**	Adjusting entry for accrued interest expense. (p. 249)	13._____	14._____
J. Supplies Expense				
K. Warranty Expense	**15-16.**	Reversing entry for accrued interest expense. (p. 250)	15._____	16._____
	17-18.	Payment of a note at maturity. (p 251)	17._____	18._____
	19-20.	Adjusting entry for warranty expense. (p. 253)	19._____	20._____
	21-22.	Paid for a repair on an item under warranty. (p. 254)	21._____	22._____

8-1 WORK TOGETHER (LO1), p. 242

Journalizing notes payable transactions

1.

CASH RECEIPTS JOURNAL

PAGE 6

DATE	ACCOUNT TITLE	DOC. NO.	POST. REF.	GENERAL DEBIT	GENERAL CREDIT	ACCOUNTS RECEIVABLE CREDIT	SALES CREDIT	SALES TAX PAYABLE CREDIT	SALES DISCOUNT DEBIT	CASH DEBIT

3.

CASH PAYMENTS JOURNAL

PAGE 9

DATE	ACCOUNT TITLE	CK. NO.	POST. REF.	GENERAL DEBIT	GENERAL CREDIT	ACCOUNTS PAYABLE DEBIT	PURCHASES DISCOUNT CREDIT	CASH CREDIT

2.

Maturity dates:

June 4, $5,000.00 Note		
	Days from the Month	Days Remaining
Term of the Note		

July 15, $8,000.00 Note		
	Days from the Month	Days Remaining
Term of the Note		

2.

Interest due at maturity:

June 4, $5,000.00 Note

Principal	×	Interest Rate	×	Time as a Fraction of Year	=	Interest for Fraction of Year
				/365		

July 15, $8,000.00 Note

Principal	×	Interest Rate	×	Time as a Fraction of Year	=	Interest for Fraction of Year
				/365		

8-1 ON YOUR OWN (LO1), p. 242

Journalizing notes payable transactions

1.

CASH RECEIPTS JOURNAL

PAGE 5

| | | | | GENERAL | | ACCOUNTS RECEIVABLE CREDIT | SALES CREDIT | SALES TAX PAYABLE CREDIT | SALES DISCOUNT DEBIT | CASH DEBIT |
DATE	ACCOUNT TITLE	DOC. NO.	POST. REF.	DEBIT	CREDIT					

3.

CASH PAYMENTS JOURNAL

PAGE 11

| | | | | GENERAL | | ACCOUNTS PAYABLE DEBIT | PURCHASES DISCOUNT CREDIT | CASH CREDIT |
DATE	ACCOUNT TITLE	CK. NO.	POST. REF.	DEBIT	CREDIT			

2.

Maturity dates:

May 16, $16,000.00 Note		
	Days from the Month	Days Remaining
Term of the Note		

August 8, $20,000.00 Note		
	Days from the Month	Days Remaining
Term of the Note		

2.

Interest due at maturity:

May 16, $16,000.00 Note

Principal	×	Interest Rate	×	Time as a Fraction of Year	=	Interest for Fraction of Year
				/365		

August 8, $20,000.00 Note

Principal	×	Interest Rate	×	Time as a Fraction of Year	=	Interest for Fraction of Year
				/365		

8-2 **WORK TOGETHER (LO2), p. 248**

Journalizing adjusting and reversing entries for prepaid expenses

1.

GENERAL JOURNAL   PAGE 13

	DATE	ACCOUNT TITLE	DOC. NO.	POST. REF.	DEBIT	CREDIT	
1							1
2							2
3							3
4							4
5							5
6							6
7							7
8							8
9							9
10							10
11							11
12							12
13							13

2.

GENERAL JOURNAL   PAGE 1

	DATE	ACCOUNT TITLE	DOC. NO.	POST. REF.	DEBIT	CREDIT	
1							1
2							2
3							3
4							4
5							5
6							6
7							7
8							8
9							9
10							10
11							11
12							12
13							13

ON YOUR OWN (LO2), p. 248

Journalizing adjusting and reversing entries for prepaid expenses

1.

GENERAL JOURNAL

PAGE 13

	DATE	ACCOUNT TITLE	DOC. NO.	POST. REF.	DEBIT	CREDIT	
1							1
2							2
3							3
4							4
5							5
6							6
7							7
8							8
9							9
10							10
11							11
12							12
13							13

2.

GENERAL JOURNAL

PAGE 1

	DATE	ACCOUNT TITLE	DOC. NO.	POST. REF.	DEBIT	CREDIT	
1							1
2							2
3							3
4							4
5							5
6							6
7							7
8							8
9							9
10							10
11							11
12							12
13							13

8-3 **WORK TOGETHER (LO4, 5), p. 255**

Journalizing adjusting and reversing entries for accrued expenses

1.

GENERAL JOURNAL

PAGE 16

DATE	ACCOUNT TITLE	DOC. NO.	POST. REF.	DEBIT	CREDIT	
						1
						2
						3
						4
						5
						6
						7
						8
						9
						10
						11
						12
						13
						14
						15

3.

CASH PAYMENTS JOURNAL

PAGE 2

DATE	ACCOUNT TITLE	CK. NO.	POST. REF.	GENERAL DEBIT	GENERAL CREDIT	ACCOUNTS PAYABLE DEBIT	PURCHASES DISCOUNT CREDIT	CASH CREDIT	
									1
									2
									3
									4
									5

2.

GENERAL JOURNAL

	DATE		ACCOUNT TITLE	DOC. NO.	POST. REF.	DEBIT	CREDIT	
1								1
2								2
3								3
4								4
5								5
6								6
7								7
8								8
9								9
10								10
11								11
12								12
13								13
14								14
15								15
16								16
17								17
18								18
19								19
20								20
21								21
22								22
23								23
24								24
25								25
26								26
27								27
28								28
29								29
30								30
31								31
32								32

8-3 **ON YOUR OWN (LO4, 5), p. 255**

Journalizing adjusting and reversing entries for accrued expenses

1.

GENERAL JOURNAL

PAGE 13

DATE	ACCOUNT TITLE	DOC. NO.	POST. REF.	DEBIT	CREDIT	
						1
						2
						3
						4
						5
						6
						7
						8
						9
						10
						11
						12
						13
						14
						15

3.

CASH PAYMENTS JOURNAL

PAGE 2

				1 GENERAL	2	3 ACCOUNTS PAYABLE DEBIT	4 PURCHASES DISCOUNT CREDIT	5 CASH CREDIT	
DATE	ACCOUNT TITLE	CK. NO.	POST. REF.	DEBIT	CREDIT				
									1
									2
									3
									4
									5

2.

GENERAL JOURNAL

PAGE 1

	DATE		ACCOUNT TITLE	DOC. NO.	POST. REF.	DEBIT	CREDIT	
1								1
2								2
3								3
4								4
5								5
6								6
7								7
8								8
9								9
10								10
11								11
12								12
13								13
14								14
15								15
16								16
17								17
18								18
19								19
20								20
21								21
22								22
23								23
24								24
25								25
26								26
27								27
28								28
29								29
30								30
31								31
32								32

8-1 **APPLICATION PROBLEM (LO1), p. 258**

Journalizing notes payable transactions

1.

CASH RECEIPTS JOURNAL

PAGE 5

			GENERAL		ACCOUNTS RECEIVABLE CREDIT	SALES CREDIT	SALES TAX PAYABLE CREDIT	SALES DISCOUNT DEBIT	CASH DEBIT
DATE	ACCOUNT TITLE	DOC. NO.	POST. REF.	DEBIT	CREDIT					

3.

CASH PAYMENTS JOURNAL

PAGE 9

				GENERAL		ACCOUNTS PAYABLE DEBIT	PURCHASES DISCOUNT CREDIT	CASH CREDIT
DATE	ACCOUNT TITLE	CK. NO.	POST. REF.	DEBIT	CREDIT			

2.

Maturity dates:

May 16, $10,000.00 Note		
	Days from the Month	Days Remaining
Term of the Note		

June 23, $4,500.00 Note		
	Days from the Month	Days Remaining
Term of the Note		

2.

Interest due at maturity:

May 16, $10,000.00 Note

Principal	×	Interest Rate	×	Time as a Fraction of Year	=	Interest for Fraction of Year
				/365		

June 23, $4,500.00 Note

Principal	×	Interest Rate	×	Time as a Fraction of Year	=	Interest for Fraction of Year
				/365		

8-2 APPLICATION PROBLEM (LO2), p. 258

Journalizing adjusting and reversing entries for prepaid expenses

1.

GENERAL JOURNAL   PAGE 13

	DATE	ACCOUNT TITLE	DOC. NO.	POST. REF.	DEBIT	CREDIT	
1							1
2							2
3							3
4							4
5							5
6							6
7							7
8							8
9							9
10							10
11							11
12							12
13							13

2.

GENERAL JOURNAL   PAGE 1

	DATE	ACCOUNT TITLE	DOC. NO.	POST. REF.	DEBIT	CREDIT	
1							1
2							2
3							3
4							4
5							5
6							6
7							7
8							8
9							9
10							10
11							11
12							12
13							13

Journalizing adjusting and reversing entries for accrued expenses

1.

GENERAL JOURNAL

PAGE 16

	DATE	ACCOUNT TITLE	DOC. NO.	POST. REF.	DEBIT	CREDIT	
1							1
2							2
3							3
4							4
5							5
6							6
7							7
8							8
9							9
10							10
11							11
12							12
13							13
14							14
15							15
16							16
17							17

CASH PAYMENTS JOURNAL

PAGE 2

	DATE	ACCOUNT TITLE	CK. NO.	POST. REF.	GENERAL DEBIT	GENERAL CREDIT	ACCOUNTS PAYABLE DEBIT	PURCHASES DISCOUNT CREDIT	CASH CREDIT	
					1	2	3	4	5	
1										1
2										2
3										3

3.

8-3 **APPLICATION PROBLEM (concluded)**

2.

GENERAL JOURNAL

	DATE		ACCOUNT TITLE	DOC. NO.	POST. REF.	DEBIT	CREDIT	
1								1
2								2
3								3
4								4
5								5
6								6
7								7
8								8
9								9
10								10
11								11
12								12
13								13
14								14
15								15
16								16
17								17
18								18
19								19
20								20
21								21
22								22
23								23
24								24
25								25
26								26
27								27
28								28
29								29
30								30
31								31
32								32

Journalizing notes payable transactions and adjusting and reversing entries

1.

CASH RECEIPTS JOURNAL

PAGE 10

				1	2	3	4	5	6	7
				GENERAL		ACCOUNTS RECEIVABLE CREDIT	SALES CREDIT	SALES TAX PAYABLE CREDIT	SALES DISCOUNT DEBIT	CASH DEBIT
DATE	ACCOUNT TITLE	DOC. NO.	POST. REF.	DEBIT	CREDIT					
1										
2										
3										
4										
5										
6										
7										
8										
9										

5.

CASH PAYMENTS JOURNAL

PAGE 9

				1	2	3	4	5
				GENERAL		ACCOUNTS PAYABLE DEBIT	PURCHASES DISCOUNT CREDIT	CASH CREDIT
DATE	ACCOUNT TITLE	CK. NO.	POST. REF.	DEBIT	CREDIT			
1								
2								
3								
4								
5								
6								
7								
8								
9								

8-M MASTERY PROBLEM (continued)

4.

August 10, $20,000 Note		
	Days from the Month	Days Remaining
Term of the Note		

October 20, $25,000 Note		
	Days from the Month	Days Remaining
Term of the Note		

November 5, $13,000 Note		
	Days from the Month	Days Remaining
Term of the Note		

4.

Interest due at maturity:

August 10, $20,000 Note

Principal	×	Interest Rate	×	Time as a Fraction of Year	=	Interest for Fraction of Year
				/365		

October 20, $25,000 Note

Principal	×	Interest Rate	×	Time as a Fraction of Year	=	Interest for Fraction of Year
				/365		

November 5, $13,000 Note

Principal	×	Interest Rate	×	Time as a Fraction of Year	=	Interest for Fraction of Year
				/365		

2.

Supporting calculations for interest accrual:

August 10, $20,000 Note

Principal	×	Interest Rate	×	Time as a Fraction of Year	=	Interest for Fraction of Year
				/365		

October 20, $25,000 Note

Principal	×	Interest Rate	×	Time as a Fraction of Year	=	Interest for Fraction of Year
				/365		

November 5, $13,000 Note

Principal	×	Interest Rate	×	Time as a Fraction of Year	=	Interest for Fraction of Year
				/365		

8-M MASTERY PROBLEM (concluded)

2.

GENERAL JOURNAL

PAGE 13

	DATE	ACCOUNT TITLE	DOC. NO.	POST. REF.	DEBIT	CREDIT	
1							1
2							2
3							3
4							4
5							5
6							6
7							7
8							8
9							9
10							10
11							11
12							12
13							13

3.

GENERAL JOURNAL

PAGE 1

	DATE	ACCOUNT TITLE	DOC. NO.	POST. REF.	DEBIT	CREDIT	
1							1
2							2
3							3
4							4
5							5
6							6
7							7
8							8
9							9
10							10
11							11
12							12
13							13

Accruing for self-insurance losses

3.

	20X1	20X2	20X3	20X4	20X5
Product claims					
Sales					
Claim ratio					

1., 2., 3.

Name	Perfect Score	Your Score
Analyzing Procedures for Unearned Revenue, Accrued Revenue, and Installment Notes Receivable	20 Pts.	
Identifying Accounting Terms	6 Pts.	
Analyzing Entries for Unearned Revenue, Accrued Revenue, and Installment Notes Receivable	20 Pts.	
Total	46 Pts.	

Part One—Analyzing Procedures for Unearned Revenue, Accrued Revenue, and Installment Notes Receivable

Directions: Place a *T* for True or an *F* for False in the Answers column to show whether each of the following statements is true or false.

Answers

1. Unearned revenue is also known as deferred revenue. (p. 264)　　1. _____

2. Unearned Rent is classified as a long-term liability. (p. 265)　　2. _____

3. A business not in the business of renting buildings should classify rental income in the Other Revenue section of the income statement. (p. 265)　　3. _____

4. If an adjusting entry creates a balance in an asset or liability account, the adjusting entry is normally reversed. (p. 266)　　4. _____

5. When making end-of-period adjusting entries, accrued interest on a note receivable is calculated from the date of the note through the maturity date of the note. (p. 267)　　5. _____

6. Interest Income is reported in the Other Revenue section of the income statement. (p. 267)　　6. _____

7. Interest Receivable is reported in the Long-Term Assets section of the balance sheet. (p. 267)　　7. _____

8. Retailers often issue a gift card to a customer returning merchandise. (p. 270)　　8. _____

9. Gift cards have a magnetic strip where the amount of the card balance can be stored. (p. 270)　　9. _____

10. The sale of a gift card results in the recognition of revenue when payment for the card is received. (p. 270)　　10. _____

11. Until a gift card is redeemed, the outstanding balance of the card is unearned revenue. (p. 270)　　11. _____

12. Laws allow retailers to charge monthly fees every month gift cards are not redeemed. (p. 270)　　12. _____

13. The redemption of a gift card reduces the amount of gift cards outstanding. (p. 271)　　13. _____

14. When a business concludes that a gift card will never be redeemed, the value of the card is no longer an asset. (p. 272)　　14. _____

15. The account Sales Returns and Allowances is often used to record the value of unredeemed cards. (p. 272)　　15. _____

16. The amount of Breakage Revenue is an estimate. (p. 272)　　16. _____

17. The total sales from gift cards is listed separately on the income statement to allow users to compare the amount of revenue from sales with the related cost of merchandise sold. (p. 272)

18. The amount of revenue recognized each month from the receipt of an installment note payment is equal to the principal portion of the payment. (p. 275)

19. When a balance sheet is prepared, the amount presented as the Current Portion of Notes Receivable is equal to the total payments the business expects to collect during the next fiscal period. (p. 276)

20. The Current Portion of Notes Receivable appears in the Current Assets section of the balance sheet. (p. 276)

Part Two—Identifying Accounting Terms

Directions: Select the one term in Column I that best fits each definition in Column II. Print the letter identifying your choice in the Answers column.

Column I	Column II	Answers
A. Accrued Revenue	1. Cash received for goods and services which have not been provided. (p. 264)	1. _____
B. Amortization Schedule		
C. Breakage	2. Revenue earned in one fiscal period but not received until a later fiscal period. (p. 267)	2. _____
D. Installment Note	3. The value of unredeemed gift cards. (p. 272)	3. _____
E. Reclassification Entry	4. A note resulting from a sale that requires monthly payments of principal and interest. (p. 274)	4. _____
F. Unearned Revenue	5. A schedule of the periodic payments on a note. (p. 275)	5. _____
	6. An entry that transfers account balances between accounts on one financial statement. (p. 276)	6. _____

Part Three—Analyzing Entries for Unearned Revenue, Accrued Revenue, and Installment Notes Receivable

Directions: For each transaction below, print in the proper Answers columns the identifying letter of the accounts to be debited and credited.

Account Titles	Transactions	Answers Debit	Credit
A. Breakage Revenue	**1-2.** Adjusting entry to recognize one month of rental use owed to the lessee. The business recognizes rental payments as revenue when payment is received. (p. 264)	1._____	2._____
B. Cash			
C. Current Portion of Notes Receivable	**3-4.** Reversing entry required for unearned rent. (p. 266)	3._____	4._____
D. Gift Cards Outstanding	**5-6.** Adjusting entry for interest earned that will be received in the next fiscal period. (p. 267)	5._____	6._____
E. Interest Income			
F. Interest Receivable	**7-8.** Reversing entry required for accrued interest income. (p. 268)	7._____	8._____
G. Notes Receivable	**9-10.** Received cash for the sale of gift cards. (p. 270)	9._____	10._____
H. Rent Income			
I. Sales	**11-12.** Customers redeemed gift cards for the sale of merchandise (ignore sales taxes). (p. 271)	11._____	12._____
J. Unearned Rent	**13-14.** Adjusting entry to recognize the value of gift cards that will never be redeemed. (p. 272)	13._____	14._____
	15-16. Sold merchandise, receiving a down payment and accepting an installment note receivable. (p. 274).	15._____	16._____
	17-18. Received cash for the monthly payment of an installment note receivable. (p. 275)	17._____	18._____
	19-20. Reclassify the value of notes receivable to be received during the next fiscal period. (p. 276)	19._____	20._____

9-1 WORK TOGETHER (LO1, 2), p. 269

Journalizing adjusting and reversing entries for unearned and accrued revenue

1.

GENERAL JOURNAL

PAGE 13

	DATE	ACCOUNT TITLE	DOC. NO.	POST. REF.	DEBIT	CREDIT	
1							1
2							2
3							3
4							4
5							5
6							6
7							7
8							8

2.

GENERAL JOURNAL

PAGE 14

	DATE	ACCOUNT TITLE	DOC. NO.	POST. REF.	DEBIT	CREDIT	
1							1
2							2
3							3
4							4
5							5
6							6
7							7
8							8

Note: Calculation not a required part of solution.

Note	Principal	×	Interest Rate	×	Fraction of Year	=	Accrued Interest Income
					/365		
					/365		

Journalizing adjusting and reversing entries for unearned and accrued revenue

1.

GENERAL JOURNAL — PAGE 19

	DATE		ACCOUNT TITLE	DOC. NO.	POST. REF.	DEBIT	CREDIT	
1								1
2								2
3								3
4								4
5								5
6								6
7								7
8								8

2.

GENERAL JOURNAL — PAGE 20

	DATE		ACCOUNT TITLE	DOC. NO.	POST. REF.	DEBIT	CREDIT	
1								1
2								2
3								3
4								4
5								5
6								6
7								7
8								8

Note: Calculation not a required part of solution.

Note	Principal	×	Interest Rate	×	Fraction of Year	=	Accrued Interest Income
					/365		
					/365		

9-2 **WORK TOGETHER (LO3, 4), p. 273**

Journalizing gift card transactions

1.

CASH RECEIPTS JOURNAL

PAGE 24

DATE	ACCOUNT TITLE	DOC. NO.	POST. REF.	GENERAL DEBIT	GENERAL CREDIT	ACCOUNTS RECEIVABLE CREDIT	SALES CREDIT	SALES TAX PAYABLE CREDIT	SALES DISCOUNT DEBIT	CASH DEBIT
			1	2	3	4	5	6	7	
1										
2										
3										
4										
5										
6										
7										
8										
9										
10										
11										
12										
13										
14										
15										
16										
17										
18										
19										
20										
21										
22										

1.

GENERAL JOURNAL PAGE 18

	DATE		ACCOUNT TITLE	DOC. NO.	POST. REF.	DEBIT	CREDIT	
1								1
2								2
3								3
4								4
5								5
6								6
7								7
8								8
9								9
10								10
11								11
12								12
13								13

2.

GENERAL JOURNAL PAGE 19

	DATE		ACCOUNT TITLE	DOC. NO.	POST. REF.	DEBIT	CREDIT	
1								1
2								2
3								3
4								4
5								5
6								6
7								7
8								8
9								9
10								10
11								11
12								12
13								13

9-2 ON YOUR OWN (LO3, 4), p. 273

Journalizing gift card transactions

1.

CASH RECEIPTS JOURNAL

PAGE 18

DATE	ACCOUNT TITLE	DOC. NO.	POST. REF.	1 GENERAL DEBIT	2 GENERAL CREDIT	3 ACCOUNTS RECEIVABLE CREDIT	4 SALES CREDIT	5 SALES TAX PAYABLE CREDIT	6 SALES DISCOUNT DEBIT	7 CASH DEBIT

1.

GENERAL JOURNAL PAGE 14

	DATE		ACCOUNT TITLE	DOC. NO.	POST. REF.	DEBIT	CREDIT	
1								1
2								2
3								3
4								4
5								5
6								6
7								7
8								8
9								9
10								10
11								11
12								12
13								13

2.

GENERAL JOURNAL PAGE 15

	DATE		ACCOUNT TITLE	DOC. NO.	POST. REF.	DEBIT	CREDIT	
1								1
2								2
3								3
4								4
5								5
6								6
7								7
8								8
9								9
10								10
11								11
12								12
13								13

9-3 WORK TOGETHER (LO6, 7), p. 279

Journalizing installment notes receivable transactions

1.

CASH RECEIPTS JOURNAL

PAGE 5

DATE	ACCOUNT TITLE	DOC. NO.	POST. REF.	GENERAL DEBIT	GENERAL CREDIT	ACCOUNTS RECEIVABLE CREDIT	SALES CREDIT	SALES TAX PAYABLE CREDIT	SALES DISCOUNT DEBIT	CASH DEBIT

Illustration for 1.

Borrower   Daniel Toney
Amount Borrowed $12,000.00
Term of Note (Months)   60
Annual Interest Rate   8%
Monthly Payment $243.32
Monthly Due Date   10th

Payment Number	Month	Beginning Balance	Interest	Principal	Ending Balance
1	January	$12,000.00	$80.00	$163.32	$11,836.68
2	February	$11,836.68	$78.91	$164.41	$11,672.27
3	March	$11,672.27	$77.82	$165.50	$11,506.77
4	April	$11,506.77	$76.71	$166.61	$11,340.16
5	May	$11,340.16	$75.60	$167.72	$11,172.44
6	June	$11,172.44	$74.48	$168.84	$11,003.60
7	July	$11,003.60	$73.36	$169.96	$10,833.64
8	August	$10,833.64	$72.22	$171.10	$10,662.54

2.

GENERAL JOURNAL

PAGE 15

	DATE	ACCOUNT TITLE	DOC. NO.	POST. REF.	DEBIT	CREDIT	
1							1
2							2
3							3
4							4
5							5
6							6
7							7
8							8
9							9
10							10
11							11
12							12
13							13

3.

GENERAL JOURNAL

PAGE 16

	DATE	ACCOUNT TITLE	DOC. NO.	POST. REF.	DEBIT	CREDIT	
1							1
2							2
3							3
4							4
5							5
6							6
7							7
8							8
9							9
10							10
11							11
12							12
13							13

9-3 **ON YOUR OWN (LO6, 7), p. 279**

Journalizing installment notes receivable transactions

1.

CASH RECEIPTS JOURNAL

PAGE 6

DATE	ACCOUNT TITLE	DOC. NO.	POST. REF.	GENERAL DEBIT	GENERAL CREDIT	ACCOUNTS RECEIVABLE CREDIT	SALES CREDIT	SALES TAX PAYABLE CREDIT	SALES DISCOUNT DEBIT	CASH DEBIT

Illustrations for 1.

	Borrower	Wayne Wood
	Amount Borrowed	$3,800.00
	Term of Note (Months)	36
	Annual Interest Rate	9%
	Monthly Payment	$120.84
	Monthly Due Date	6th

Payment Number	Month	Beginning Balance	Interest	Principal	Ending Balance
1	December	$3,800.00	$28.50	$92.34	$3,707.66
2	January	$3,707.66	$27.81	$93.03	$3,614.63
3	February	$3,614.63	$27.11	$93.73	$3,520.90
4	March	$3,520.90	$26.41	$94.43	$3,426.47
5	April	$3,426.47	$25.70	$95.14	$3,331.33
6	May	$3,331.33	$24.98	$95.86	$3,235.47
7	June	$3,235.47	$24.27	$96.57	$3,138.90
8	July	$3,138.90	$23.54	$97.30	$3,041.60

	Borrower	Patrick Morgan
	Amount Borrowed	$4,000.00
	Term of Note (Months)	36
	Annual Interest Rate	9%
	Monthly Payment	$127.20
	Monthly Due Date	22nd

Payment Number	Month	Beginning Balance	Interest	Principal	Ending Balance
1	April	$4,000.00	$30.00	$ 97.20	$3,902.80
2	May	$3,902.80	$29.27	$ 97.93	$3,804.87
3	June	$3,804.87	$28.54	$ 98.66	$3,706.21
4	July	$3,706.21	$27.80	$ 99.40	$3,606.81
5	August	$3,606.81	$27.05	$100.15	$3,506.66
6	September	$3,506.66	$26.30	$100.90	$3,405.76
7	October	$3,405.76	$25.54	$101.66	$3,304.10
8	November	$3,304.10	$24.78	$102.42	$3,201.68

9-3   ON YOUR OWN (concluded)

2.

GENERAL JOURNAL   PAGE 18

	DATE		ACCOUNT TITLE	DOC. NO.	POST. REF.	DEBIT	CREDIT	
1								1
2								2
3								3
4								4
5								5
6								6
7								7
8								8
9								9
10								10
11								11
12								12
13								13

3.

GENERAL JOURNAL   PAGE 19

	DATE		ACCOUNT TITLE	DOC. NO.	POST. REF.	DEBIT	CREDIT	
1								1
2								2
3								3
4								4
5								5
6								6
7								7
8								8
9								9
10								10
11								11
12								12
13								13

9-1 APPLICATION PROBLEM (LO1, 2), p. 283

Journalizing adjusting and reversing entries for unearned and accrued revenue

1., 3.

GENERAL JOURNAL

	DATE	ACCOUNT TITLE	DOC. NO.	POST. REF.	DEBIT	CREDIT	
1							1
2							2
3							3
4							4
5							5
6							6
7							7
8							8

2., 4.

GENERAL JOURNAL

	DATE	ACCOUNT TITLE	DOC. NO.	POST. REF.	DEBIT	CREDIT	
1							1
2							2
3							3
4							4
5							5
6							6
7							7
8							8

Note: Calculation not a required part of solution.

Note	Principal	×	Interest Rate	×	Fraction of Year	=	Accrued Interest Income
					/365		
					/365		

9-2 **APPLICATION PROBLEM (LO3, 4), p. 283**

Journalizing gift card transactions

1.

CASH RECEIPTS JOURNAL

PAGE 16

			GENERAL		ACCOUNTS RECEIVABLE CREDIT	SALES CREDIT	SALES TAX PAYABLE CREDIT	SALES DISCOUNT DEBIT	CASH DEBIT
DATE	ACCOUNT TITLE	DOC. NO.	POST. REF.	DEBIT	CREDIT					
				1	2	3	4	5	6	7
1										
2										
3										
4										
5										
6										
7										
8										
9										
10										
11										
12										
13										
14										
15										
16										
17										
18										
19										
20										
21										
22										

1.

GENERAL JOURNAL PAGE 12

	DATE		ACCOUNT TITLE	DOC. NO.	POST. REF.	DEBIT	CREDIT	
1								1
2								2
3								3
4								4
5								5
6								6
7								7
8								8
9								9
10								10
11								11
12								12
13								13

2.

GENERAL JOURNAL PAGE 13

	DATE		ACCOUNT TITLE	DOC. NO.	POST. REF.	DEBIT	CREDIT	
1								1
2								2
3								3
4								4
5								5
6								6
7								7
8								8
9								9
10								10
11								11
12								12
13								13

9-3 **APPLICATION PROBLEM (LO6, 7), p. 284**

Journalizing installment notes receivable transactions

1.

CASH RECEIPTS JOURNAL

PAGE 7

				1 GENERAL DEBIT	2 GENERAL CREDIT	3 ACCOUNTS RECEIVABLE CREDIT	4 SALES CREDIT	5 SALES TAX PAYABLE CREDIT	6 SALES DISCOUNT DEBIT	7 CASH DEBIT
DATE	ACCOUNT TITLE	DOC. NO.	POST. REF.							

Illustrations for 1.

Borrower	Berk Hyde
Amount Borrowed	$62,350.00
Term of Note (Months)	60
Annual Interest Rate	8%
Monthly Payment	$1,264.23
Monthly Due Date	5th

Payment Number	Month	Beginning Balance	Interest	Principal	Ending Balance
1	March	$62,350.00	$415.67	$848.56	$61,501.44
2	April	$61,501.44	$410.01	$854.22	$60,647.22
3	May	$60,647.22	$404.31	$859.92	$59,787.30
4	June	$59,787.30	$398.58	$865.65	$58,921.65
5	July	$58,921.65	$392.81	$871.42	$58,050.23
6	August	$58,050.23	$387.00	$877.23	$57,173.00
7	September	$57,173.00	$381.15	$883.08	$56,289.92
8	October	$56,289.92	$375.27	$888.96	$55,400.96

Borrower	Altoria Johnwick
Amount Borrowed	$48,620.00
Term of Note (Months)	60
Annual Interest Rate	8%
Monthly Payment	$985.84
Monthly Due Date	12th

Payment Number	Month	Beginning Balance	Interest	Principal	Ending Balance
1	February	$48,620.00	$324.13	$661.71	$47,958.29
2	March	$47,958.29	$319.72	$666.12	$47,292.17
3	April	$47,292.17	$315.28	$670.56	$46,621.61
4	May	$46,621.61	$310.81	$675.03	$45,946.58
5	June	$45,946.58	$306.31	$679.53	$45,267.05
6	July	$45,267.05	$301.78	$684.06	$44,582.99
7	August	$44,582.99	$297.22	$688.62	$43,894.37
8	September	$43,894.37	$292.63	$693.21	$43,201.16
9	October	$43,201.16	$288.01	$697.83	$42,503.33
10	November	$42,503.33	$283.36	$702.48	$41,800.85

9-3 **APPLICATION PROBLEM (concluded)**

2.

GENERAL JOURNAL   PAGE 20

	DATE	ACCOUNT TITLE	DOC. NO.	POST. REF.	DEBIT	CREDIT	
1							1
2							2
3							3
4							4
5							5
6							6
7							7
8							8
9							9
10							10
11							11
12							12
13							13

3.

GENERAL JOURNAL   PAGE 21

	DATE	ACCOUNT TITLE	DOC. NO.	POST. REF.	DEBIT	CREDIT	
1							1
2							2
3							3
4							4
5							5
6							6
7							7
8							8
9							9
10							10
11							11
12							12
13							13

Journalizing unearned revenue, accrued revenue, and gift card and installment note receivable transactions

1.

GENERAL JOURNAL

PAGE 20

DATE	ACCOUNT TITLE	DOC. NO.	POST. REF.	DEBIT	CREDIT	
						1
						2
						3
						4
						5
						6

CASH RECEIPTS JOURNAL

PAGE 24

				1	2	3	4	5	6	7	
				GENERAL		ACCOUNTS RECEIVABLE CREDIT	SALES CREDIT	SALES TAX PAYABLE CREDIT	SALES DISCOUNT DEBIT	CASH DEBIT	
DATE	ACCOUNT TITLE	DOC. NO.	POST. REF.	DEBIT	CREDIT						
											1
											2
											3
											4
											5
											6
											7
											8
											9
											10
											11
											12
											13

9-M MASTERY PROBLEM (continued)

Illustrations for 1.

Borrower	Lisa Renfroe
Amount Borrowed	$2,650.00
Term of Note (Months)	36
Annual Interest Rate	12%
Monthly Payment	$88.02
Monthly Due Date	24th

Payment Number	Month	Beginning Balance	Interest	Principal	Ending Balance
1	September	$2,650.00	$26.50	$61.52	$2,588.48
2	October	$2,588.48	$25.88	$62.14	$2,526.34
3	November	$2,526.34	$25.26	$62.76	$2,463.58
4	December	$2,463.58	$24.64	$63.38	$2,400.20
5	January	$2,400.20	$24.00	$64.02	$2,336.18
6	February	$2,336.18	$23.36	$64.66	$2,271.52
7	March	$2,271.52	$22.72	$65.30	$2,206.22
8	April	$2,206.22	$22.06	$65.96	$2,140.26

Borrower	Rose Cribbs
Amount Borrowed	$3,280.00
Term of Note (Months)	36
Annual Interest Rate	12%
Monthly Payment	$108.94
Monthly Due Date	31st

Payment Number	Month	Beginning Balance	Interest	Principal	Ending Balance
1	June	$3,280.00	$32.80	$76.14	$3,203.86
2	July	$3,203.86	$32.04	$76.90	$3,126.96
3	August	$3,126.96	$31.27	$77.67	$3,049.29
4	September	$3,049.29	$30.49	$78.45	$2,970.84
5	October	$2,970.84	$29.71	$79.23	$2,891.61
6	November	$2,891.61	$28.92	$80.02	$2,811.59
7	December	$2,811.59	$28.12	$80.82	$2,730.77
8	January	$2,730.77	$27.31	$81.63	$2,649.14

2.

GENERAL JOURNAL

	DATE	ACCOUNT TITLE	DOC. NO.	POST. REF.	DEBIT	CREDIT	
1							1
2							2
3							3
4							4
5							5
6							6
7							7

3.

GENERAL JOURNAL

	DATE	ACCOUNT TITLE	DOC. NO.	POST. REF.	DEBIT	CREDIT	
1							1
2							2
3							3

4.

GENERAL JOURNAL

	DATE	ACCOUNT TITLE	DOC. NO.	POST. REF.	DEBIT	CREDIT	
1							1
2							2
3							3
4							4
5							5
6							6
7							7

Note: Calculation not a required part of solution.

Note	Principal	×	Interest Rate	×	Fraction of Year	=	Accrued Interest Income
					/365		
					/365		

9-C CHALLENGE PROBLEM (LO3), p. 285

Journalizing sales and gift card transactions from a point-of-sale system

CASH RECEIPTS JOURNAL

PAGE 5

	DATE	ACCOUNT TITLE	DOC. NO.	POST. REF.	GENERAL DEBIT	GENERAL CREDIT	ACCOUNTS RECEIVABLE CREDIT	SALES CREDIT	SALES TAX PAYABLE CREDIT	SALES DISCOUNT DEBIT	CASH DEBIT	
					1	2	3	4	5	6	7	
1												1
2												2
3												3
4												4
5												5
6												6
7												7
8												8
9												9
10												10
11												11
12												12
13												13
14												14
15												15
16												16
17												17
18												18
19												19
20												20
21												21

REINFORCEMENT ACTIVITY 2, p. 287

Processing Accounting Data for a Corporation

1.

GENERAL JOURNAL

PAGE 12

	DATE		ACCOUNT TITLE	DOC. NO.	POST. REF.	DEBIT	CREDIT	
1								1
2								2
3								3
4								4
5								5
6								6
7								7
8								8
9								9
10								10
11								11
12								12
13								13
14								14
15								15
16								16
17								17
18								18
19								19
20								20
21								21
22								22
23								23
24								24
25								25
26								26
27								27
28								28

REINFORCEMENT ACTIVITY 2 (continued)

2., 3., 4.

GENERAL JOURNAL

	DATE		ACCOUNT TITLE	DOC. NO.	POST. REF.	DEBIT	CREDIT	
1								1
2								2
3								3
4								4
5								5
6								6
7								7
8								8
9								9
10								10
11								11
12								12
13								13
14								14
15								15
16								16
17								17
18								18
19								19
20								20
21								21
22								22
23								23
24								24
25								25
26								26
27								27
28								28
29								29
30								30
31								31
32								32

REINFORCEMENT ACTIVITY 2 (continued)

1.

CASH RECEIPTS JOURNAL

PAGE 15

	DATE	ACCOUNT TITLE	DOC. NO.	POST. REF.	GENERAL DEBIT	GENERAL CREDIT	ACCOUNTS RECEIVABLE CREDIT	SALES CREDIT	SALES TAX PAYABLE CREDIT	SALES DISCOUNT DEBIT	CASH DEBIT	
					1	2	3	4	5	6	7	
1												1
2												2
3												3
4												4
5												5
6												6
7												7
8												8
9												9
10												10
11												11
12												12
13												13
14												14
15												15
16												16
17												17
18												18
19												19
20												20
21												21

1.

CASH PAYMENTS JOURNAL

PAGE 20

DATE	ACCOUNT TITLE	CK. NO.	POST. REF.	GENERAL DEBIT	GENERAL CREDIT	ACCOUNTS PAYABLE DEBIT	PURCHASES DISCOUNT CREDIT	CASH CREDIT

	Appraised Value	Percentage of Total Appraised Value	Assigned Cost
Land			
Building			
Total			

REINFORCEMENT ACTIVITY 2 (continued)

3.

Stock Item: C-362

Purchases			FIFO Method	
Date	Units Purchased	Unit Price	Units	Cost
Beginning Inventory	33	$30.95		
May	50	33.15		
August	50	32.08		
September	50	32.66		
November	10	33.21		
December	10	34.15		
Totals				

Stock Item: A-342

Purchases			FIFO Method	
Date	Units Purchased	Unit Price	Units	Cost
Beginning Inventory	16	$82.50		
January	25	82.50		
March	25	84.50		
June	30	84.75		
July	30	85.15		
October	30	86.50		
Totals				

Stock Item: B-164

Purchases			FIFO Method	
Date	Units Purchased	Unit Price	Units	Cost
Beginning Inventory	16	$1,251.25		
January	10	1,184.24		
February	5	850.00		
Totals				

3.

Stock Item	Quantity of Units on Hand	Market Price per Unit	Total Market Price	FIFO Cost	Lower of Cost of Market
C-362	26	$ 35.50			
A-342	42	84.50			
B-164	16	1,062.25			
			Totals		

REINFORCEMENT ACTIVITY 2 (continued)

4.

Borrower			David Lander		
Amount Borrowed			$2,480.00		
Term of Note (Months)			12		
Annual Interest Rate			12%		
Monthly Payment			$220.34		
Monthly Due Date			31st		

Payment Number	Month	Beginning Balance	Interest	Principal	Ending Balance
1	September	$2,480.00	$24.80	$195.54	$2,284.46
2	October	$2,284.46	$22.84	$197.50	$2,086.96
3	November	$2,086.96	$20.87	$199.47	$1,887.49
4	December	$1,887.49	$18.87	$201.47	$1,686.02
5	January	$1,686.02	$16.86	$203.48	$1,482.54
6	February	$1,482.54	$14.83	$205.51	$1,277.03
7	March	$1,277.03	$12.77	$207.57	$1,069.46
8	April	$1,069.46	$10.69	$209.65	$ 859.81

Borrower			Danielle Petrus		
Amount Borrowed			$4,200.00		
Term of Note (Months)			12		
Annual Interest Rate			10%		
Monthly Payment			$369.25		
Monthly Due Date			23rd		

Payment Number	Month	Beginning Balance	Interest	Principal	Ending Balance
1	May	$4,200.00	$35.00	$334.25	$3,865.75
2	June	$3,865.75	$32.21	$337.04	$3,528.71
3	July	$3,528.71	$29.41	$339.84	$3,188.87
4	August	$3,188.87	$26.57	$342.68	$2,846.19
5	September	$2,846.19	$23.72	$345.53	$2,500.66
6	October	$2,500.66	$20.84	$348.41	$2,152.25
7	November	$2,152.25	$17.94	$351.31	$1,800.94
8	December	$1,800.94	$15.01	$354.24	$1,446.70
9	January	$1,446.70	$12.06	$357.19	$1,089.51
10	February	$1,089.51	$ 9.08	$360.17	$ 729.34

REINFORCEMENT ACTIVITY 2 (concluded)

	Lender		Platt Equipment		
	Borrower		Franklin Auto Parts, Inc.		
	Amount Borrowed		$40,000.00		
	Term of Note (Months)		60		
	Annual Interest Rate		8%		
	Monthly Payment		$811.06		
	Monthly Due Date		31st		

Payment Number	Month	Beginning Balance	Interest	Principal	Ending Balance
1	June	$40,000.00	$266.67	$544.39	$39,455.61
2	July	$39,455.61	$263.04	$548.02	$38,907.59
3	August	$38,907.59	$259.38	$551.68	$38,355.91
4	September	$38,355.91	$255.71	$555.35	$37,800.56
5	October	$37,800.56	$252.00	$559.06	$37,241.50
6	November	$37,241.50	$248.28	$562.78	$36,678.72
7	December	$36,678.72	$244.52	$566.54	$36,112.18
8	January	$36,112.18	$240.75	$570.31	$35,541.87
9	February	$35,541.87	$236.95	$574.11	$34,967.76
10	March	$34,967.76	$233.12	$577.94	$34,389.82
11	April	$34,389.82	$229.27	$581.79	$33,808.03
12	May	$33,808.03	$225.39	$585.67	$33,222.36
13	June	$33,222.36	$221.48	$589.58	$32,632.78
14	July	$32,632.78	$217.55	$593.51	$32,039.27

Name	Perfect Score	Your Score
Identifying Accounting Terms	18 Pts.	
Analyzing Transactions for Organizing a Corporation	12 Pts.	
Analyzing Concepts for Organizing a Corporation	10 Pts.	
Total	40 Pts.	

Part One—Identifying Accounting Terms

Directions: Select the one term in Column I that best fits each definition in Column II. Print the letter identifying your choice in the Answers column.

Column I	Column II	Answers
A. articles of incorporation	**1.** The owner of one or more shares of stock. (p. 294)	**1.** _____
B. board of directors	**2.** A group of persons elected by the stockholders to govern. (p. 295)	**2.** _____
C. charter	**3.** A legal document that identifies basic characteristics of a corporation, which is a part of the application submitted to a state to become a corporation. (p. 295)	**3.** _____
D. conversion option	**4.** The legal right for a business to conduct operations as a corporation. (p. 295)	**4.** _____
E. conversion price	**5.** A class of stock that gives preferred shareholders preference over common shareholders in dividends along with other rights. (p. 296)	**5.** _____
F. conversion ratio		
G. convertible preferred stock	**6.** Written evidence of the number of shares that each stockholder owns in a corporation. (p. 296)	**6.** _____
H. double taxation	**7.** A share of stock that has par value. (p. 296)	**7.** _____
I. initial public offering	**8.** No-par-value stock that is assigned a value by a corporation. (p. 297)	**8.** _____
J. limited liability corporation	**9.** The taxation of earnings to the corporation and to the stockholders when they receive dividends. (p. 298)	**9.** _____
K. par-value stock	**10.** A form of business organization that offers its owners (known as members) the limited liability afforded to corporate stockholders. (p. 298)	**10.** _____
L. preferred stock		
M. privately held corporation	**11.** A corporation owned by a small number of individuals. (p. 303)	**11.** _____
N. publicly held corporation	**12.** The initial issue of a security on a public exchange. (p. 303)	**12.** _____
O. registration statement	**13.** A corporation having its stock traded on public exchanges. (p. 303)	**13.** _____
P. stated-value stock	**14.** The document submitted to the SEC for permission to sell a security on a public exchange. (p. 303)	**14.** _____
Q. stock certificate		
R. stockholder	**15.** The ability of a security to be traded for a specified number of shares of another security. (p. 307)	**15.** _____

Column I	Column II	Answers
	16. The number of shares of common stock received when a security is converted. (p. 307)	16._____
	17. Preferred stock that can be exchanged for a specified number of common shares. (p. 307)	17._____
	18. The par or stated value of the preferred stock divided by the conversion ratio. (p. 307)	18._____

Part Two—Analyzing Transactions for Organizing a Corporation

Directions: For each transaction below, print in the proper Answers column the identifying letters of the accounts to be debited and credited.

Account Titles	Transactions	Answers Debit	Credit
A. Capital Stock—Common	1-2. Received $2,500 cash for 200 shares of $10.00 par-value common stock. (p. 299)	1._____	2._____
B. Capital Stock—Preferred			
C. Cash	3-4. Received $6,000 cash for 1,000 shares of no-par-value common stock. (p. 300)	3._____	4._____
D. Inventory	5-6. Received $5,000 cash for 40 shares of $10.00 stated-value common stock. (p. 301)	5._____	6._____
E. Paid-In Capital in Excess of Par Value—Common			
	7-8. Received $2,000 cash for 20 shares of 6%, $100.00 par-value preferred stock at par value. (p. 304)	7._____	8._____
F. Paid-In Capital in Excess of Par Value—Preferred			
G. Paid-In Capital in Excess of Stated Value—Common	9-10. Received $3,000 cash for 25 shares of 6%, $100.00 par-value preferred stock at $120 per share. (p. 305)	9._____	10._____
	11-12. Issued 280 shares of 6%, $100.00 par-value preferred stock in exchange for inventory at an agreed value of $30,000. (p. 306)	11._____	12._____

Part Three—Analyzing Concepts for Organizing a Corporation

Directions: Place a *T* for True or an *F* for False in the Answers column to show whether each of the following statements is true or false.

Answers

1. Changing ownership of stock is referred to as a stock certificate. (p. 296)   1. _____

2. Double taxation is a disadvantage of organizing a business as an LLC. (p. 298)   2. _____

3. The credit to the capital stock account of no-par common stock equals the total cash or other assets received. (p. 300)   3. _____

4. The initial issue of a security on a public exchange is referred to as an IPO. (p. 303)   4. _____

5. The annual report a publicly held corporation submits to the SEC is the 10-K. (p. 303)   5. _____

6. Investors demanding a dividend rate higher than that offered by the preferred stock will pay more than the par value. (p. 305)   6. _____

7. The payment of dividends on preferred stock is guaranteed by the board of directors. (p. 305)   7. _____

8. When par-value or stated-value stock is sold, the credit to the capital stock account always equals the total par or stated value of the stock issue. (p. 305)   8. _____

9. A conversion option adds value to preferred stock and enables the corporation to issue the stock with a lower dividend rate. (p. 307)   9. _____

10. A $100.00 par-value convertible preferred stock with a conversion ratio of 20 has a conversion price of $5.00. (p. 307)   10. _____

10-1 WORK TOGETHER (LO4), p. 302

Issuing common stock

Assumption A: $1.00 par-value common stock

CASH RECEIPTS JOURNAL PAGE 6

				1	2	3	4	5	6	7	
				GENERAL		ACCOUNTS RECEIVABLE CREDIT	SALES CREDIT	SALES TAX PAYABLE CREDIT	SALES DISCOUNT DEBIT	CASH DEBIT	
DATE	ACCOUNT TITLE	DOC. NO.	POST. REF.	DEBIT	CREDIT						
											1
											2
											3
											4

Assumption B: no-par-value common stock

CASH RECEIPTS JOURNAL PAGE 6

				1	2	3	4	5	6	7	
				GENERAL		ACCOUNTS RECEIVABLE CREDIT	SALES CREDIT	SALES TAX PAYABLE CREDIT	SALES DISCOUNT DEBIT	CASH DEBIT	
DATE	ACCOUNT TITLE	DOC. NO.	POST. REF.	DEBIT	CREDIT						
											1
											2
											3
											4

Assumption C: $1.00 stated-value common stock

CASH RECEIPTS JOURNAL PAGE 6

				1	2	3	4	5	6	7	
				GENERAL		ACCOUNTS RECEIVABLE CREDIT	SALES CREDIT	SALES TAX PAYABLE CREDIT	SALES DISCOUNT DEBIT	CASH DEBIT	
DATE	ACCOUNT TITLE	DOC. NO.	POST. REF.	DEBIT	CREDIT						
											1
											2
											3
											4

Issuing common stock

Assumption A: $5.00 par-value common stock

CASH RECEIPTS JOURNAL

PAGE 15

					1 GENERAL	2 GENERAL	3 ACCOUNTS RECEIVABLE CREDIT	4 SALES CREDIT	5 SALES TAX PAYABLE CREDIT	6 SALES DISCOUNT DEBIT	7 CASH DEBIT
DATE	ACCOUNT TITLE	DOC. NO.	POST. REF.		DEBIT	CREDIT					
1												1
2												2
3												3
4												4

Assumption B: no-par-value common stock

CASH RECEIPTS JOURNAL

PAGE 15

					1 GENERAL	2 GENERAL	3 ACCOUNTS RECEIVABLE CREDIT	4 SALES CREDIT	5 SALES TAX PAYABLE CREDIT	6 SALES DISCOUNT DEBIT	7 CASH DEBIT
DATE	ACCOUNT TITLE	DOC. NO.	POST. REF.		DEBIT	CREDIT					
1												1
2												2
3												3
4												4

Assumption C: $5.00 stated-value common stock

CASH RECEIPTS JOURNAL

PAGE 15

					1 GENERAL	2 GENERAL	3 ACCOUNTS RECEIVABLE CREDIT	4 SALES CREDIT	5 SALES TAX PAYABLE CREDIT	6 SALES DISCOUNT DEBIT	7 CASH DEBIT
DATE	ACCOUNT TITLE	DOC. NO.	POST. REF.		DEBIT	CREDIT					
1												1
2												2
3												3
4												4

10-2 WORK TOGETHER (LO6), p. 309

Journalizing preferred stock transactions

CASH RECEIPTS JOURNAL

PAGE 14

				1 GENERAL		3	4	5	6	7
DATE	ACCOUNT TITLE	DOC. NO.	POST. REF.	DEBIT	CREDIT	ACCOUNTS RECEIVABLE CREDIT	SALES CREDIT	SALES TAX PAYABLE CREDIT	SALES DISCOUNT DEBIT	CASH DEBIT

GENERAL JOURNAL

PAGE 12

DATE	ACCOUNT TITLE	DOC. NO.	POST. REF.	DEBIT	CREDIT

Journalizing preferred stock transactions

CASH RECEIPTS JOURNAL

PAGE 2

						1	2		3	4	5	6	7
DATE	ACCOUNT TITLE	DOC. NO.	POST. REF.			GENERAL		ACCOUNTS RECEIVABLE CREDIT	SALES CREDIT	SALES TAX PAYABLE CREDIT	SALES DISCOUNT DEBIT	CASH DEBIT	
						DEBIT	CREDIT						

GENERAL JOURNAL

PAGE 3

				1	2	3	4	5	6	7	8	9
DATE	ACCOUNT TITLE	DOC. NO.	POST. REF.	DEBIT				CREDIT				

10-1 APPLICATION PROBLEM (LO4), p. 313

Issuing common stock

Assumption A: $0.10 par-value common stock

CASH RECEIPTS JOURNAL

PAGE 7

				1 GENERAL	2 GENERAL	3 ACCOUNTS RECEIVABLE	4 SALES	5 SALES TAX PAYABLE	6 SALES DISCOUNT	7 CASH	
DATE	ACCOUNT TITLE	DOC. NO.	POST. REF.	DEBIT	CREDIT	CREDIT	CREDIT	CREDIT	DEBIT	DEBIT	
											1
											2
											3
											4

Assumption B: no-par-value common stock

CASH RECEIPTS JOURNAL

PAGE 7

				1 GENERAL	2 GENERAL	3 ACCOUNTS RECEIVABLE	4 SALES	5 SALES TAX PAYABLE	6 SALES DISCOUNT	7 CASH	
DATE	ACCOUNT TITLE	DOC. NO.	POST. REF.	DEBIT	CREDIT	CREDIT	CREDIT	CREDIT	DEBIT	DEBIT	
											1
											2
											3
											4

Assumption C: $0.10 stated-value common stock

CASH RECEIPTS JOURNAL

PAGE 7

				1 GENERAL	2 GENERAL	3 ACCOUNTS RECEIVABLE	4 SALES	5 SALES TAX PAYABLE	6 SALES DISCOUNT	7 CASH	
DATE	ACCOUNT TITLE	DOC. NO.	POST. REF.	DEBIT	CREDIT	CREDIT	CREDIT	CREDIT	DEBIT	DEBIT	
											1
											2
											3
											4

Journalizing preferred stock transactions

CASH RECEIPTS JOURNAL

PAGE 5

				GENERAL		ACCOUNTS RECEIVABLE CREDIT	SALES CREDIT	SALES TAX PAYABLE CREDIT	SALES DISCOUNT DEBIT	CASH DEBIT
DATE	ACCOUNT TITLE	DOC. NO.	POST. REF.	DEBIT	CREDIT					
											1
											2
											3
											4
											5
											6
											7
											8
											9

GENERAL JOURNAL

PAGE 7

DATE	ACCOUNT TITLE	DOC. NO.	POST. REF.	DEBIT	CREDIT
						1
						2
						3
						4
						5
						6
						7
						8
						9

10-M MASTERY PROBLEM (LO4, 6), p. 314

Journalizing stock transactions

GENERAL JOURNAL

PAGE 4

DATE	ACCOUNT TITLE	DOC. NO.	POST. REF.	DEBIT	CREDIT	
						1
						2
						3
						4
						5
						6
						7
						8
						9

CASH RECEIPTS JOURNAL

PAGE 4

				1 GENERAL DEBIT	2 GENERAL CREDIT	3 ACCOUNTS RECEIVABLE CREDIT	4 SALES CREDIT	5 SALES TAX PAYABLE CREDIT	6 SALES DISCOUNT DEBIT	7 CASH DEBIT	
DATE	ACCOUNT TITLE	DOC. NO.	POST. REF.								
											1
											2
											3
											4
											5
											6
											7
											8
											9
											10

Journalizing stock transactions

GENERAL JOURNAL

PAGE 2

DATE	ACCOUNT TITLE	DOC. NO.	POST. REF.	DEBIT	CREDIT	
						1
						2
						3
						4
						5
						6
						7
						8
						9
						10
						11
						12
						13
						14

CASH RECEIPTS JOURNAL

PAGE 4

				1 GENERAL		3 ACCOUNTS RECEIVABLE CREDIT	4 SALES CREDIT	5 SALES TAX PAYABLE CREDIT	6 SALES DISCOUNT DEBIT	7 CASH DEBIT	
DATE	ACCOUNT TITLE	DOC. NO.	POST. REF.	DEBIT	2 CREDIT						
											1
											2
											3
											4
											5
											6
											7

Name	Perfect Score	Your Score
Analyzing Transactions for Dividends, Treasury Stock, and Marketable Securities	22 Pts.	
Identifying Accounting Terms	7 Pts.	
Analyzing Concepts for Dividends, Treasury Stock, and Marketable Securities	10 Pts.	
Total	39 Pts.	

Part One—Analyzing Transactions for Dividends, Treasury Stock, and Marketable Securities

Directions: For each transaction below, print in the proper Answers column the identifying letters of the accounts to be debited and credited.

Account Titles	Transactions	Answers Debit	Credit
A. Capital Stock—Common	**1-2.** Declared an annual cash dividend on common and preferred stock. (p. 320)	1._____	2._____
B. Cash	**3-4.** Paid cash for annual cash dividend previously declared. (p. 320)	3._____	4._____
C. Dividend Revenue			
D. Dividends—Common	**5-6.** Declared a stock dividend payable next month. The current market price of the stock is greater than its par value. (p. 321)	5._____	6._____
E. Dividends—Preferred			
F. Dividends Payable			
G. Gain on Sale of Investments	**7-8.** Issued common stock in payment of a previously declared stock dividend. (p. 322)	7._____	8._____
H. Marketable Securities	**9-10.** Closed the Stock Dividends account. (p. 323)	9._____	10._____
I. Paid-In Capital from Sale of Treasury Stock	**11-12.** Paid cash for 100 shares of the corporation's own par-value common stock. (p. 325)	11._____	12._____
J. Paid-In Capital in Excess of Par Value—Common			
K. Retained Earnings	**13-14.** Received cash for 50 shares of treasury stock at $6.00 per share. Treasury stock was bought for $5.00 per share. (p. 326)	13._____	14._____
L. Stock Dividends			
M. Stock Dividends Distributable	**15-16.** Received cash for 50 shares of the remaining treasury stock at $4.00 per share. Treasury stock was bought for $5.00 per share. (p. 327)	15._____	16._____
N. Treasury Stock			
	17-18. Purchased 50 shares of another corporation's stock. (p. 330)	17._____	18._____
	19-20. Received a cash dividend from an investment in the stock of another corporation. (p. 332)	19._____	20._____
	21-22. Sold stock of another corporation for $50.00 per share. The stock was purchased as an investment for $35.00 per share. (p. 333)	21._____	22._____

Part Two—Identifying Accounting Terms

Directions: Select the one term in Column I that best fits each definition in Column II. Print the letter identifying your choice in the Answers column.

Column I	Column II	Answers
A. buyback	**1.** Action by a board of directors to distribute corporate earnings to stockholders. (p. 318)	1._____
B. date of declaration	**2.** The date on which a board of directors votes to distribute a dividend. (p. 318)	2._____
C. date of payment	**3.** The date that determines which stockholders are to receive dividends. (p. 318)	3._____
D. date of record	**4.** The date on which dividends are actually to be paid to stockholders. (p. 318)	4._____
E. declaring a dividend	**5.** The payment of a dividend with the stock of the corporation. (p. 321)	5._____
F. stock dividend	**6.** A corporation's own stock that has been issued and reacquired. (p. 325)	6._____
G. treasury stock	**7.** A program approved by a board of directors authorizing the corporation to repurchase its stock. (p. 325)	7._____

Part Three—Analyzing Concepts for Dividends, Treasury Stock, and Marketable Securities

Directions: Place a *T* for True or an *F* for False in the Answers column to show whether each of the following statements is true or false.

Answers

1. A corporation has no obligation to distribute retained earnings to stockholders until the board of directors has declared a dividend. (p. 318)

   1. _____

2. A dividend is normally paid several weeks after the date of record. (p. 318)

   2. _____

3. The total amount of dividends to be paid are allocated first to common stock, then to preferred stock. (p. 319)

   3. _____

4. No journal entry is recorded on the date of record. (p. 320)

   4. _____

5. The total amount of a stock dividend is calculated using the number of shares issued multiplied by the par or stated value of the stock. (p. 321)

   5. _____

6. A stock dividend typically results in an increase in the market price per share. (p. 323)

   6. _____

7. A buyback often occurs when a corporation believes that its stock is overvalued by the stock market. (p. 325)

   7. _____

8. Treasury stock is not an asset of the corporation. (p. 326)

   8. _____

9. Marketable securities are an asset of the corporation. (p. 330)

   9. _____

10. Dividend Revenue is classified as other revenue on the income statement. (p. 332)

    10. _____

11-1 **WORK TOGETHER (LO1, 2), p. 324**

Journalizing dividend transactions

GENERAL JOURNAL

PAGE 5

DATE	ACCOUNT TITLE	DOC. NO.	POST. REF.	DEBIT	CREDIT	
						1
						2
						3
						4
						5
						6
						7
						8
						9
						10
						11
						12
						13
						14
						15

CASH PAYMENTS JOURNAL

PAGE 7

				GENERAL		ACCOUNTS PAYABLE DEBIT	PURCHASES DISCOUNT CREDIT	CASH CREDIT	
DATE	ACCOUNT TITLE	CK. NO.	POST. REF.	DEBIT	CREDIT				
									1
									2
									3
									4
									5

Supporting Calculations

April 1 Cash Dividend

July 1 Stock Dividend

11-1 **ON YOUR OWN (LO1, 2), p. 324**

Journalizing dividend transactions

GENERAL JOURNAL

PAGE 7

	DATE	ACCOUNT TITLE	DOC. NO.	POST. REF.	DEBIT	CREDIT	
1							1
2							2
3							3
4							4
5							5
6							6
7							7
8							8
9							9
10							10
11							11
12							12
13							13
14							14
15							15

CASH PAYMENTS JOURNAL

PAGE 12

	DATE	ACCOUNT TITLE	CK. NO.	POST. REF.	GENERAL DEBIT	GENERAL CREDIT	ACCOUNTS PAYABLE DEBIT	PURCHASES DISCOUNT CREDIT	CASH CREDIT	
1										1
2										2
3										3
4										4
5										5

Supporting Calculations

July 1 Cash Dividend

August 15 Stock Dividend

Journalizing treasury stock transactions

11-2 WORK TOGETHER (LO5), p. 329

CASH RECEIPTS JOURNAL

PAGE 12

				GENERAL		ACCOUNTS RECEIVABLE CREDIT	SALES CREDIT	SALES TAX PAYABLE CREDIT	SALES DISCOUNT DEBIT	CASH DEBIT
DATE	ACCOUNT TITLE	DOC. NO.	POST. REF.	DEBIT	CREDIT					
1										
2										
3										
4										
5										
6										
7										
8										
9										

CASH PAYMENTS JOURNAL

PAGE 2

				GENERAL		ACCOUNTS PAYABLE DEBIT	PURCHASES DISCOUNT CREDIT	CASH CREDIT
DATE	ACCOUNT TITLE	CK. NO.	POST. REF.	DEBIT	CREDIT			
1								
2								
3								
4								
5								
6								
7								
8								
9								

Journalizing treasury stock transactions

CASH RECEIPTS JOURNAL

PAGE 16

			1	2	3	4	5	6	7
DATE	ACCOUNT TITLE	DOC. NO.	POST. REF.	GENERAL DEBIT	GENERAL CREDIT	ACCOUNTS RECEIVABLE CREDIT	SALES CREDIT	SALES TAX PAYABLE CREDIT	SALES DISCOUNT DEBIT	CASH DEBIT

CASH PAYMENTS JOURNAL

PAGE 4

				1	2	3	4	5
DATE	ACCOUNT TITLE	CK. NO.	POST. REF.	GENERAL DEBIT	GENERAL CREDIT	ACCOUNTS PAYABLE DEBIT	PURCHASES DISCOUNT CREDIT	CASH CREDIT

11-3 WORK TOGETHER (LO6), p. 334

Journalizing the purchase and sale of the capital stock of other corporations

CASH PAYMENTS JOURNAL

PAGE 3

DATE	ACCOUNT TITLE	CK. NO.	POST. REF.	GENERAL DEBIT	GENERAL CREDIT	ACCOUNTS PAYABLE DEBIT	PURCHASES DISCOUNT CREDIT	CASH CREDIT

CASH RECEIPTS JOURNAL

PAGE 8

DATE	ACCOUNT TITLE	DOC. NO.	POST. REF.	GENERAL DEBIT	GENERAL CREDIT	ACCOUNTS RECEIVABLE CREDIT	SALES CREDIT	SALES TAX PAYABLE CREDIT	SALES DISCOUNT DEBIT	CASH DEBIT

Journalizing the purchase and sale of the capital stock of other corporations

CASH PAYMENTS JOURNAL

PAGE 1

| | | | | GENERAL | | ACCOUNTS PAYABLE DEBIT | PURCHASES DISCOUNT CREDIT | CASH CREDIT |
DATE	ACCOUNT TITLE	CK. NO.	POST. REF.	DEBIT	CREDIT			

CASH RECEIPTS JOURNAL

PAGE 6

| | | | | GENERAL | | ACCOUNTS RECEIVABLE CREDIT | SALES CREDIT | SALES TAX PAYABLE CREDIT | SALES DISCOUNT DEBIT | CASH DEBIT |
DATE	ACCOUNT TITLE	DOC. NO.	POST. REF.	DEBIT	CREDIT					

Name _____ Date _____ Class _____

11-1 **APPLICATION PROBLEM (LO1, 2), p. 336**

Journalizing dividend transactions

GENERAL JOURNAL

PAGE 1

	DATE	ACCOUNT TITLE	DOC. NO.	POST. REF.	DEBIT	CREDIT	
1							1
2							2
3							3
4							4
5							5
6							6
7							7
8							8
9							9
10							10
11							11
12							12
13							13
14							14
15							15

CASH PAYMENTS JOURNAL

PAGE 2

	DATE	ACCOUNT TITLE	CK. NO.	POST. REF.	GENERAL DEBIT	GENERAL CREDIT	ACCOUNTS PAYABLE DEBIT	PURCHASES DISCOUNT CREDIT	CASH CREDIT	
					1	2	3	4	5	
1										1
2										2
3										3
4										4
5										5

Supporting Calculations

January 1 Cash Dividend

April 1 Cash Dividend

May 15 Stock Dividend

11-2 **APPLICATION PROBLEM (LO5), p. 336**

Journalizing treasury stock transactions

CASH RECEIPTS JOURNAL

PAGE 12

				GENERAL		ACCOUNTS RECEIVABLE CREDIT	SALES CREDIT	SALES TAX PAYABLE CREDIT	SALES DISCOUNT DEBIT	CASH DEBIT	
DATE	ACCOUNT TITLE	DOC. NO.	POST. REF.	DEBIT	CREDIT						
				1	2	3	4	5	6	7	
1											1
2											2
3											3
4											4
5											5
6											6
7											7
8											8
9											9

CASH PAYMENTS JOURNAL

PAGE 2

				GENERAL		ACCOUNTS PAYABLE DEBIT	PURCHASES DISCOUNT CREDIT	CASH CREDIT	
DATE	ACCOUNT TITLE	CK. NO.	POST. REF.	DEBIT	CREDIT				
				1	2	3	4	5	
1									1
2									2
3									3
4									4
5									5
6									6
7									7
8									8
9									9

Journalizing the purchase and sale of the capital stock of other corporations

CASH PAYMENTS JOURNAL

PAGE 15

DATE	ACCOUNT TITLE	CK. NO.	POST. REF.	GENERAL DEBIT	GENERAL CREDIT	ACCOUNTS PAYABLE DEBIT	PURCHASES DISCOUNT CREDIT	CASH CREDIT
1								
2								
3								
4								
5								
6								
7								
8								
9								

CASH RECEIPTS JOURNAL

PAGE 10

DATE	ACCOUNT TITLE	DOC. NO.	POST. REF.	GENERAL DEBIT	GENERAL CREDIT	ACCOUNTS RECEIVABLE CREDIT	SALES CREDIT	SALES TAX PAYABLE CREDIT	SALES DISCOUNT DEBIT	CASH DEBIT
1										
2										
3										
4										
5										
6										
7										
8										
9										

11-M MASTERY PROBLEM (LO1, 2, 5, 6), p. 337

Journalizing dividend, treasury stock, and investment transactions

GENERAL JOURNAL

PAGE 4

DATE	ACCOUNT TITLE	DOC. NO.	POST. REF.	DEBIT	CREDIT	
						1
						2
						3
						4
						5
						6
						7
						8
						9
						10

CASH RECEIPTS JOURNAL

PAGE 6

DATE	ACCOUNT TITLE	DOC. NO.	POST. REF.	GENERAL DEBIT	GENERAL CREDIT	ACCOUNTS RECEIVABLE CREDIT	SALES CREDIT	SALES TAX PAYABLE CREDIT	SALES DISCOUNT DEBIT	CASH DEBIT	
											1
											2
											3
											4
											5
											6
											7
											8
											9

CASH PAYMENTS JOURNAL

PAGE 7

					GENERAL		ACCOUNTS PAYABLE DEBIT	PURCHASES DISCOUNT CREDIT	CASH CREDIT
DATE	ACCOUNT TITLE	CK. NO.	POST. REF.	DEBIT	CREDIT				
				1	2	3	4	5	

1						1
2						2
3						3
4						4
5						5
6						6
7						7
8						8
9						9
10						10
11						11
12						12
13						13
14						14
15						15
16						16
17						17
18						18
19						19
20						20
21						21
22						22
23						23

11-M **MASTERY PROBLEM (concluded)**

Supporting Calculations

July 1 Cash Dividend

August 6 Stock Dividend

Journalizing stock and dividend transactions

GENERAL JOURNAL

PAGE 1

DATE	ACCOUNT TITLE	DOC. NO.	POST. REF.	DEBIT	CREDIT	
						1
						2
						3
						4
						5
						6
						7
						8
						9
						10
						11
						12
						13
						14
						15

CASH RECEIPTS JOURNAL

PAGE 4

				1	2	3	4	5	6	7	
				GENERAL		ACCOUNTS RECEIVABLE CREDIT	SALES CREDIT	SALES TAX PAYABLE CREDIT	SALES DISCOUNT DEBIT	CASH DEBIT	
DATE	ACCOUNT TITLE	DOC. NO.	POST. REF.	DEBIT	CREDIT						
											1
											2
											3
											4
											5

11-C CHALLENGE PROBLEM (continued)

CASH PAYMENTS JOURNAL

PAGE 3

DATE	ACCOUNT TITLE	CK. NO.	POST. REF.	GENERAL DEBIT	GENERAL CREDIT	ACCOUNTS PAYABLE DEBIT	PURCHASES DISCOUNT CREDIT	CASH CREDIT
1								
2								
3								
4								
5								
6								
7								
8								
9								
10								
11								
12								
13								
14								
15								
16								
17								
18								
19								
20								
21								
22								
23								

Supporting Calculations

January 5 Stock Dividend

Supporting Calculations

Preferred Dividend Payments

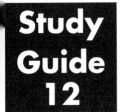

Name	Perfect Score	Your Score
Identifying Accounting Terms	13 Pts.	
Analyzing Transactions for Bonds	20 Pts.	
Analyzing Concepts for Bonds	12 Pts.	
Total	45 Pts.	

Study Guide 12

Part One—Identifying Accounting Terms

Directions: Select the one term in Column I that best fits each definition in Column II. Print the letter identifying your choice in the Answers column.

Column I	Column II	Answers
A. bond	1. A long-term promise to pay a specified amount on a specified date and to pay interest at stated intervals. (p. 342)	1._____
B. bond amortization	2. All bonds representing the total amount of a loan. (p. 342)	2._____
C. bond issue	3. The amount to be paid to a bondholder at the bond maturity date. (p. 343)	3._____
D. call option	4. The rate of interest used to calculate periodic interest payments on a bond. (p. 343)	4._____
E. callable bond	5. The market interest rate at the time bonds are issued. (p. 346)	5._____
F. carrying value	6. Reducing the amount of a bond discount or premium over time. (p. 347)	6._____
G. effective interest rate	7. The face value of a bond adjusted for any unamortized discount or premium. (p. 347)	7._____
H. face value	8. Paying the amounts owed to bondholders for a bond issue. (p. 350)	8._____
I. institutional investors	9. Bonds that all mature on the same date. (p. 350)	9._____
J. retiring a bond issue	10. Portions of a bond issue that mature on different dates. (p. 350)	10._____
K. serial bonds	11. The right of a corporation to repurchase its security for a specified price. (p. 350)	11._____
L. stated interest rate	12. A bond that can be called before its maturity date. (p. 350)	12._____
M. term bonds	13. Organizations that manage the investments of individual investors. (p. 355)	13._____

Part Two—Analyzing Transactions for Bonds

Directions: For each transaction below, print in the proper Answers column the identifying letters of the accounts to be debited and credited.

Account Titles	Transactions	Answers Debit	Answers Credit
A. Bonds Payable	**1-2.** Received cash for the issuance of 5%, $5,000 face-value bonds issued to yield 5.3%. (p. 343)	1._____	2._____
B. Cash			
C. Discount on Bonds Payable	**3-4.** Received cash for the issuance of 5%, $5,000 face-value bonds issued to yield 4.8%. (p. 344)	3._____	4._____
D. Gain on Sale of Investments			
E. Interest Expense	**5-6.** Paid cash for the semiannual interest payment for bonds issued at a discount. (p. 347)	5._____	6._____
F. Interest Revenue	**7-8.** Paid cash for the semiannual interest payment for bonds issued at a premium. (p. 348)	7._____	8._____
G. Investment Securities	**9-10.** Retired a bond at its face value. (p. 350)	9._____	10._____
H. Loss on Redemption of Bonds	**11-12.** Redeemed a $100,000 bond issue with a call option of 102%. The bonds had a carrying value of $94,000. (p. 351)	11._____	12._____
I. Premium on Bonds Payable	**13-14.** Purchased another corporation's $1,000 face-value bonds at $975. (p. 355)	13._____	14._____
	15-16. Received the semiannual interest payment on $5,000 bonds purchased for $4,875. (p. 357)	15._____	16._____
	17-18. Received the semiannual interest payment on $5,000 bonds purchased for $5,250. (p. 358)	17._____	18._____
	19-20. Received $215,000 cash from the sale of a $200,000 investment in the bonds of another corporation. (p. 359)	19._____	20._____

Part Three—Analyzing Concepts for Bonds

Directions: Place a *T* for True or an *F* for False in the Answers column to show whether each of the following statements is true or false.

Answers

1. An advantage of borrowing additional capital is that stockholders' equity is not spread over additional shares of stock. (p. 342)

   1. _____

2. The stated interest rate of a bond issue rarely equals the market interest rate on the day the bonds are issued. (p. 343)

   2. _____

3. If the market interest rate on a bond is below the stated interest rate, investors are not willing to pay full price for a bond that yields a below-market rate. (p. 343)

   3. _____

4. Interest expense is calculated based on the carrying value of the bonds, multiplied by the effective interest rate. (p. 347)

   4. _____

5. The amount of interest expense on bonds issued at a discount will decrease each year. (p. 347)

   5. _____

6. A call option protects a corporation from increases in market interest rates. (p. 351)

   6. _____

7. The redemption amount for a bond is almost always above the carrying value, resulting in a loss. (p. 351)

   7. _____

8. If the market price of the corporation's common stock rises above the conversion price, bondholders will not be willing to convert their bonds to common stock. (p. 352)

   8. _____

9. IFRS requires that the estimated value of the conversion option be recorded in a separate account from Bonds Payable. (p. 352)

   9. _____

10. A bond issued at a premium will also be purchased by the investor at a premium. (p. 355)

   10. _____

11. The carrying value of the bonds purchased at a discount will gradually increase to equal the bonds' total face value. (p. 357)

   11. _____

12. A corporation in the restaurant business would record a loss on the sale of investments as an Other Expense. (p. 359)

   12. _____

12-1 **WORK TOGETHER (LO2), p. 345**

Journalizing bond transactions

CASH RECEIPTS JOURNAL

PAGE 7

			GENERAL		ACCOUNTS RECEIVABLE CREDIT	SALES CREDIT	SALES TAX PAYABLE CREDIT	SALES DISCOUNT DEBIT	CASH DEBIT
DATE	ACCOUNT TITLE	DOC. NO.	POST. REF.	DEBIT	CREDIT				
				1	2	3	4	5	6	7

Journalizing bond transactions

CASH RECEIPTS JOURNAL

PAGE 8

				GENERAL		ACCOUNTS RECEIVABLE CREDIT	SALES CREDIT	SALES TAX PAYABLE CREDIT	SALES DISCOUNT DEBIT	CASH DEBIT
DATE	ACCOUNT TITLE	DOC. NO.	POST. REF.	DEBIT	CREDIT					
1										
2										
3										
4										
5										
6										
7										
8										
9										
10										
11										
12										
13										
14										
15										
16										
17										
18										
19										
20										
21										
22										

12-2 WORK TOGETHER (LO3), p. 349

Journalizing bond interest payments

CASH PAYMENTS JOURNAL

PAGE 20

				GENERAL		ACCOUNTS PAYABLE DEBIT	PURCHASES DISCOUNT CREDIT	CASH CREDIT
DATE	ACCOUNT TITLE	CK. NO.	POST. REF.	DEBIT	CREDIT			
				1	2	3	4	5
1								
2								
3								
4								
5								
6								
7								
8								
9								
10								
11								
12								
13								
14								
15								
16								
17								
18								
19								
20								
21								

Supporting Calculations

June 30 Interest Payment

December 31 Interest Payment

12-2 ON YOUR OWN (LO3), p. 349

Journalizing bond interest payments

CASH PAYMENTS JOURNAL

PAGE 12

			GENERAL		ACCOUNTS PAYABLE DEBIT	PURCHASES DISCOUNT CREDIT	CASH CREDIT
DATE	ACCOUNT TITLE	CK. NO.	POST. REF.	DEBIT	CREDIT			

				1	2	3	4	5
1								
2								
3								
4								
5								
6								
7								
8								
9								
10								
11								
12								
13								
14								
15								
16								
17								
18								
19								
20								
21								

Supporting Calculations

June 30 Interest Payment

December 31 Interest Payment

12-3 **WORK TOGETHER (LO4, 5), p. 354**

Redeeming and calling a bond issue

CASH PAYMENTS JOURNAL

PAGE 6

DATE	ACCOUNT TITLE	CK. NO.	POST. REF.	GENERAL DEBIT	GENERAL CREDIT	ACCOUNTS PAYABLE DEBIT	PURCHASES DISCOUNT CREDIT	CASH CREDIT
1								
2								
3								
4								
5								
6								
7								
8								
9								
10								
11								
12								
13								
14								
15								
16								
17								
18								
19								
20								
21								

Supporting Calculations

July 1 Redemption

October 1 Redemption

12-3 **ON YOUR OWN (LO4, 5), p. 354**

Redeeming and calling a bond issue

CASH PAYMENTS JOURNAL

PAGE 10

DATE	ACCOUNT TITLE	CK. NO.	POST. REF.	GENERAL DEBIT	GENERAL CREDIT	ACCOUNTS PAYABLE DEBIT	PURCHASES DISCOUNT CREDIT	CASH CREDIT

Supporting Calculations

October 1 Redemption

November 1 Redemption

Journalizing bond investment transactions

12-4 WORK TOGETHER (LO7, 8, 9), p. 360

CASH PAYMENTS JOURNAL

PAGE 5

				1 GENERAL		3 ACCOUNTS PAYABLE DEBIT	4 PURCHASES DISCOUNT CREDIT	5 CASH CREDIT
DATE	ACCOUNT TITLE	CK. NO.	POST. REF.	DEBIT	CREDIT			
								1
								2
								3
								4
								5
								6
								7
								8
								9

CASH RECEIPTS JOURNAL

PAGE 3

				1 GENERAL		3 ACCOUNTS RECEIVABLE CREDIT	4 SALES CREDIT	5 SALES TAX PAYABLE CREDIT	6 SALES DISCOUNT DEBIT	7 CASH DEBIT
DATE	ACCOUNT TITLE	DOC. NO.	POST. REF.	DEBIT	CREDIT					
										1
										2
										3
										4
										5
										6
										7
										8
										9

Supporting Calculations

PlatMat Corporation Interest Payment

OpeLin Industries Interest Payment

OpeLin Bond Sale

12-4 ON YOUR OWN (LO7, 8, 9), p. 360

Journalizing bond investment transactions

CASH PAYMENTS JOURNAL

PAGE 7

				GENERAL		ACCOUNTS PAYABLE DEBIT	PURCHASES DISCOUNT CREDIT	CASH CREDIT
DATE	ACCOUNT TITLE	CK. NO.	POST. REF.	DEBIT	CREDIT			
				1	2	3	4	5
1								
2								
3								
4								
5								
6								
7								
8								
9								

CASH RECEIPTS JOURNAL

PAGE 4

				GENERAL		ACCOUNTS RECEIVABLE CREDIT	SALES CREDIT	SALES TAX PAYABLE CREDIT	SALES DISCOUNT DEBIT	CASH DEBIT
DATE	ACCOUNT TITLE	DOC. NO.	POST. REF.	DEBIT	CREDIT					
				1	2	3	4	5	6	7
1										
2										
3										
4										
5										
6										
7										
8										
9										

Supporting Calculations

Greatlin Industries Interest Payment

PESC Corporation Interest Payment

PESC Corporation Bond Sale

12-1 APPLICATION PROBLEM (LO2), p. 362

Journalizing bond transactions

CASH RECEIPTS JOURNAL

DATE	ACCOUNT TITLE	DOC. NO.	POST. REF.	GENERAL DEBIT	GENERAL CREDIT	ACCOUNTS RECEIVABLE CREDIT	SALES CREDIT	SALES TAX PAYABLE CREDIT	SALES DISCOUNT DEBIT	CASH DEBIT

Journalizing bond interest payments

CASH PAYMENTS JOURNAL

PAGE 18

DATE	ACCOUNT TITLE	CK. NO.	POST. REF.	GENERAL DEBIT	GENERAL CREDIT	ACCOUNTS PAYABLE DEBIT	PURCHASES DISCOUNT CREDIT	CASH CREDIT	
									1
									2
									3
									4
									5
									6
									7
									8
									9
									10
									11
									12
									13
									14
									15
									16
									17
									18
									19
									20
									21

12-2 APPLICATION PROBLEM (concluded)

Supporting Calculations

July 1 Interest Payment

August 1 Interest Payment

Redeeming and calling a bond issue

CASH PAYMENTS JOURNAL

PAGE 9

DATE	ACCOUNT TITLE	CK. NO.	POST. REF.	GENERAL DEBIT	GENERAL CREDIT	ACCOUNTS PAYABLE DEBIT	PURCHASES DISCOUNT CREDIT	CASH CREDIT	
									1
									2
									3
									4
									5
									6
									7
									8
									9
									10
									11
									12
									13
									14
									15
									16
									17
									18
									19
									20
									21

12-3 APPLICATION PROBLEM (concluded)

Supporting Calculations

April 1 Redemption

July 1 Redemption

Journalizing bond investment transactions

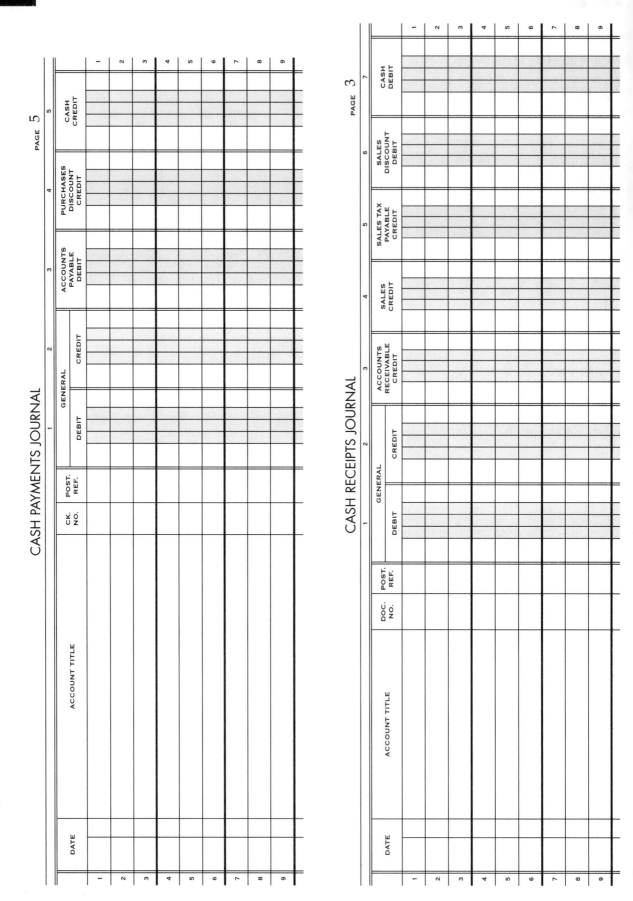

CASH PAYMENTS JOURNAL   PAGE 5

CASH RECEIPTS JOURNAL   PAGE 3

12-4 APPLICATION PROBLEM (concluded)

Supporting Calculations

March 1 Interest Payment

April 1 Interest Payment

April 1 Bond Sale

Journalizing bond transactions

CASH RECEIPTS JOURNAL

PAGE 6

			1	2	3	4	5	6	7
DATE	ACCOUNT TITLE	DOC. NO.	POST. REF.	GENERAL DEBIT	GENERAL CREDIT	ACCOUNTS RECEIVABLE CREDIT	SALES CREDIT	SALES TAX PAYABLE CREDIT	SALES DISCOUNT DEBIT	CASH DEBIT

1										
2										
3										
4										
5										
6										

CASH PAYMENTS JOURNAL

PAGE 3

				1	2	3	4	5
DATE	ACCOUNT TITLE	CK. NO.	POST. REF.	GENERAL DEBIT	GENERAL CREDIT	ACCOUNTS PAYABLE DEBIT	PURCHASES DISCOUNT CREDIT	CASH CREDIT

1								
2								
3								
4								
5								
6								
7								
8								
9								
10								
11								
12								

12-M MASTERY PROBLEM (continued)

Supporting Calculations

April 27 Interest Payment

July 1 Interest Payment

July 1 Redemption

October 1 Interest Revenue

October 1 Bond Sale

12-C   CHALLENGE PROBLEM (LO3, 5), p. 364

Journalizing bond transactions

CASH PAYMENTS JOURNAL

PAGE 3

	DATE	ACCOUNT TITLE	CK. NO.	POST. REF.	GENERAL DEBIT	GENERAL CREDIT	ACCOUNTS PAYABLE DEBIT	PURCHASES DISCOUNT CREDIT	CASH CREDIT	
					1	2	3	4	5	
1										1
2										2
3										3
4										4
5										5
6										6
7										7
8										8
9										9
10										10
11										11
12										12
13										13
14										14
15										15
16										16
17										17
18										18
19										19
20										20
21										21

Supporting Calculations

April 1 Interest Payment

June 23 Interest Payment

June 23 Redemption

Study Guide 13

Name		Perfect Score	Your Score
	Identifying Accounting Terms	24 Pts.	
	Analyzing Financial Analysis Practices	22 Pts.	
	Analyzing Financial Information	15 Pts.	
	Total	61 Pts.	

Part One—Identifying Accounting Terms

Directions: Select the one term in Column I that best fits each definition in Column II. Print the letter identifying your choice in the Answers column.

Column I	Column II	Answers
A. capital expenditures	1. Financial statements that provide information for multiple fiscal periods. (p. 368)	1._____
B. cash equivalents	2. Short-term, liquid investments that are readily convertible to cash and which mature in three months or less. (p. 371)	2._____
C. common equity per share	3. The amount of total current assets less total current liabilities. (p. 373)	3._____
D. comparative financial statements	4. A ratio that measures the relationship of current assets to current liabilities. (p. 374)	4._____
E. comprehensive income	5. Cash and other current assets that can be converted quickly into cash. (p. 374)	5._____
F. current ratio	6. A ratio that measures the relationship of quick assets to current liabilities. (p. 374)	6._____
G. debt ratio	7. Total liabilities divided by total assets. (p. 375)	7._____
H. dividend yield	8. The ratio found by dividing stockholders' equity by total assets. (p. 375)	8._____
I. earnings per share (EPS)	9. The amount of common stockholders' equity belonging to a single share of common stock. (p. 376)	9._____
J. EBIT	10. Earnings before interest expense and taxes. (p. 376)	10._____
K. equity ratio	11. The number of times a company can cover its interest expense with its earnings. (p. 376)	11._____
L. free cash flow	12. Gross profit as a percent of net sales. (p. 378)	12._____
M. gross margin	13. Income from operations as a percent of net sales. (p. 379)	13._____
N. interest coverage ratio	14. The relationship between net income and average total assets. (p. 381)	14._____
O. market value of a share of stock	15. The relationship between net income and average stockholders' equity. (p. 382)	15._____
P. operating margin	16. Measure equal to cash flows from operations less cash used for capital expenditures. (p. 383)	16._____
Q. permanent difference	17. Purchases of plant assets used in the operation of a business. (p. 383)	17._____

Column I	Column II	Answers
R. price-earnings ratio	**18.** Net income after federal income tax divided by the number of outstanding shares of stock. (p. 387)	**18.** _____
S. quick assets	**19.** The price at which a share of stock may be sold on the stock market at any given time. (p. 388)	**19.** _____
T. quick ratio	**20.** The relationship between the market value per share and earnings per share of a stock. (p. 388)	**20.** _____
U. rate earned on average stockholders' equity	**21.** The relationship between dividends per share and market price per share. (p. 389)	**21.** _____
V. rate earned on average total assets	**22.** A difference between net income and taxable income only for that year and that is never balanced out in a future year. (p. 391)	**22.** _____
W. temporary difference	**23.** A difference between net income and taxable income for more than one period that reverses out over the entire period. (p. 391)	**23.** _____
X. working capital	**24.** All changes in equity for the period except changes caused by owner investments and owner distributions. (p. 392)	**24.** _____

Part Two—Analyzing Financial Analysis Practices

Directions: Place a *T* for True or *F* for False in the Answers column to show whether each of the following statements is true or false.

Answers

1. The Securities and Exchange Commission requires public companies to submit quarterly and annual reports. (p. 368)

   1. _____

2. To be useful, financial statements must be prepared by using the same accounting principles in each period. (p. 368)

   2. _____

3. On a balance sheet, accounts receivable are listed at gross value. (p. 371)

   3. _____

4. A business can only get capital from owners' investments and retained earnings. (p. 373)

   4. _____

5. Plant assets are also known as working capital. (p. 373)

   5. _____

6. The current ratio can be too high, indicating more capital invested in current assets than is needed to run the business. (p. 374)

   6. _____

7. Quick assets include cash, inventory, and accounts receivable. (p. 374)

   7. _____

8. The debt ratio is a profitability ratio. (p. 375)

   8. _____

9. The debt and equity ratios show the mix of capital provided by capital borrowed and capital provided by stockholders. (p. 375)

   9. _____

10. The sum of the debt ratio and the equity ratio equals 100%. (p. 375)

    10. _____

11. Gross margin is a profitability ratio. (p. 378)

    11. _____

12. The ratio of the money earned relative to the amount of the investment is known as the *return on investment*. (p. 378)

    12. _____

13. Operating margin is a better measure of a company's profitability than a ratio using net income. (p. 379)

    13. _____

14. A decrease in the accounts receivable turnover ratio from 7.5 times to 6.0 times is considered a favorable trend. (p. 385)

    14. _____

15. An inventory turnover ratio considerably lower than the acceptable range would indicate that the company is at risk for lost sales because some items could be out of stock. (p. 386)

    15. _____

16. A low P/E ratio could mean that the stock is undervalued and would indicate a good time to buy the shares. (p. 388)

    16. _____

17. An example of a permanent difference between net income and taxable income is interest revenue on a tax-exempt bond. (p. 391)

    17. _____

18. Accrued items often lead to temporary differences between taxable income and net income. (p. 392)

    18. _____

19. The largest temporary difference is often associated with accounts receivable. (p. 392)

    19. _____

20. Companies must disclose comprehensive income only as a separate statement. (p. 392)

    20. _____

21. An item that appears in the upper part of an income statement is closely related to the purpose of the company and is likely to recur. (p. 393)

    21. _____

22. When a company discontinues a segment, the revenues and expenses of that segment are included in income from operations. (p. 393)

    22. _____

Part Three—Analyzing Financial Information

Directions: For each of the following items, select the choice that best completes the statement. Print the letter identifying your choice in the Answers column.

1. If quick assets are $100,000.00, current assets are $200,000.00, and current liabilities are $50,000.00, the current ratio is (A) 4.0 times (B) 2.0 times (C) 1.0 time (D) none of the above. (p. 374)

1. _____

2. If quick assets are $100,000.00, current assets are $200,000.00, and current liabilities are $50,000.00, the quick ratio is (A) 4.0 times (B) 2.0 times (C) 1.0 time (D) none of the above. (p. 374)

2. _____

3. If total assets are $200,000.00, total stockholders' equity is $120,000.00, and total liabilities are $80,000.00, the debt ratio is (A) 250% (B) 60% (C) 40% (D) none of the above. (p. 375)

3. _____

4. If total assets are $200,000.00, total stockholders' equity is $120,000.00, and total liabilities are $80,000.00, the equity ratio is (A) 250% (B) 60% (C) 40% (D) none of the above. (p. 375)

4. _____

5. If the preferred stockholders' share of total stockholders' equity is $50,000.00, total stockholders' equity is $200,000.00, and there are 60,000 shares of common stock outstanding, the common equity per share is (A) $3.33 (B) $3.00 (C) $2.50 (D) $0.83. (p. 376)

5. _____

6. If net income is $100,000.00, interest expense is $25,000.00, tax expense is $13,000.00, and gross profit is $75,000.00, EBIT is (A) $213,333.33 (B) $200,000.00 (C) $175,000.00 (D) $138,000.00. (p. 376)

6. _____

7. If EBIT is $200,000.00 and interest expense is $25,000.00, the interest coverage ratio is (A) 9.0 (B) 8.0 (C) 1.0 (D) 0.125. (p. 376)

7. _____

8. If gross profit is $200,000.00, income from operations is $150,000.00, net income is $50,000,00, and net sales are $250,000,00, the operating margin is (A) 80.0% (B) 60.0% (C) 40.0% (D) 20.0%. (p. 379)

8. _____

9. If the beginning total assets are $225,000.00, ending total assets are $175,000.00, and net income is $26,000.00, the rate earned on average total assets is (A) 14.9% (B) 13.0% (C) 11.6% (D) 6.5%. (p. 381)

9. _____

10. If cash flow from operating activities is $150,000.00, cash flow from investing activities is $225,000.00, cash flow from financing activities is $200,000.00, and capital expenditures are $50,000.00, free cash flow is (A) $525,000.00 (B) $175,000.00 (C) $150,000.00 (D) $100,000.00. (p. 383)

10. _____

11. If average accounts receivable are $80,000.00 and net sales are $200,000.00, the accounts receivable turnover ratio is (A) 2.5 (B) 0.6 (C) 0.4 (D) none of the above. (p. 385)

11. _____

12. If average merchandise inventory is $40,000.00, net sales are $100,000.00, and the cost of merchandise sold is $80,000.00, the inventory turnover ratio is (A) 2.5 (B) 0.8 (C) 0.5 (D) none of the above. (p. 386)

12. _____

13. If a company has no outstanding preferred stock, net income after income tax is $75,000.00, and shares of stock outstanding are 25,000, the earnings per share is (A) $25.00 (B) $3.00 (C) 30 cents (D) none of the above. (p. 386)

13. _____

14. If earnings per share are $10.00 and the market price of stock is $100.00 per share, the price-earnings ratio is (A) 20 times (B) 10 times (C) 0.1 time (D) none of the above. (p. 388)

14. _____

15. If the common dividend per share is $0.30 and the market price per share is $10.00, the dividend yield is (A) 33.3% (B) 30.0% (C) 3.0% (D) 0.03%. (p. 389)

15. _____

13-1 WORK TOGETHER (LO3, 4), p. 377

Analyzing short- and long-term financial strength

	Current Year	Prior Year
Total current assets	$1,610,000.00	$1,425,000.00
Total quick assets	485,000.00	502,000.00
Total assets	2,409,000.00	2,222,000.00
Total current liabilities	624,000.00	678,000.00
Total liabilities	1,004,000.00	994,500.00
Total stockholders' equity	1,405,000.00	1,227,500.00
Total interest expense	9,500.00	7,800.00
Total federal income tax	27,770.00	22,614.00
Net income	104,468.00	85,070.00
Shares of common stock outstanding	90,000	84,750
Shares of preferred stock outstanding, $100 par	1,200	1,000

1., 2.

Ratio	Target Range		Actual Ratio		Favorable Trend	Favorable Result
	Low	High	Current Year	Prior Year		
Working Capital	$950,000.00	$1,100,000.00				
Current ratio	2.0	3.5				
Quick ratio	0.9	1.3				
Debt ratio	38.0%	42.0%				
Equity ratio	58.0%	62.0%				
Common equity per share	$15.50	$20.00				
Interest coverage ratio	16.0	19.0				

1a. Working capital:

1b. Current ratio:

1c. Quick ratio:

1d. Debt ratio:

1e. Equity ratio:

1f. Common equity per share:

13-1 WORK TOGETHER (concluded)

1g. Interest coverage ratio:

3.

_____

_____

_____

13-1 ON YOUR OWN (LO3, 4), p. 377

Analyzing short- and long-term financial strength

	Current Year	Prior Year
Total current assets	$1,210,000.00	$1,100,000.00
Total quick assets	603,750.00	544,000.00
Total assets	1,837,500.00	1,537,500.00
Total current liabilities	465,000.00	308,000.00
Total liabilities	1,185,000.00	732,000.00
Total stockholders' equity	652,500.00	805,500.00
Total interest expense	22,600.00	16,750.00
Total federal income tax	26,440.00	26,181.00
Net income	99,466.00	98,490.00
Shares of common stock outstanding	90,000	84,750
Shares of preferred stock outstanding, $100 par	1,300	1,200

1., 2.

Ratio	Target Range Low	Target Range High	Actual Ratio Current Year	Actual Ratio Prior Year	Favorable Trend	Favorable Result
Working Capital	$600,000.00	$900,000.00				
Current ratio	2.0	3.0				
Quick ratio	0.9	1.4				
Debt ratio	45.0%	55.0%				
Equity ratio	48.0%	55.0%				
Common equity per share	$5.50	$9.50				
Interest coverage ratio	9.0	14.0				

1a. Working capital:

1b. Current ratio:

1c. Quick ratio:

1d. Debt ratio:

1e. Equity ratio:

1f. Common equity per share:

13-1 **ON YOUR OWN (concluded)**

1g. Interest coverage ratio:

3.

_____

_____

_____

13-2 WORK TOGETHER (LO5), p. 384

Calculating profitability measures

	Current Year	Prior Year
Gross profit	$401,900.00	$354,925.00
Net sales	648,750.00	555,000.00
Income from operations	60,300.00	47,300.00
Net income	58,388.00	44,400.00
Beginning total assets	623,200.00	486,800.00
Ending total assets	647,000.00	623,200.00
Beginning total stockholders' equity	424,897.00	268,853.00
Ending total stockholders' equity	380,453.00	424,897.00
Cash flow from operating activities	75,250.000	72,550.000
Capital expenditures	28,350.000	25,500.000

1., 2.

Ratio	Target Range		Actual Ratio		Favorable Trend	Favorable Result
	Low	High	Current Year	Prior Year		
Gross margin	53.0%	60.0%				
Operating margin	8.0%	10.0%				
Rate earned on average total assets	8.5%	9.5%				
Rate earned on average total stockholders' equity	10.5%	18.5%				
Free cash flows	$46,500.00	$49,000.00				

a. Gross margin:

b. Operating margin:

1c. Rate earned on average total assets:

1d. Rate earned on average stockholders' equity:

1e. Free cash flow:

3.

_____

_____

_____

_____

_____

_____

13-2 ON YOUR OWN (LO5), p. 384

Calculating profitability measures

	Current Year	Prior Year
Gross profit	$165,338.00	$234,740.00
Net sales	685,920.00	781,485.00
Income from operations	83,910.00	137,453.00
Net income	56,400.00	87,990.00
Beginning total assets	408,278.00	764,922.00
Ending total assets	427,250.00	408,278.00
Beginning total stockholders' equity	301,500.00	280,362.00
Ending total stockholders' equity	321,500.00	301,500.00
Cash flow from operating activities	126,741.00	133,682.00
Capital expenditures	52,500.00	50,950.00

1., 2.

Ratio	Target Range		Actual Ratio		Favorable Trend	Favorable Result
	Low	High	Current Year	Prior Year		
Gross margin	29.0%	32.0%				
Operating margin	15.5%	17.8%				
Rate earned on average total assets	14.0%	16.0%				
Rate earned on average total stockholders' equity	28.00%	31.50%				
Free cash flows	$79,000.00	$84,000.00				

1a. Gross margin:

1b. Operating margin:

1c. Rate earned on average total assets:

1d. Rate earned on average stockholders' equity:

1e. Free cash flow:

3.

_____

_____

_____

_____

_____

_____

13-3 WORK TOGETHER (LO6, 7), p. 390

Calculating and analyzing efficiency measures and market ratios

	Current Year	Prior Year
Net sales	$4,320,000.00	$4,105,500.00
Net income	397,500.00	348,967.00
Cost of merchandise sold	2,857,500.00	2,721,947.00
Beginning accounts receivable (book value)	472,500.00	455,700.00
Ending accounts receivable (book value)	532,500.00	472,500.00
Beginning inventory	375,000.00	353,853.00
Ending inventory	412,500.00	375,000.00
Preferred dividends	60,000.00	60,000.00
Common dividends	90,000.00	93,125.00
Market price, common stock	39.50	45.00
Market price, preferred stock	100.00	100.00
Shares of preferred stock outstanding ($50.00, 6%)	20,000	20,000
Shares of common stock outstanding	75,000	74,500

1., 2.

Ratio	Target Range		Actual Ratio		Favorable Trend	Favorable Result
	Low	High	Current Year	Prior Year		
Accounts receivable turnover ratio	9.1	12.0				
Days' sales in accounts receivable	30 days	40 days				
Inventory turnover ratio	7.0	7.4				
Days' sales in inventory	49 days	52 days				
Earnings per share	$4.00	$5.50				
Price-earnings ratio	N/A	N/A				
Common dividend yield	2.0%	3.0%				
Preferred dividend yield	2.5%	3.5%				

1a. Accounts receivable turnover ratio:

1b. Days' sales in accounts receivable:

1c. Inventory turnover ratio:

1d. Days' sales in inventory:

1e. Earnings per share:

13-3 WORK TOGETHER (concluded)

1f. Price-earnings ratio:

1g. Dividend yield:

Common stock:

Preferred stock:

3.

_____

_____

_____

_____

_____

_____

_____

_____

Calculating and analyzing efficiency measures and market ratios

	Current Year	Prior Year
Net sales	$4,320,000.00	$3,980,100.00
Net income	294,000.00	244,274.00
Cost of merchandise sold	2,100,000.00	1,990,500.00
Beginning accounts receivable (book value)	356,250.00	425,250.00
Ending accounts receivable (book value)	393,750.00	356,250.00
Beginning inventory	225,000.00	288,300.00
Ending inventory	210,000.00	225,000.00
Preferred dividends	30,000.00	28,500.00
Common dividends	33,750.000	30,000.000
Market price, common stock	36.00	35.00
Market price, preferred stock	75.00	75.00
Shares of preferred stock outstanding ($50.00, 6%)	10,000	9,500
Shares of common stock outstanding	56,250	60,000

1., 2.

Ratio	Target Range		Actual Ratio		Favorable Trend	Favorable Result
	Low	High	Current Year	Prior Year		
Accounts receivable turnover ratio	11	12.0				
Days' sales in accounts receivable	30 days	33 days				
Inventory turnover ratio	9.0	10				
Days' sales in inventory	37 days	41 days				
Earnings per share	$4.75	$5.50				
Price-earnings ratio	N/A	N/A				
Common dividend yield	1.8%	2.0%				
Preferred dividend yield	3.5%	4.5%				

1a. Accounts receivable turnover ratio:

13-3 ON YOUR OWN (continued)

1b. Days' sales in accounts receivable:

1c. Inventory turnover ratio:

1d. Days' sales in inventory:

1e. Earnings per share:

1f. Price-earnings ratio:

1g. Dividend yield:

Common stock:

Preferred stock:

3.

_____

_____

_____

_____

_____

_____

_____

13-4 WORK TOGETHER (LO8), p. 394

Calculating permanent and temporary differences in net income and taxable income

	Permanent	Temporary
1. Depreciation of office furniture	_____	_____
Interest income	_____	_____

2.

3.

4.

13-4 ON YOUR OWN (LO8), p. 394

Calculating permanent and temporary differences in net income and taxable income

	Permanent	Temporary
1. Rent revenue	_____	_____
Interest revenue	_____	_____

2.

3.

13-1 APPLICATION PROBLEM (LO3, 4), p. 396

Analyzing short- and long-term financial strength

	Current Year	Prior Year
Total current assets	$436,760.00	$357,040.00
Total quick assets	173,050.00	172,250.00
Total assets	639,150.00	536,540.00
Total current liabilities	209,250.00	176,500.00
Total liabilities	273,250.00	256,500.00
Total stockholders' equity	365,900.00	280,040.00
Total interest expense	14,720.00	12,600.00
Total federal income tax	24,930.00	16,062.00
Net income	93,786.00	60,425.00
Shares of common stock outstanding	50,000	40,000
Shares of preferred stock outstanding, $50 par	4,000	4,000

1., 2.

Ratio	Target Range		Actual Ratio		Favorable Trend	Favorable Result
	Low	High	Current Year	Prior Year		
Working Capital	$200,000.00	$230,000.00				
Current ratio	1.8	2.1				
Quick ratio	0.7	1.0				
Debt ratio	40.0%	45.0%				
Equity ratio	55.0%	60.0%				
Common equity per share	$3.35	$3.50				
Interest coverage ratio	7.0	10.0				

1a. Working capital:

1b. Current ratio:

1c. Quick ratio:

1d. Debt ratio:

1e. Equity ratio:

1f. Common equity per share:

1g. Interest coverage ratio:

3.

_____

_____

_____

_____

_____

_____

_____

13-2 APPLICATION PROBLEM (LO5), p. 396

Calculating profitability measures

	Current Year	Prior Year
Gross profit	$ 375,588.00	$ 264,540.00
Net sales	1,249,176.00	1,097,472.00
Income from operations	231,098.00	155,250.00
Net income	58,388.00	44,400.00
Beginning total assets	804,804.00	795,300.00
Ending total assets	958,716.00	804,804.00
Beginning total stockholders' equity	420,048.00	418,241.00
Ending total stockholders' equity	548,832.00	420,048.00
Cash flow from operating activities	70,066.00	68,547.00
Capital expenditures	52,750.00	32,100.00

1., 2.

Ratio	Target Range		Actual Ratio		Favorable Trend	Favorable Result
	Low	High	Current Year	Prior Year		
Gross margin	22.0%	24.0%				
Operating margin	17.2%	18.7%				
Rate earned on average total assets	6.0%	7.0%				
Rate earned on average total stockholders' equity	11.5%	12.5%				
Free cash flows	$32,000.00	$37,000.00				

1a. Gross margin:

1b. Operating margin:

1c. Rate earned on average total assets:

1d. Rate earned on average stockholders' equity:

1e. Free cash flow:

3.

_____

_____

_____

_____

_____

_____

_____

_____

13-3 APPLICATION PROBLEM (LO6, 7), p. 397

Calculating and analyzing efficiency measures and market ratios

	Current Year	Prior Year
Net sales	$1,651,200.00	$1,254,120.00
Net income	149,920.00	135,680.00
Cost of merchandise sold	987,480.00	792,424.00
Beginning accounts receivable (book value)	194,312.00	165,450.00
Ending accounts receivable (book value)	161,312.00	194,312.00
Beginning inventory	138,350.00	140,435.00
Ending inventory	155,384.00	138,350.00
Preferred dividends	80,000.00	80,000.00
Common dividends	21,000.000	21,600.000
Market price, common stock	30.00	25.50
Market price, preferred stock	85.00	86.00
Shares of preferred stock outstanding ($100.00, 8%)	10,000	10,000
Shares of common stock outstanding	21,000	18,000

1., 2.

Ratio	Target Range Low	Target Range High	Actual Ratio Current Year	Actual Ratio Prior Year	Favorable Trend	Favorable Result
Accounts receivable turnover ratio	9.1	12.0				
Days' sales in accounts receivable	30 days	40 days				
Inventory turnover ratio	5.0	6.0				
Days' sales in inventory	61 days	73 days				
Earnings per share	$3.00	$3.50				
Price-earnings ratio	N/A	N/A				
Common dividend yield	3.8%	4.8%				
Preferred dividend yield	9.0%	10.0%				

1a. Accounts receivable turnover ratio:

1b. Days' sales in accounts receivable:

1c. Inventory turnover ratio:

1d. Days' sales in inventory:

1e. Earnings per share:

1f. Price-earnings ratio:

1g. Dividend yield:

Common

Preferred

3.

_____

_____

_____

_____

_____

_____

_____

13-4 APPLICATION PROBLEM (LO8), p. 397

Calculating permanent and temporary differences in net income and taxable income

	Permanent	Temporary
1. Depreciation of office furniture	_____	_____
Interest income	_____	_____
Rent expense	_____	_____

2.

3.

4.

Analyzing financial statements

	Current Year	Prior Year
Beginning accounts receivable (book value)	$ 84,400.00	$ 86,320.00
Ending accounts receivable (book value)	70,792.00	84,400.00
Beginning inventory	259,648.00	256,278.00
Ending inventory	268,624.00	259,648.00
Total current assets	483,000.00	523,168.00
Total quick assets	97,712.00	163,416.00
Beginning total assets	783,728.00	785,445.00
Ending total assets	733,160.00	783,728.00
Total current liabilities	196,776.00	224,480.00
Total liabilities	376,776.00	410,080.00
Beginning total stockholders' equity	373,648.00	378,112.00
Ending total stockholders' equity	356,384.00	373,648.00
Net sales	1,030,320.00	1,225,864.00
Cost of merchandise sold	730,504.00	814,944.00
Gross profit	299,816.00	410,920.00
Income from operations	51,576.00	96,232.00
Total interest expense	24,824.00	21,120.00
Total federal income tax	6,044.00	15,824.00
Net income	22,736.00	59,529.00
Cash flow from operating activities	60,180.000	78,100.000
Capital expenditures	29,775.000	51,000.000
Preferred dividends	5,000.00	5,000.00
Common dividends	44,800.000	45,000.000
Market price, common stock	10.00	20.00
Market price, preferred stock	58.00	68.00
Shares of preferred stock outstanding ($100.00, 5%)	1,000	1,000
Shares of common stock outstanding	16,000	15,000

13-M MASTERY PROBLEM (continued)

1., 2.

Ratio	Target Range		Actual Measure		Favorable Trend	Favorable Result
	Low	High	Current Year	Prior Year		
Working Capital	$290,000.00	$300,000.00				
Current ratio	2.3	2.7				
Quick ratio	0.7	1.0				
Debt ratio	49.0%	52.0%				
Equity ratio	48.0%	51.0%				
Common equity per share	$17.50	$18.50				
Interest coverage ratio	3.0	4.5				
Gross margin	30.0%	34.0%				
Operating margin	6.0%	8.0%				
Rate earned on average total assets	5.0%	8.0%				
Rate earned on average total stockholders' equity	10.0%	16.0%				
Free cash flows	$32,000.00	$37,000.00				
Accounts receivable turnover ratio	14.0	15.0				
Days' sales in accounts receivable	24 days	26 days				
Inventory turnover ratio	3.2	4.0				
Days' sales in inventory	91 days	114 days				
Earnings per share	$3.40	$3.65				
Price-earnings ratio	N/A	N/A				
Common dividend yield	25.0%	28.0%				
Preferred dividend yield	7.8%	8.8%				

1. Working capital:

2. Current ratio:

3. Quick ratio:

4. Debt ratio:

5. Equity ratio:

6. Common equity per share:

7. Interest coverage ratio:

8. Gross margin:

9. Operating margin:

10. Rate earned on average total assets:

13-M MASTERY PROBLEM (continued)

11. Rate earned on average stockholders' equity:

12. Free cash flow:

13. Accounts receivable turnover ratio:

14. Days' sales in accounts receivable:

15. Inventory turnover ratio:

16. Days' sales in inventory:

17. Earnings per share:

18. Price-earnings ratio:

19. Dividend yield:

Common

Preferred

13-C CHALLENGE PROBLEM (LO3), p. 398

Calculating the effect of transactions on the current ratio

1. a.

b.

c.

d.

e.

2.

_____

_____

_____

_____

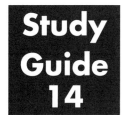

Name		Perfect Score	Your Score
Study Guide 14	Analyzing Procedures and Concepts Related to the Statement of Cash Flows	20 Pts.	
	Analyzing a Statement of Cash Flows	32 Pts.	
	Total	52 Pts.	

Part One—Analyzing Procedures and Concepts Related to the Statement of Cash Flows

Directions: Place a *T* for True or *F* for False in the Answers column to show whether each of the following statements is true or false.

Answers

1. Cash flow analysis helps owners, creditors, and other interested parties determine a company's potential to produce cash in the future. (p. 402)   1. _____

2. The statement of cash flows is prepared on an accrual basis. (p. 402)   2. _____

3. Only the cash flows from operating activities differ between the direct and indirect methods of preparing the statement of cash flows. (p. 403)   3. _____

4. The total cash provided by (used for) operating activities equals the same amount, regardless of which method is used to prepare the statement of cash flows. (p. 403)   4. _____

5. Activities in the operating activities section of the statement of cash flows can be indirectly determined by making adjustments to net income. (p. 403)   5. _____

6. Depreciation expense is not recognized on the income statement, since no cash is used. (p. 404)   6. _____

7. Amortization expense is a noncash expense and is treated in a manner similar to depreciation expense on the statement of cash flows. (p. 404)   7. _____

8. An increase in a noncash current asset is a source of cash. (p. 405)   8. _____

9. If Accounts Receivable declined during the year, it is considered a source of cash. (p. 405)   9. _____

10. A decrease in a current liability represents a use of cash. (p. 407)   10. _____

11. If cash from operating activities increases during the year, the statement of cash flows reports it as *Cash used by operating activities*. (p. 409)   11. _____

12. Increases in accumulated depreciation are ignored when preparing the statement of cash flows. (p. 412)   12. _____

13. Decreases in long-term assets are generally considered a *source of cash*. (p. 412)   13. _____

14. Cash flows resulting from a company's financing activities are identified by analyzing changes in long-term assets presented on the comparative balance sheet. (p. 413)   14. _____

15. One purpose of financing activities is to maintain an adequate balance in the cash account. (p. 413)   15. _____

16. To analyze the financing activities of a corporation, the comparative balance sheet and comparative income statement must be analyzed. (p. 413)   16. _____

17. Net income does not affect the financing activities of the business. (p. 413)   17. _____

18. Decreases in long-term liabilities and the payment of cash dividends generally result in cash inflows. (p. 413) 18. _____

19. The net change in cash is determined by totaling the cash provided by (or used for) operating activities, investing activities, and financing activities. (p. 414) 19. _____

20. Similar to the current ratio, the operating cash flow ratio indicates how likely the company is to be able to pay off current liabilities with its cash flows from operations. (p. 415) 20. _____

Part Two—Analyzing a Statement of Cash Flows

Directions: The parts of the statement of cash flows below are identified with capital letters. Decide the location of each of the following items. Print the letter identifying your choice in the Answers column.

Answers

1. Date of the statement of cash flows.   1. _____
2. Heading of the investing activities section.   2. _____
3. Statement name.   3. _____
4. Explanation of first cash flow resulting from an investing activity.   4. _____
5. Amount of net increase or decrease in cash.   5. _____
6. The amount of net income/net loss.   6. _____
7. Words *Cash provided by/used for investing activities.*   7. _____
8. Words *Depreciation expense.*   8. _____
9. Words *Net increase/decrease in cash.*   9. _____
10. Words *Cash provided by/used for operating activities.*   10. _____
11. Business name.   11. _____
12. Amount of first cash flow resulting from an investing activity.   12. _____
13. Words *Cash balance, end of period.*   13. _____
14. Amount of ending Cash balance.   14. _____
15. Amount of cash provided by/used for investing activities.   15. _____
16. Heading of operating activities section.   16. _____
17. Amount of first cash flow resulting from a financing activity.   17. _____
18. Amount of depreciation expense.   18. _____
19. Heading of financing activities section.   19. _____
20. Words *Changes in current assets and liabilities.*   20. _____
21. Explanation of first change in current asset.   21. _____
22. Words *Net income* or *Net loss.*   22. _____
23. Words *Cash balance, beginning of period.*   23. _____
24. Amount of first change in current asset.   24. _____
25. Explanation of first cash flow resulting from a financing activity.   25. _____
26. Words *Adjustments to net income* or *Adjustments to net loss.*   26. _____
27. Amount of cash provided by/used for financing activities.   27. _____
28. Amount of total adjustments to net income/net loss.   28. _____
29. Amount of beginning Cash balance.   29. _____
30. Words *Total adjustments to net income* or *Total adjustments to net loss.* 30. _____
31. Words *Cash provided by/used for financing activities.*   31. _____
32. Amount of cash provided by/used for operating activities.   32. _____

14-1 WORK TOGETHER (LO3, 4), p. 410

Preparing the operating activities section of a statement of cash flows

Western Wear, Inc.
Comparative Balance Sheet
December 31, 20X2 and 20X1

	20X2	20X1	Increase (Decrease)
ASSETS			
Current Assets:			
Cash	49 3 8 0 00	20 5 0 0 00	28 8 8 0 00
Accounts Receivable (book value)	77 5 0 0 00	80 0 0 0 00	(2 5 0 0 00)
Supplies	3 0 0 0 00	2 7 5 0 00	2 5 0 00
Merchandise Inventory	49 0 0 0 00	46 0 0 0 00	3 0 0 0 00
Total Current Assets	178 8 8 0 00	149 2 5 0 00	29 6 3 0 00
Plant Assets:			
Office Equipment	22 5 0 0 00	19 5 0 0 00	3 0 0 0 00
Store Furniture	49 0 0 0 00	46 0 0 0 00	3 0 0 0 00
Building	70 0 0 0 00	70 0 0 0 00	———
Land	———	12 5 0 0 00	(12 5 0 0 00)
Less Accum. Depr.—Equipment and Land	20 4 5 0 00	6 8 0 0 00	13 6 5 0 00
Total Plant Assets (book value)	121 0 5 0 00	141 2 0 0 00	(20 1 5 0 00)
Total Assets	299 9 3 0 00	290 4 5 0 00	9 4 8 0 00
LIABILITIES			
Current Liabilities:			
Notes Payable	11 5 0 0 00	10 5 0 0 00	1 0 0 0 00
Accounts Payable	23 5 0 0 00	22 5 0 0 00	1 0 0 0 00
Sales Tax Payable	3 0 0 00	4 0 0 00	(1 0 0 00)
Total Current Liabilities	35 3 0 0 00	33 4 0 0 00	1 9 0 0 00
Long-Term Liabilities:			
Mortgage Payable	62 5 0 0 00	70 0 0 0 00	(7 5 0 0 00)
Bonds Payable	40 0 0 0 00	35 0 0 0 00	5 0 0 0 00
Total Long-Term Liabilities	102 5 0 0 00	105 0 0 0 00	(2 5 0 0 00)
Total Liabilities	137 8 0 0 00	138 4 0 0 00	(6 0 0 00)
STOCKHOLDERS' EQUITY			
Total Stockholders' Equity	162 1 3 0 00	152 0 5 0 00	10 0 8 0 00
Total Liabilities and Stockholders' Equity	299 9 3 0 00	290 4 5 0 00	9 4 8 0 00

1. a., b., c., d.

Account	20X2	20X1	Current Asset or Current Liability	Increase (Decrease)	Source or Use of Cash
Accounts Receivable (book value)					
Supplies					
Merchandise Inventory					
Notes Payable					
Accounts Payable					
Sales Tax Payable					

14-1 ON YOUR OWN (LO3, 4), p. 410

Preparing the operating activities section of a statement of cash flows

Southern Gulf Corporation
Comparative Balance Sheet
December 31, 20X2 and 20X1

	20X2	20X1	Increase (Decrease)
ASSETS			
Current Assets:			
Cash	132 6 0 0 00	140 0 0 0 00	(7 4 0 0 00)
Accounts Receivable (book value)	188 0 0 0 00	180 0 0 0 00	8 0 0 0 00
Prepaid Insurance	4 0 0 0 00	6 0 0 0 00	(2 0 0 0 00)
Merchandise Inventory	184 0 0 0 00	220 0 0 0 00	(36 0 0 0 00)
Total Current Assets	508 6 0 0 00	546 0 0 0 00	(37 4 0 0 00)
Plant Assets:			
Office Equipment	92 0 0 0 00	52 0 0 0 00	40 0 0 0 00
Office Furniture	36 0 0 0 00	24 0 0 0 00	12 0 0 0 00
Building	470 0 0 0 00	420 0 0 0 00	50 0 0 0 00
Land	——	24 0 0 0 00	(24 0 0 0 00)
Less Accum. Depr.—Equipment and Land	49 0 0 0 00	39 2 0 0 00	9 8 0 0 00
Total Plant Assets (book value)	549 0 0 0 00	480 8 0 0 00	68 2 0 0 00
Total Assets	1057 6 0 0 00	1026 8 0 0 00	30 8 0 0 00
LIABILITIES			
Current Liabilities:			
Notes Payable	33 0 0 0 00	36 0 0 0 00	(3 0 0 0 00)
Accounts Payable	76 0 0 0 00	68 0 0 0 00	8 0 0 0 00
Total Current Liabilities	109 0 0 0 00	104 0 0 0 00	5 0 0 0 00
Long-Term Liabilities:			
Mortgage Payable	356 0 0 0 00	372 0 0 0 00	(16 0 0 0 00)
Bonds Payable	80 0 0 0 00	100 0 0 0 00	(20 0 0 0 00)
Total Long-Term Liabilities	436 0 0 0 00	472 0 0 0 00	(36 0 0 0 00)
Total Liabilities	545 0 0 0 00	576 0 0 0 00	(31 0 0 0 00)
STOCKHOLDERS' EQUITY			
Total Stockholders' Equity	512 6 0 0 00	450 8 0 0 00	61 8 0 0 00
Total Liabilities and Stockholders' Equity	1057 6 0 0 00	1026 8 0 0 00	30 8 0 0 00

1. a., b., c., d.

Account	20X2	20X1	Current Asset Current Liability	Increase (Decrease)	Source or Use of Cash
Accounts Receivable (book value)					
Prepaid Insurance					
Merchandise Inventory					
Notes Payable					
Accounts Payable					

14-2 WORK TOGETHER (LO5, 6, 7, 8), p. 417

Completing the statement of cash flows

1.

Account	Current Year	Prior Year	Long-Term Asset or Long-Term Liability	Increase (Decrease)	Source or Use of Cash
Office Equipment					
Store Furniture					
Building					
Land (no gain on sale)					
Mortgage Payable					
Bonds Payable					

3.

Activity	Amount	Source or Use of Cash
Sale of additional common stock	$10,000.00	
Payment of cash dividend	5,000.00	

Western Wear, Inc.

Statement of Cash Flows

For Year Ended December 31, 20X2

2.

WT 14-1

2.

WT 14-2

4.

5.

6. Operating cash flow ratio   =

Cash flow margin ratio   =

Name _____ Date _____ Class _____

Completing the statement of cash flows

1.

Account	20X2	20X1	Long-Term Asset or Long-Term Liability	Increase (Decrease)	Source or Use of Cash
Office Equipment					
Office Furniture					
Building					
Land (no gain on sale)					
Mortgage Payable					
Bonds Payable					

3.

Activity	Amount	Source or Use of Cash
Sale of additional common stock	$40,000.00	
Payment of cash dividend	20,000.00	

Southern Gulf Corporation

Statement of Cash Flows

For Year Ended December 31, 20X2

2.

OYO 14-1

2.

4.

OYO 14-2

5.

6. Operating cash flow ratio =

    Cash flow margin ratio =

14-1 APPLICATION PROBLEM (LO3, 4), p. 419

Preparing the operating activities section of a statement of cash flows

1.

Item	Amount	Source or Use of Cash
Net income		

2.

Item	Amount	Source or Use of Cash
Depreciation expense		

3.

Account	Current Year	Prior Year	Current Asset or Current Liability	Increase (Decrease)	Source or Use of Cash
Accounts Receivable (book value)					
Merchandise Inventory					
Supplies					
Accounts Payable					

APPLICATION PROBLEM (LO5, 6, 7, 8), p. 419

Completing the statement of cash flows

1.

Account	Current Year	Prior Year	Long-Term Asset or Long-Term Liability	Increase (Decrease)	Source or Use of Cash
Office Equipment					
Office Furniture					
Land					

2.

Activity	Amount	Source or Use of Cash
Sale of additional common stock		
Payment of cash dividend		

5.

Item	Amount
Net increase in Cash	

6.

Item	Amount
Cash balance, beginning of period	

7.

Item	Amount
Cash balance, end of period	

14-1/14-2 **APPLICATION PROBLEM (concluded)**

NLC Corporation

Statement of Cash Flows

For Year Ended December 31, 20X2

4.

APPLICATION PROBLEM 14-1

3.

APPLICATION PROBLEM 14-2

4.

8., 9.

10. Operating cash flow ratio   =

Cash flow margin ratio   =

Preparing a statement of cash flows

Alpine Corporation

Comparative Income Statement

For Years Ended December 31, 20X2 and 20X1

	20X2	20X1	Increase (Decrease)
Net Sales	570 124 00	596 176 00	(26 052 00)
Cost of Merchandise Sold	233 628 00	240 899 00	(7 271 00)
Gross Profit on Operations	336 496 00	355 277 00	(18 781 00)
Operating Expenses:			
Depreciation Expense	12 057 00	11 409 00	648 00
Other Operating Expenses	297 098 49	289 384 46	7 714 03
Total Operating Expenses	309 155 49	300 793 46	8 362 03
Net Income before Federal Income Tax Expense	27 340 51	54 483 54	(27 143 03)
Less Federal Income Tax Expense	5 741 51	11 441 54	(5 700 03)
Net Income after Federal Income Tax Expense	21 599 00	43 042 00	(21 443 00)

Alpine Corporation

Comparative Statement of Stockholders' Equity

For Years Ended December 31, 20X2 and 20X1

	20X2	20X1	Increase (Decrease)
Capital Stock:			
$15.00 Per Share			
Balance, January 1	120 000 00	120 000 00	—
Additional Capital Stock Issued	12 000 00	—	12 000 00
Balance, December 31	132 000 00	120 000 00	12 000 00
Retained Earnings:			
Balance, January 1	74 389 00	47 347 00	27 042 00
Net Income after Federal Income Tax	21 599 00	43 042 00	(21 443 00)
Total	95 988 00	90 389 00	5 599 00
Less Dividend Payment	22 000 00	16 000 00	6 000 00
Balance, December 31	73 988 00	74 389 00	(401 00)
Total Stockholders' Equity, December 31	205 988 00	194 389 00	11 599 00

14-M MASTERY PROBLEM (continued)

Alpine Corporation

Comparative Balance Sheet

December 31, 20X2 and 20X1

	20X2	20X1	Increase (Decrease)
ASSETS			
Current Assets:			
Cash	51 014 00	25 219 00	25 795 00
Accounts Receivable (book value)	207 174 00	231 010 00	(23 836 00)
Supplies	1 001 00	1 262 00	(261 00)
Merchandise Inventory	71 636 00	74 760 00	(3 124 00)
Total Current Assets	330 825 00	332 251 00	(1 426 00)
Plant Assets:			
Equipment	57 856 00	49 856 00	8 000 00
Less Accum. Depreciation—Equipment	26 200 00	14 143 00	12 057 00
Total Plant Assets (book value)	31 656 00	35 713 00	(4 057 00)
Total Assets	362 481 00	367 964 00	(5 483 00)
LIABILITIES			
Current Liabilities:			
Notes Payable	11 203 00	12 460 00	(1 257 00)
Accounts Payable	89 299 00	103 251 00	(13 952 00)
Total Current Liabilities	100 502 00	115 711 00	(15 209 00)
Long-Term Liabilities:			
Mortgage Payable	55 991 00	57 864 00	(1 873 00)
Total Liabilities	156 493 00	173 575 00	(17 082 00)
STOCKHOLDERS' EQUITY			
Total Stockholders' Equity	205 988 00	194 389 00	11 599 00
Total Liabilities and Stockholders' Equity	362 481 00	367 964 00	(5 483 00)

1.

Item	Amount	Source or Use of Cash
Net income		

Item	Amount	Source or Use of Cash
Depreciation expense		

2.

Account	20X2	20X1	Current Asset or Current Liability	Increase (Decrease)	Source or Use of Cash
Accounts Receivable (book value)					
Supplies					
Merchandise Inventory					
Notes Payable					
Accounts Payable					

3., 4.

Account	20X2	20X1	Long-Term Asset or Long-Term Liability	Increase (Decrease)	Source or Use of Cash
Equipment					
Mortgage Payable					

5.

Activity	Amount	Source or Use of Cash
Sale of additional common stock		
Payment of cash dividend		

14-M **MASTERY PROBLEM (continued)**

Alpine Corporation

Statement of Cash Flows

For Year Ended December 31, 20X2

6.

7.

8.

10. Operating cash flow ratio   =

      Cash flow margin ratio   =

11.

_____

_____

_____

_____

_____

_____

_____

_____

_____

_____

14-C CHALLENGE PROBLEM (LO3, 4, 5, 6, 7), p. 421

Preparing a statement of cash flows with amortization expense

Southwest Electronics, Inc.

Comparative Income Statement

For Years Ended December 31, 20X2 and 20X1

	20X2	20X1	Increase (Decrease)
Net Sales	336 597 00	320 110 00	16 487 00
Cost of Merchandise Sold	154 218 00	135 537 00	18 681 00
Gross Profit on Operations	182 379 00	184 573 00	(2 194 00)
Operating Expenses:			
Depreciation Expense	13 650 00	4 700 00	8 950 00
Other Operating Expenses	168 744 00	172 178 00	(3 434 00)
Amortization Expense	4 710 00	4 710 00	——
Total Operating Expenses	187 104 00	181 588 00	5 516 00
Net Income	(4 725 00)	2 985 00	(7 710 00)

Southwest Electronics, Inc.

Comparative Statement of Stockholders' Equity

For Years Ended December 31, 20X2 and 20X1

	20X2	20X1	Increase (Decrease)
Capital Stock:			
$10.00 Per Share			
Balance, January 1	153 565 00	153 565 00	——
Additional Capital Stock Issued	7 000 00	——	7 000 00
Balance, December 31	160 565 00	153 565 00	7 000 00
Retained Earnings:			
Balance, January 1	7 985 00	5 000 00	2 985 00
Net Income (Net Loss)	(4 725 00)	2 985 00	(7 710 00)
Balance, December 31	3 260 00	7 985 00	(4 725 00)
Total Stockholders' Equity, December 31	163 825 00	161 550 00	2 275 00

Southwest Electronics, Inc.

Comparative Balance Sheet

December 31, 20X2 and 20X1

	20X2	20X1	Increase (Decrease)
ASSETS			
Current Assets:			
Cash	23 355 00	20 385 00	2 970 00
Notes Receivable	10 130 00	6 325 00	3 805 00
Accounts Receivable (book value)	56 550 00	67 500 00	(10 950 00)
Supplies	2 500 00	800 00	1 700 00
Merchandise Inventory	91 050 00	46 600 00	44 450 00
Total Current Assets	183 585 00	141 610 00	41 975 00
Plant Assets:			
Office Equipment	27 810 00	22 660 00	5 150 00
Office Furniture	6 605 00	5 000 00	1 605 00
Building	32 500 00	———	32 500 00
Land	50 000 00	75 000 00	(25 000 00)
Less Accum. Depreciation—Equipment	20 450 00	6 800 00	13 650 00
Total Plant Assets (book value)	96 465 00	95 860 00	605 00
Intangible Assets:			
Patents	14 130 00	18 840 00	(4 710 00)
Total Assets	294 180 00	256 310 00	37 870 00
LIABILITIES			
Current Liabilities:			
Notes Payable	7 780 00	11 205 00	(3 425 00)
Accounts Payable	57 425 00	52 950 00	4 475 00
Salaries Payable	4 850 00	5 350 00	(500 00)
Total Current Liabilities	70 055 00	69 505 00	550 00
Long-Term Liabilities:			
Mortgage Payable	60 300 00	25 255 00	35 045 00
Total Liabilities	130 355 00	94 760 00	35 595 00
STOCKHOLDERS' EQUITY			
Total Stockholders' Equity	163 825 00	161 550 00	2 275 00
Total Liabilities and Stockholders' Equity	294 180 00	256 310 00	37 870 00

14-C **CHALLENGE PROBLEM (concluded)**

Southwest Electronics, Inc.

Statement of Cash Flows

For Year Ended December 31, 20X2

REINFORCEMENT ACTIVITY 3, p. 424

Processing and Analyzing Accounting Data for a Corporation

1.

GENERAL JOURNAL

PAGE 12

	DATE	ACCOUNT TITLE	DOC. NO.	POST. REF.	DEBIT	CREDIT	
17							17
18							18
19							19
20							20
21							21
22							22
23							23
24							24
25							25
26							26
27							27
28							28
29							29
30							30
31							31
32							32
33							33
34							34
35							35
36							36
37							37
38							38
39							39
40							40
41							41
42							42
43							43
44							44
45							45
46							46

REINFORCEMENT ACTIVITY 3 (continued)

1.

CASH RECEIPTS JOURNAL

PAGE 15

				1	2	3	4	5	6	7
				GENERAL		ACCOUNTS RECEIVABLE CREDIT	SALES CREDIT	SALES TAX PAYABLE CREDIT	SALES DISCOUNT DEBIT	CASH DEBIT
DATE	ACCOUNT TITLE	DOC. NO.	POST. REF.	DEBIT	CREDIT					

1.

CASH PAYMENTS JOURNAL

PAGE 20

				1	2	3	4	5
				GENERAL		ACCOUNTS PAYABLE DEBIT	PURCHASES DISCOUNT CREDIT	CASH CREDIT
DATE	ACCOUNT TITLE	CK. NO.	POST. REF.	DEBIT	CREDIT			

REINFORCEMENT ACTIVITY 3 (continued)

2.

Peterson Pet Supply, Inc.

Income Statement

For Years Ended December 31, 20X3, 20X2, and 20X1

	20X3	20X2	20X1
Net Sales	625 5 5 5 22	597 5 4 6 78	545 2 1 0 10
Cost of Merchandise Sold:	396 3 2 1 84	387 4 6 5 98	360 0 0 0 00
Gross Profit	229 2 3 3 38	210 0 8 0 80	185 2 1 0 10
Operating Expenses:			
Selling, General and Administrative	129 5 5 5 55	116 5 4 4 41	101 3 6 5 36
Depreciation	40 0 0 0 00	38 0 0 0 00	35 0 0 0 00
Total Operating Expenses	169 5 5 5 55	154 5 4 4 41	136 3 6 5 36
Income from Operations	59 6 7 7 83	55 5 3 6 39	48 8 4 4 74
Other Revenue and Expenses:			
Interest Income	8 9 7 0 10	8 5 4 3 65	7 5 1 4 44
Interest Expense	(9 6 6 8 33)	(7 8 5 0 00)	(5 5 5 4 15)
Total Other Revenue and Expenses	(6 9 8 23)	6 9 3 65	1 9 6 0 29
Net Income before Federal Income Tax	58 9 7 9 60	56 2 3 0 04	50 8 0 5 03
Less: Federal Income Tax Expense	12 3 8 5 72	11 8 0 8 31	10 6 6 9 06
Net Income	46 5 9 3 88	44 4 2 1 73	40 1 3 5 97

2.

Peterson Pet Supply, Inc.

Statement of Stockholders' Equity

For Years Ended December 31, 20X3, 20X2, and 20X1

	20X3	20X2	20X1
Paid-In Capital:			
Common Stock, $10.00 Par Value:			
Balance, January 1	750 0 0 0 00	650 0 0 0 00	650 0 0 0 00
Additional Common Stock Issued	250 0 0 0 00	100 0 0 0 00	—
Balance, December 31	1000 0 0 0 00	750 0 0 0 00	650 0 0 0 00
Preferred Stock, 8%, $100.00 Par Value:			
Balance, January 1	50 0 0 0 00	50 0 0 0 00	50 0 0 0 00
Additional Preferred Stock Issued	20 0 0 0 00	—	—
Balance, December 31	70 0 0 0 00	50 0 0 0 00	50 0 0 0 00
Total Capital Stock Issued	1070 0 0 0 00	800 0 0 0 00	700 0 0 0 00
Additional Paid-In Capital:			
Paid-In Capital in Excess of Par Value—Common	210 0 0 0 00	150 0 0 0 00	94 6 0 8 38
Paid-In Capital in Excess of Par Value—Preferred	5 5 0 0 00	1 5 0 0 00	1 5 0 0 00
Paid-In Capital from Sale of Treasury Stock	15 2 0 0 00	12 3 5 9 18	—
Total Additional Paid-In Capital	230 7 0 0 00	163 8 5 9 18	96 1 0 8 38
Total Paid-In Capital	1300 7 0 0 00	963 8 5 9 18	796 1 0 8 38
Retained Earnings:			
Balance, January 1, 20--	56 5 9 1 97	53 6 7 0 24	30 5 3 4 27
Net Income after Federal Income Tax	46 5 9 3 88	44 4 2 1 73	40 1 3 5 97
Less Preferred Dividends Declared	(5 6 0 0 00)	(4 0 0 0 00)	(4 0 0 0 00)
Less Common Dividends Declared	(57 0 0 0 00)	(37 5 0 0 00)	(13 0 0 0 00)
Balance, December 31	40 5 8 5 85	56 5 9 1 97	53 6 7 0 24
Treasury Stock			
Balance, December 31	29 0 0 0 00	30 0 0 0 00	20 0 0 0 00
Total Stockholders' Equity, December 31, 20--	1312 2 8 5 85	990 4 5 1 15	829 7 7 8 62
Common Shares Outstanding	100 0 0 0 00	75 0 0 0 00	65 0 0 0 00
Preferred Shares Outstanding	7 0 0 00	5 0 0 00	5 0 0 00
Treasury Shares	2 9 0 0 00	3 0 0 0 00	2 0 0 0 00

REINFORCEMENT ACTIVITY 3 (continued)

2.

Peterson Pet Supply, Inc.

Balance Sheet

December 31, 20X3 and 20X2

	20X3	20X2
Assets		
Current Assets:		
Cash and Cash Equivalents	47 2 7 7 30	45 3 7 8 52
Marketable Securities	73 6 2 6 38	69 7 4 6 36
Accounts Receivable (book value)	66 7 0 6 43	55 6 4 7 10
Merchandise Inventory	69 0 6 6 40	95 2 1 4 25
Other Current Assets	98 9 4 4 98	79 9 8 7 61
Total Current Assets	355 6 2 1 49	345 9 7 3 84
Investment Securities	438 4 0 0 00	120 0 0 0 00
Land	75 0 0 0 00	100 0 0 0 00
Building	300 0 0 0 00	300 0 0 0 00
Accumulated Depreciation—Building	(50 0 0 0 00)	(40 0 0 0 00)
Office Equipment	170 0 0 0 00	120 0 0 0 00
Accumulated Depreciation—Office Equipment	(40 0 0 0 00)	(35 0 0 0 00)
Store Equipment	385 0 0 0 00	350 0 0 0 00
Accumulated Depreciation—Store Equipment	(75 0 0 0 00)	(50 0 0 0 00)
Total Assets	1559 0 2 1 49	1210 9 7 3 84
Liabilities		
Current Liabilities:		
Accounts Payable	52 9 3 9 05	54 2 2 5 68
Sales Tax Payable	1 6 1 6 05	1 5 4 5 22
Accrued Salaries and Related Expenses	26 1 8 3 69	25 7 0 0 40
Federal Income Tax Payable	5 1 0 3 49	4 8 3 0 06
Other Current Liabilities	55 8 9 3 36	59 2 2 1 33
Total Current Liabilities	141 7 3 5 64	145 5 2 2 69
Long-Term Liabilities:		
Bonds Payable, net	105 0 0 0 00	75 0 0 0 00
Total Liabilities	246 7 3 5 64	220 5 2 2 69
Stockholders' Equity		
Paid-In Capital	1300 7 0 0 00	963 8 5 9 18
Retained Earnings	40 5 8 5 85	56 5 9 1 97
Treasury Stock	(29 0 0 0 00)	(30 0 0 0 00)
Total Stockholders' Equity	1312 2 8 5 85	990 4 5 1 15
Total Liabilities and Stockholders' Equity	1559 0 2 1 49	1210 9 7 3 84

2.

REINFORCEMENT ACTIVITY 3 (continued)

3.

Ratio	Target Range		Actual Measure			Favorable Trend	Favorable Result
	Low	High	20X3	20X2	20X1		
a. Profitability ratios:							
1. Gross margin	37.0%	39.0%					
2. Operating margin	9.0%	10.0%					
3. Rate earned on average total assets	4.5%	5.5%					
4. Rate earned on average stockholders' equity	4.5%	5.0%					
b. Efficiency ratios:							
1. Accounts receivable turnover	9.7	10.7					
2. Inventory turnover	3.0	5.0					
c. Short-term financial strength ratios:							
1. Working capital	$2,10,000.00	$2,15,000.00					
2. Current ratio	2.4	2.6					
3. Quick ratio	1.2	1.6					
d. Long-term financial strength ratios:							
1. Debt ratio	13.0%	18.0%					
2. Equity ratio	82.0%	87.0%					
3. Common equity per share	12.50	13.00					
4. Interest coverage ratio	8.0	8.4					
e. Market ratios:							
1. Earnings per share	$0.60	$0.70					
2. Price-earnings ratios	N/A	N/A					
3. Dividend yield	3.8%	4.7%					
f. Cash ratios:							
1. Free cash flow	$60,000.00	$70,000.00					
2. Operating cash flow ratio	0.4	0.5					
3. Cash flow margin ratio	0.1	0.4					

REINFORCEMENT ACTIVITY 3 (continued)

Supporting Calculations:

(a) Profitability ratios:

(1) Gross margin:

20X3:

20X2:

20X1:

(2) Operating margin:

20X3:

20X2:

20X1:

(3) Rate earned on average total assets:

20X3:

20X2:

(4) Rate earned on average stockholders' equity:

20X3:

20X2:

(b) Efficiency ratios:

(1) Accounts receivable turnover:

20X3:

20X2:

(2) Inventory turnover:

20X3:

20X2:

REINFORCEMENT ACTIVITY 3 (continued)

(c) Short-term financial strength ratios:

(1) Working capital:

20X3:

20X2:

(2) Current ratio:

20X3:

20X2:

(3) Quick ratio:

20X3:

20X2:

(d) Long-term financial strength ratios:

(1) Debt ratio:

20X3:

20X2:

(2) Equity ratio:

20X3:

20X2:

(3) Common equity per share:

20X3:

20X2:

20X1:

(4) Interest coverage ratio:

20X3:

20X2:

20X1:

REINFORCEMENT ACTIVITY 3 (continued)

(e) Market ratios:

(1) Earnings per share:

20X3:

20X2:

20X1:

(2) Price-earnings ratio:

20X3:

20X2:

20X1:

(3) Dividend yield—common stock:

20X3:

20X2:

20X1:

(f) Cash ratios:

(1) Free cash flow:

20X3:

20X2:

(2) Operating cash flow ratio:

20X3:

20X2:

(3) Cash flow margin ratio:

20X3:

20X2:

REINFORCEMENT ACTIVITY 3 (concluded)

4.

CASH RECEIPTS JOURNAL

PAGE 1

DATE	ACCOUNT TITLE	DOC. NO.	POST. REF.	GENERAL DEBIT	GENERAL CREDIT	ACCOUNTS RECEIVABLE CREDIT	SALES CREDIT	SALES TAX PAYABLE CREDIT	SALES DISCOUNT DEBIT	CASH DEBIT
				1	2	3	4	5	6	7

4.

CASH PAYMENTS JOURNAL

PAGE 1

DATE	ACCOUNT TITLE	CK. NO.	POST. REF.	GENERAL DEBIT	GENERAL CREDIT	ACCOUNTS PAYABLE DEBIT	PURCHASES DISCOUNT CREDIT	CASH CREDIT
				1	2	3	4	5